PREFACE

This book is intended for beginning students in all branches of engineering. It should also be of interest to high school students who are considering a career in engineering and wish to learn more about the nature and challenges of the engineering profession.

The book begins with a brief history of engineering, which examines the roots of engineering and traces its development to the present day. The second chapter defines engineering and describes the functions and career paths for various branches of engineering.

Chapter 3 describes the professional responsibilities of engineers, the legal framework for the practice of engineering through registration and licensing, the purpose and importance of engineering societies, and the code of ethics that protects the integrity of the profession.

The fourth chapter deals with creativity and the learning process, offering suggestions on how to be a successful engineering student and how to develop and nurture creativity in engineering practice.

Chapter 5 discusses the engineering design method and describes techniques commonly used by engineers to solve problems.

The sixth chapter describes the ways that successful engineers communicate with their supervisors, their peers, and the public. It includes sections on the engineer as a writer, as a speaker, and as a presiding officer, as well as the rudiments of graphical communication.

Chapter 7 gives recommended procedures for the handling of engineering data and discusses the application of common mathematical procedures to the solution of engineering problems.

Chapter 8 is a case study of Atlanta's Freedom Parkway Project, which, because of public opposition, extended over 30 years. The protracted controversy surrounding this project involved five mayors, six transportation commissioners, seven governors, and a former president of the United States. The case study demonstrates clearly that engineering is much more than solving mathematical equations and that engineers must be concerned about the possible harmful effects of their designs on people and the earth's environment.

Chapter 9 is a case study that examines the circumstances and events leading to the aftermath of one of the most dramatic engineering failures of this century: the space shuttle *Challenger* accident. The chapter focuses not only on the engineering failure that led to the loss of the *Challenger* crew but also on the breakdown in communication and engineering ethics that allowed the shuttle to be launched despite unacceptable risks to human life.

In this, the third edition of this book, the material has been thoroughly updated, and several areas have been expanded. For example, in Chapter 2, new sections are devoted to emerging specialties in bioengineering, computer engineering, and microelectromechanical systems (MEMS). Incorporating material written by Dr. J. David Irwin and published in *On Becoming an Engineer* by the IEEE Press, the chapter describes initial career profiles for 28 beginning engineering graduates.

Chapter 3 gives a more complete description of Canada's Ritual of the Calling of an Engineer and adds a new section on the framework of engineering ethics. The chapter includes the Code of Ethics of the National Society of Professional Engineers in its entirety and adds six new case studies from NSPE's Board of Ethical Review.

Chapter 4 has new sections on personality and learning styles, and characteristics of creative people.

Chapter 5 gives an expanded treatment of learning from failures and a new section on working in teams.

The material in Chapter 6 has been extensively expanded and modernized. It includes new material on how engineers find information, and how they evaluate and process information and turn it into reliable knowledge. It describes the use of the World Wide Web and discusses how to evaluate Web sources. It describes sources of information such as databases and print reference sources, and gives examples of Web resources that engineers can use. The material on graphical communications has been thoroughly revised and updated, and includes discussions of computer aided design (CAD), simulation, and virtual reality.

Many people and organizations contributed to the development of this book. I am indebted to editor Joe Hayton and the other professionals at John Wiley & Sons, Inc. and at Argosy Publishing who brought this book into being. The contributions of several colleagues and friends, which were acknowledged in the first two editions, extend to this edition as well. For this edition, I especially appreciate the contributions of Dr. Nelson Baker, who updated the material on graphical communications and the help of Professor Greg Raschke, who prepared the section on information and communications resources. I am also grateful to the many people who provided information and gave of their time to help me with the case study on the Freedom Parkway. They are named and in some instances quoted in the chapter.

Finally, I thank the many organizations and individuals that supplied information, photographs, and sketches for the book. Direct credit is given in the book for these contributions.

Paul H. Wright

CONTENTS

CHAPTER 5/THE ENGINEERING APPROACH TO PROBLEM SOLVING

CHAPTER 6/ENGINEERING COMMUNICATIONS

CHAPTER 7/ENGINEERING CALCULATIONS

CHAPTER 8/A CASE STUDY—
ATLANTA'S FREEDOM PARKWAY PROJECT

CHAPTER 9/A CASE STUDY—
THE SPACE SHUTTLE *CHALLENGER* ACCIDENT

INDEX

An Exemplary Engineering Achievement

The housing for the Fermi National Accelerator Laboratory at the Argonne Laboratory, Batavia, Illinois, provides a surrealistic setting for advanced nuclear experiments that have produced particular energies as high as 500 billion electron volts. (Courtesy of the American Council of Engineering Companies.)

CHAPTER ONE

HISTORY OF ENGINEERING

1.1 INTRODUCTION

Engineering was not spoken into existence by royal decree or created by legislative fiat. It has evolved and developed as a practical art and a profession over more than 50 centuries of recorded history. In a broad sense, its roots can be traced to the dawn of civilization itself, and its progress parallels the progress of mankind.

Our ancient forebears attempted to control and use the materials and forces of nature for public benefit just as we do today. They studied and observed the laws of nature and developed a knowledge of mathematics and science that was not possessed by the common people. They applied this knowledge with discretion and judgment in ways that satisfied beneficial social needs with ports, roads, buildings, irrigation and flood control facilities, and other creative works.

Historical studies of engineering teach us respect for the past and its achievements. They help us to view the present in light of the past—to discern trends and to evaluate the reasons for the great changes that have punctuated human progress. By examining the roots of engineering, we are able to sense the broad flow of history and to view the present as a part of that flow. This helps us to put the present in its context and to take a better view of our goals, aspirations, and actions (1).

Our objective in this chapter, then, is to briefly trace the development of engineering from earliest recorded times to the present day. This, of course, is a large undertaking, and with limited space available, we can only briefly outline the highlights of engineering history. The reader is encouraged to consult the references listed at the end of this chapter for a more complete treatment of this important subject.

1.2   ENGINEERING IN THE EARLY CIVILIZATIONS: THE MESOPOTAMIANS

Significant engineering achievements must be credited to the ancient dwellers of Mesopotamia, the land between the Tigris and Euphrates Rivers, currently the country of Iraq. In this area, the wheeled cart is said to have first appeared (2). In southern Mesopotamia, at the beginning of recorded history, the ancient and mysterious Sumerian people constructed canals, temples, and city walls that comprised the world's first engineering works (3).

The land of Mesopotamia was open to attack from the north, east, and west, and its history is a confused record of conquests and occupations by neighboring peoples (4). The most prominent rulers of ancient Mesopotamia were the Babylonians and the Assyrians.

Records inscribed on clay tablets have been discovered and deciphered, providing an insight into life in that area thousands of years ago. These records show that as early as 2000 B.C., an angle measuring device called the astrolabe was being used for astronomical observations. This instrument, which consisted of a graduated circle and a sighting arm, was based on the 60-unit numerical system used by the Mesopotamians. That system has been retained in time and angle measurements to the present day.

The most unusual class of structure left by the Mesopotamians was the *ziggurat*, a temple tower built in honor of their gods. The ziggurat was a terraced pyramid of brick with staircases, setbacks, and a shrine or chapel at the top. The Tower of Babel mentioned in the Old Testament is believed to have been this type of structure.

Hammurabi, the great king who ruled Babylonia for 43 years (circa 1850 to 1750 B.C.) compiled a comprehensive new code of law that bears his name. This famous code provided penalties for those who permitted poor construction practices and is considered to be a forerunner of today's building codes.

The Code of Hammurabi provided an important message dealing with quality assurance and professional responsibility and exacted extremely severe penalties for its breach. It read:

> *If a builder build a house for a man and do not make its construction firm and the house which he has built collapse and cause the death of the owner of the house—that builder shall be put to death.*
>
> *If it cause the death of the son of the owner of the house—they shall put to death a son of the builder.*
>
> *If it cause the death of the slave of the owner of the house—he shall give to the owner of the house a slave of equal value.*
>
> *If it destroy property, he shall restore whatever it destroyed, and because he did not make the house which he built firm and it collapsed, he shall rebuild the house which collapsed at his own expense.*

If a builder build a house for a man and do not make its construction meet the requirements and a wall fall in, that builder shall strengthen the wall at his own expense.

It is not surprising that the people who populated the valleys of the Tigris and Euphrates developed significant irrigation and flood control works. Today, in Iraq, evidence of abandoned canals can still be traced by lines of embankments, lakes, and streams. The Nahrwan, a 400-foot wide canal extended generally parallel to the Tigris River over a distance of 200 miles (3), irrigating an area averaging 18 miles in width (5). Imposing masonry dams were used by the Mesopotamians to divert small tributaries into the canal.

During the reign of King Sennacherib, the Assyrians completed (circa 700 B.C.) the first notable example of a public water supply. They built a 30-mile-long feeder canal bringing fresh water from the hills of Mount Tas to the existing Khosr River, by which the water flowed an additional 15 miles into Ninevah. At Jerwan, an elevated cut-stone aqueduct was built to carry the open canal over a small stream. This famous structure was 863 feet long, 68 feet wide, and 28 feet at the highest point (6). It supported a channel that was approximately 50 feet wide and about 5 feet deep (2). The channel was underlain by a thick layer of concrete, the first known use of this construction material.

1.3   ENGINEERING IN THE EARLY CIVILIZATIONS: THE EGYPTIANS

In the ancient Egyptian civilization, experts in planning and construction emerged. These engineering forerunners held top positions as the trusted advisors of the Egyptian kings. The man who held this position was a general construction expert who was known as the king's "chief of works." (See Figure 1.1.)

These ancient engineers/architects practiced the earliest known form of surveying, developed effective irrigation systems, and built remarkable edifices of stone. The annual flooding of the Nile created a need for reestablishing land boundaries. To perform these surveys, Egyptian engineers used sections of rope that had been soaked in water, dried, and then coated with a wax material to insure constant length. (See Figure 1.2.) They may have also used primitive surveying instruments, but none has been found (7).

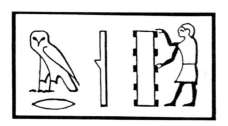

Figure 1.1   *Hieroglyphs from Ancient Egypt translated "chief of works." (Courtesy of the American Society of Civil Engineers.)*

Figure 1.2 *Survey party and officials using coiled "measuring rope" as portrayed in wall painting of an Egyptian superintendent, about 2000 B.C. (Courtesy of the American Society of Civil Engineers.)*

It is known that as early as 3300 B.C., the Egyptians developed and maintained an extensive system of dykes, canals, and drainage systems (*8*). A great mass of people populated the narrow fertile valley of the Nile, and irrigation works were needed to maintain the large population and exploit the skill of agriculture. The river also served as the principal means of transportation because horses, wheeled vehicles, and roads were unknown in Egypt until about 1785 B.C. (*8*).

The engineers of ancient Egypt sought to build the tallest, broadest, and most durable structures the world would ever see. Their palaces, temples, and tombs were designed as symbols of triumphant and everlasting power.

The best known works of the Egyptian builders are the pyramids. The first pyramid was the Step Pyramid at Sakkara, built by Imhotep as a burial place for the ruler Zoser in about 2980 B.C. (see Figure 1.3). The design of pyramids evolved from tombs known as mastabas, as Figure 1.4 illustrates. The ancient Egyptians regarded the king's tomb as a house where he actually lived after death, and some of the more elaborate mastabas contained several rooms and storage cells where food and weapons were placed in close proximity to the dead ruler and his family. Zoser's Step Pyramid is actually six mastabas, the second built on top of the first, the third on top of the second, and so forth. It is conjectured that Imhotep may have built the mastabas one on top of the other to prevent tomb robbers from digging, as they commonly did, into the edifice from the top (*8*).

Three pyramids still stand on the West bank of the Nile River at Giza as reminders of the outstanding engineering skills of the Egyptians. The largest pyramid, known as the Great Pyramid or the Pyramid of Cheops, is approximately 481 feet high, and its base covers 13 acres (*2*). The pyramid is constructed of more than 2 million blocks of stone with the average weight of 2.5 tons. Some of the interior blocks weigh up to 30 tons.

Herodotus, the Greek historian who visited Egypt in the fifth century B.C., reported that it took 100,000 men 20 years working in three-month relays to

Figure 1.3   *The Step Pyramid at Sakkara, built by Imhotep for the ruler Zoser in 2980 B.C. (Courtesy of the Library of Congress.)*

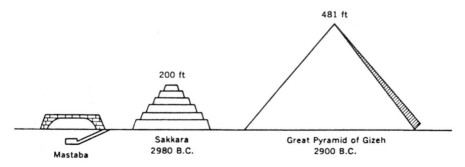

Figure 1.4   *Sketch showing the evolution of the pyramid. (Source: J. K. Finch, "The Engineer Through the Ages: Egypt, Part I," Civil Engineering, February 1957.)*

build the pyramid (*6*). The stone blocks were floated to the site by a causeway that had been built for that purpose. Using ropes, levers, rollers, wooden sledges, earth ramps, and copper chisels, the Egyptian workers built the pyramid with precise and exacting engineering standards. The low courses of this remarkable structure are set with joints measuring one ten-thousandth of an inch wide.

1.4   CONTRIBUTIONS OF THE GREEKS

Beginning about 600 B.C., the Greek way of life and thought became dominant in the eastern Mediterranean area. The Greeks are best remembered for their abstract logic and their ability to theorize and to synthesize the knowledge of the past (*1*). Their advances in art, literature, and philosophy were great, tending to overshadow their contributions to engineering. They tended to focus mainly on theory and placed little value on experimentation and verification and on practical application. In fact, the great Greek thinkers expressed the viewpoint that any application of the fruits of the mind to material needs was not worthy of dignity or respect (*9*).

Nevertheless, the Greek *architecton* made the first notable advance toward professional stature. He was recognized as a master builder and construction expert with knowledge and experience beyond the scope of the average citizen.

The Greek peninsula was so cut up by mountain ranges that land communication was difficult. The Greeks turned to the sea to become the first great harbor builders. Herodotus described a great breakwater or mole that was constructed to protect the harbor at Samos. The breakwater was 400 yards long and was built in water 120 feet deep (*3*). This represents the first recorded construction of an artificial harbor, and it was to become a prototype in harbor planning even into modern times (*10*).

The Greeks' interest in navigation later led to the building of the first lighthouse in the world, the Pharos at the port of Alexandria (*10*). This 370-foot-high structure, built about 300 B.C., was known as one of the Seven Wonders of the Ancient World.

Another great work built on the island of Samos was a 3300-foot-long tunnel cut through a 900-foot hill under the direction of the architecton Eupalinus of Megara (*3, 10*). The main tunnel, which was hand-chiseled through solid limestone, was about 5.5 feet in width and height. At the bottom of the main tunnel, a trench was cut 30 feet deep and 3 feet wide. In this trench, water was brought through clay pipes to the city. The tunnel construction was carried out from both ends, but the surveying methods used to perform this work are not known.

During the Golden Age of Greece, the ruler Pericles undertook a huge building program designed to make Athens the most beautiful city on earth. He retained the services of leading artists and building experts of the time to build temples, shrines, and statues on the Acropolis, the flat-topped rock overlooking the city. The ruins of these works today provide one of the world's most remarkable sights.

The builders of the Greek temples must have used timber frames and manual hoists that were equipped with capstans and pulleys similar to those used in modern times (*10*). By their use of columns and beams, the designers showed a level of structural understanding not demonstrated by builders of the past.

1.5   CONTRIBUTIONS OF THE ROMANS

The most famous engineers of antiquity, the Romans, devoted more of their resources to public works than did their predecessors (*3*). With cheap labor, including thousands of slaves, and abundant raw materials, they built arenas, roads, aqueducts, temples, town halls, baths, and public forums.

Scholars divide Roman history into two main periods: (*1*) the Republic, which extended from 535 B.C., the legendary date of Rome's founding, until 24 B.C.; and (*2*) the Empire, which extended from 24 B.C. until A.D. 476 (*11*). The Republic was an age of conquest and exploitation of Rome's extensive colonial possessions, a time when Roman engineering achievements were confined largely to Italy. The Empire was a relatively peaceful period in which public works were extended into the colonies; remains of some of these engineering facilities can be found today in Spain, France, North Africa, and the Near East (*12*).

In contrast to the Greeks, the Romans were practical builders who relied more on experience than on mathematical logic and science. Their works were simple in design yet impressive in scale and bold in execution (*12*). By and large, their works emphasized function rather than the artistic or aesthetic.

Roman builders are credited with making significant contributions to engineering, which include developing improved methods of construction, discovering and using hydraulic cement, and devising a number of construction machines such as pile drivers, treadmill hoists, and wooden bucket wheels. The latter machines, illustrated in Figure 1.5, were used for dewatering mines and construction sites.

Some of the most famous of Roman engineering works are briefly described below:

The Circus Maximus was a race course where games and contests were held. It is believed to have been either built or greatly enlarged by Tarquinius

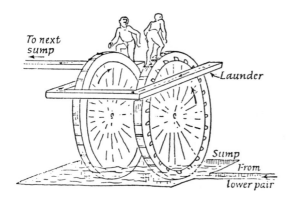

Figure 1.5   *Wooden bucket wheels used to dewater mines. (After* Engineering in the Ancient World, *by J. C. Landels, University of California Press, Berkeley and Los Angeles, 1978.)*

Priscus, an ancient king of Etruscan and Greek ancestry who ruled Rome in the sixth century B.C. (*11*).

The Appian Way was the first and most famous link in a road network that radiated from Rome. Named for Appius Claudius, the Censor of Rome in 312 B.C., the road was noted for its direct alignment, high embankments, and superior pavement structure. Figure 1.6 shows a section of the Appian Way as it appears today.

Aqua Appia, also named for Appius Claudius, was the first major aqueduct built in Rome. It was a low-level, largely underground work built in a tunnel or by cut-and-cover construction (*12*).

The Pantheon was a temple of extraordinary stateliness. Agrippa, a brilliant engineer and the adopted son of Augustus, built the Pantheon circa 17 B.C. It suffered two fires and was rebuilt by Hadrian who ruled during the period A.D. 117–138. The internal diameter of the Pantheon is equal to its height of 141 feet. It is crowned with a coffered semispherical concrete vault. Preserved to the present day, the Pantheon embodies Rome's most imaginative engineering works (*11*).

The Alcantara Bridge, built in Spain by the engineer Gaius Julius Lacer in A.D. 98, is still in use (see Figure 1.7). It has six arches of dry stone and a total length of 600 feet. The roadway is 175 feet above the river (*6*).

The Pont du Gard was part of an ancient aqueduct that supplied water to Nimes in the south of France. Built under the direction of Agrippa during the reign of Augustus (circa 27 B.C. to A.D. 14), this imposing structure was built of dry masonry construction, except for the water channel on top. It is about 160 feet high, and its larger arches have a span of approximately 80 feet (*13*). The Pont du Gard is illustrated in Figure 1.8.

Figure 1.6   *The Appian Way. (Courtesy of the Italian State Tourist Office.)*

Figure 1.7 *The Alcantara Bridge in Spain, built in the year A.D. 98, is still in use. (Photograph by Josep Giaganoiro, courtesy of the Spanish National Tourist Office.)*

Figure 1.8 *The Pont du Gard.* (Source: Theodore Schreiber, Atlas of Classical Antiquities, *Macmillan Publishing Company, 1895.*)

1.6   ENGINEERING IN THE MIDDLE AGES

During the approximately eight centuries following the fall of the Roman Empire, the period known as the Middle Ages, there were relatively few advances in engineering. There was, however, some engineering progress during this period, notably in structural design and in the development of energy-saving and power-enhancing machines and devices.

Perhaps the most interesting structures of the Middle Ages were the Gothic cathedrals. These structures have been called some "of the lightest, most daring 'skeleton stone' construction ever attempted by man" (*2*). These tall and elegant structures, with stained glass windows, pointed central arches, and high thin walls supported along the side by half arches called flying buttresses, evidence a high level of structural competence for the engineer/architects who designed them and the master craftsmen who built them.

During a period in which large landowners sought to protect themselves and their properties, massive fortress homes or castles were built. The fortress-home was characterized by thick walls, tall protective towers, and an encircling wide ditch spanned by a single bridge. With the invention of gunpowder and cannons (circa A.D. 1500), the construction of medieval castles came to an end.

During the Middle Ages, engineers sought to strengthen or supplement the productive powers of humans and animals by devising and improving labor-saving machines. The wind mill was developed during this era, and water mills were improved and used in new ways. Water wheels for mill drive were in use all over Europe by A.D. 700 (*14*). Other mechanical advances that appeared in Europe during medieval times include the spinning wheel and a hinged rudder for ships (*1*). By A.D. 900, the Vikings had developed the art of shipbuilding and discovered Greenland (*14*).

The title *engineer* first came into use during the Middle Ages (circa A.D. 1000–1200). The origin of the words "engine" and "ingeneous" is from the Latin words "in generare", meaning "to create" (*14*). Thus the person who created or designed engines of war—battering rams, catapults, assault towers, and the like—came to be known as the *ingeniator* or "engine-er".

Many of the improved engineering devices, materials, and techniques of the Middle Ages appeared first in the Far East, notably in China. These advancements included the invention of gunpowder and the development of processes for the making of paper, the casting of iron, and the manufacture of textiles (*2*).

1.7   THE ADVANCEMENT OF SCIENCE: CIRCA A.D. 1300–1750

During the late Middle Ages, significant advances were made in transportation and communications, fostering scientific discovery and accelerating the spread of knowledge. In the thirteenth century, Italian architect-engineers gave impetus to a modern era of canal building by their invention of the canal lock. Soon thereafter, networks of canals were constructed throughout Europe for inland water travel. During this period, advances were also made in navigation and shipbuilding, and docks and harbors for ocean transport were built.

Johann Gutenberg invented the movable type mold and is credited with the printing of the first book about 1450.[1] This made possible wide dissemination of information on many subjects, including science and engineering. By the year 1500, books were being published on surveying, hydraulics, chemistry, mining and metallurgy, and other scientific and engineering subjects.

The advancement of science during the fifteenth, sixteenth, and seventeenth centuries had a great impact on the technological and industrial developments that followed, and the contributions of the scientists of that time continue to be felt to the present day. Some of those scientists and their contributions to scientific knowledge are as follows.

- **Leonardo da Vinci (1452–1519).**   A great artist, architect, and experimental scientist of the Italian Renaissance, he displayed genius in many areas. He is remembered more for his conceptual designs than for practical engineering works.

- **Nicolaus Copernicus (1473–1543).**   An astronomer of German and Polish descent, he founded modern astronomy with his theory that the earth is a moving planet.

- **Galileo (1564–1642).**   An Italian astronomer and physicist, he formulated the scientific method of gaining knowledge. Galileo made the first practical use of the telescope to study astronomy, and he is credited with the discovery of a famous law of falling bodies.

- **Robert Boyle (1627–1691).**   Boyle was an Irish chemist and physicist who studied the compression and expansion of air and other gases and discovered that the volume of gas at a constant temperature varies inversely with its pressure (Boyle's law).

- **Robert Hooke (1635–1703).**   An English experimental scientist, he formulated a theory of elasticity known as Hooke's law. The law states that the amount an elastic body deforms is directly proportional to the force or stress acting on it.

- **Sir Isaac Newton (1642–1727).**   An English scientist and mathematician, he invented calculus, discovered the secrets of light and color, and formulated the law of universal gravitation.

- **Thomas Newcomen (1663–1729).**   An English inventor, Newcomen built one of the first practical steam engines in 1712. His atmospheric pressure steam engine was used to pump water from British mines for almost 75 years before it was replaced by James Watt's more efficient engine.

1.8   ADVANCEMENTS IN ENGINEERING: A.D. 1750–1900

During the 150 years leading up to the twentieth century, there was progress in mining, manufacturing, and transportation. During the 1760s, James Watt

---

[1] Pictorial book printing was known in Japan as early as A.D. 765 and even earlier in China (*14*).

devised and produced a working model of a vastly improved steam engine. With the support of manufacturer Matthew Boulton, he built hundreds of the engines (2). By 1800, five hundred of the Boulton and Watt engines were in use in Britain, pumping out mines and driving the machinery in iron works and in textile mills (1).

Up until the mid-1700s, charcoal had been used for the smelting of iron ore. Due to a shortage of wood for the making of charcoal, iron manufacturers began using coke, the lighter, more porous form of coal, for the smelting process. The increased demand for coke created a need to free the coal mines of water and led to the development of steam-driven mine pumps. The new source of power soon began to be used for the driving of machinery in the ironworks and for the operation of new blowing machines to aid the smelting process (1, 2).

Experiments with steam engines to drive boats were being made in Britain and in America, and the first commercially successful river paddle steamship, Robert Fulton's *Clermont*, appeared in America in 1807 (16). Then, in 1823, Englishman George Stephenson established a locomotive firm in Newcastle and, two years later, demonstrated the feasibility of steam-powered railroad transportation (17).

Great progress was made in transportation during the period 1780–1900. An extensive network of canals was constructed in England during the latter two decades of the eighteenth century. The great period of canal construction in the United States occurred during the first half of the nineteenth century. Examples of canals constructed during this time are (18):

1817–1825   The Erie Canal, 364 miles long, connecting Erie, Pennsylvania, and Buffalo, New York.

1828–1836   The Ohio Canal, extending from Cleveland to Portsmouth on the Ohio River.

1828–1850   The Chesapeake and Ohio Canal, extending from Washington, DC, to Cumberland, Maryland.

Soon after Stephenson's demonstration of the feasibility of railroad transportation, there was remarkable growth in railroad systems. In the United States, the railroad route mileage increased from 35,000 miles at the end of the Civil War to 193,000 miles in 1900 (17). By the beginning of the twentieth century, the railroad system in the United States had for all practical purposes been completed.

During this period, there were advances in the technology of road building. The most famous road builder of this era was John Macadam (1756–1836) from Scotland, who developed a method of road construction by compacting layers of broken stone. In addition to building about 180 miles of turnpikes, Macadam wrote several books on road construction. A Scotch contemporary of Macadam, Thomas Telford, advocated building roads by using large flat stones set on edge and wedged together to form a solid base that was surfaced with broken stone and gravel. Telford supervised the construction of about 920 miles of roads and 1200 bridges during the early years of the nineteenth century (2).

From the standpoint of engineering achievements in the nineteenth century, the development of electricity as a source of power ranks as one of the most significant. That achievement is largely attributable to the efforts of numerous scientists and engineers during the latter half of the nineteenth century. It was, however, built on the foundation of discoveries of physicists of the early 1800s, who defined the fundamental nature of electricity: men such as George Simon Ohm of Germany, Alessandra Volta of Italy, and Charles Coloumb and André Ampère of France.

Some of the highlights of the development of electric power follow. Some of the dates are approximate.

1827   Alessandra Volta devised the first electric battery.

1830   Sir Humphrey Davy discovered electromagnetism and the arc light.

1831   Michael Faraday demonstrated the process of magnetic induction.

1880   Thomas A. Edison invented a practical incandescent bulb and discovered that lamps could be connected in parallel, permitting one or more to be turned off without disconnecting the whole system.

1882   Edison's Pearl Street electric generating station was placed in operation in New York City.

1888   Nikola Telsa secured patents for an induction motor and for a new polyphase alternating current system.

1888   After organizing the Westinghouse Electric Company in 1886, George Westinghouse was granted a contract to provide generators for the Niagara hydroelectric project, the first such project in history.

By the end of the nineteenth century, applications of electric power were well established and proliferating. Communication by telegraph, demonstrated by Samuel F. B. Morse in 1843, had been established between North America and Europe by means of submarine cables. One-half million telephones were in use (2), and electric lighting for homes and industries was in growing demand. Electricity was being used to drive trains and street cars and to run the machines of new industries.

The nineteenth century also witnessed greater recognition of engineering as a profession. John Smeaton of Great Britain, the first to use the title civil engineer, was highly regarded in scientific circles. He helped create, in 1771, an engineering society with aspirations and traditions similar to those of the Royal Society, of which he was a member.

In 1818, a group of young English engineers established the Institution of Civil Engineers and elected Thomas Telford its first president. The Institution of Mechanical Engineers was formed in 1847, and George Stephenson served as its first president.

In America, by 1908, five prominent engineering societies, representing civil, mechanical, electrical, chemical and mining and metallurgical engineering, had been formed:

American Society of Civil Engineers (1852)

American Institute of Mining, Metallurgical, and Petroleum Engineers (1871)

American Society of Mechanical Engineers (1880)

Institute of Electrical and Electronics Engineers (1884)

American Institute of Chemical Engineers (1908)

1.9   ENGINEERING IN THE TWENTIETH CENTURY

During the first decade of the twentieth century, there were a number of significant technological developments that were destined to have a great impact on our civilization. At the turn of the twentieth century, inventors and engineers were engaged frantically in attempts to achieve heavier-than-air flight. Success came in 1903 when Wilbur and Orville Wright flew their airplane on a journey that lasted 12 seconds and covered a distance of 120 feet (18) (see Figure 1.9.). Since that initial flight, air transportation has grown to dominate long distance public carrier transport, accounting in 1998 for 91 percent of intercity public passenger-miles of travel in the United States (19). Today, commercial airliners routinely achieve travel speeds of 550 miles per hour, and transoceanic air travel by supersonic aircraft has been achieved at speeds up to 1450 miles per hour (18). More than 3000 airports have been built in the United States to accommodate air travel, including approximately 2200 general aviation airports that serve smaller private airplanes. The busiest airport in 1999, Atlanta Hartsfield, accommodated more than 78 million arriving and departing passengers.

A variety of "horseless carriages" had been devised by 1900, and by 1904, motor vehicles were being built in considerable numbers. Henry Ford contributed greatly to the development and popularity of automobiles by intro-

Figure 1.9   *The Wright brothers' first flight. (Courtesy of the Library of Congress.)*

ducing modern mass production and affordable vehicle costs. By the end of the twentieth century, nearly 9 of every 10 households in the country had a motor vehicle available. More than one-half of the U.S. households had two or more motor vehicles available for use. A 3.8-million-mile highway system has been developed to accommodate motor vehicle travel. The most remarkable component of this road network is the 45,500-mile Interstate Highway System, which was built at a cost of over $100 billion. That system, which was initiated in 1956, accommodates about 23 percent of all vehicular mileage of travel.

In the early 1900s, engineers and scientists introduced several advances in the treatment of water and sewage, including (20):

Rapid sand filters in reinforced concrete tanks were introduced in New Jersey.

Karl Imhoff demonstrated a large-scale sludge settling and digestion tank that replaced septic tank usage except for small installations.

Liquid chlorine was first used as a water disinfectant in Fort Meyer, Virginia.

The success of these and other pioneering advancements in environmental engineering is demonstrated by the decline in annual deaths by typhoid fever from about 10,000 in 1906 to approximately 200 twenty years later (20). See Figure 1.10.

The first giant construction project to be completed in modern times was the Panama Canal, which opened in 1914. The canal is about 50 miles in length. It has three sets of locks, each of which has a length of 1000 feet, a width of 110 feet, and a depth of approximately 70 feet. Before it opened, a ship sailing from New York to San Francisco had to travel more than 13,000 miles around the tip of South America. The canal shortened that journey to about 5200 miles.

Remarkable progress has been achieved in this century in the construction of innumerable bridges and buildings. Illustrations of the achievements in structural design and construction include:

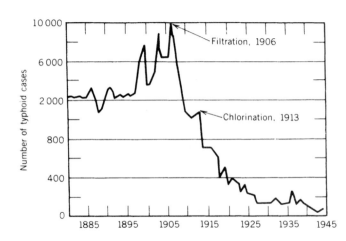

Figure 1.10   *Incidence of typhoid fever in Philadelphia, 1880–1945, showing effects of filtration and chlorination. (Source:* Civil Engineering, *American Society of Civil Engineers, October 1977.) Reproduced by permission of ASCE.*

1931   The Empire State Building, New York City, with a height of 1250 feet. At the time of its construction, it was the world's tallest building by 20 stories.

1931   The George Washington Bridge, New York City, with a length of 3500 feet. When it opened, its span nearly doubled the prior record (see Figure 1.11).

1974   The Sears Tower, Chicago, Illinois, with a height of 1450 feet.

Other twentieth century engineering achievements focused on water resources. One example of this progress is the Hoover Dam, which was completed in 1936. At the time of its construction, this pioneering concrete dam with a height of 726 feet was the world's highest. Another example of progress in water resources management was the remarkable flood control, navigation, and power projects of the Tennessee Valley Authority (TVA). Created in 1933, the TVA brought to the Tennessee Valley flood control, cheap power, and industrial growth.

Shortly after World War II, design and feasibility studies were made on the generation of electrical energy by nuclear means. The first nuclear power generating station was placed in operation in 1967 (*1*). Nuclear power had become economically competitive with fossil fuel power, and by 1998, 104 nuclear units were generating 674 billion kilowatt hours of electricity in the United States, accounting for 21 percent of the nation's energy production (*21*).

Typically, in a commercial nuclear power generating station, heat is generated by the fission of a nuclear material such as uranium 235. The heat is removed by a steam generator, and the steam is used to drive a turbine and an alternator that generates electricity. Two major challenges have faced the designers of nuclear power stations: (1) providing appropriate safeguards (e.g., adequate shielding, closed-cycle cooling systems) against radioactive emissions; and (2) devising a protective containment structure to limit the effects of an explosion. Figure 1.12 illustrates a modern nuclear power generating station.

The twentieth century has been characterized by unparalleled technological development and change. The quickening pace of discovery is, perhaps, most

Figure 1.11   *The George Washington Bridge. (Courtesy of the Port Authority of New York and New Jersey.)*

Figure 1.12   *Consolidated Edison's Indian Point Nuclear Power Plant. (Courtesy of Consolidated Edison.)*

apparent in the field of electronics. In this century, the primitive transmission of signals has been replaced by modern communications networks with massive switching systems using electronic components (*1*). Since the invention of the transistor in 1947, semiconductor devices have in large measure replaced vacuum tubes as amplifying devices for electronic signals. The transistor and semiconductor diode have led to great reductions in the size of electronic equipment. The advent of inexpensive integrated circuits, mass produced on tiny silicon chips, has brought revolutionary changes in electronic design (see Figure 1.13). Along with miniaturization, such devices have provided reliable and rapid transmission of signals through circuits and led to the development of faster switching circuits and digital computers (*1, 14*).

Figure 1.13   *64-kB random access memory held in fingertips. (Courtesy of IBM Corporation.)*

Because of space limitations, we have only been able to briefly describe a few of the extraordinary achievements of engineers during the twentieth century. It is hoped that the examples described will convey to the reader some of the excitement and challenges associated with an engineering career. Looking to the future, engineers will face a host of complex problems of far-reaching consequence, including:

1. Discovery, development and utilization of alternative sources of energy to replace the world's dwindling supplies of coal and petroleum.

2. Development of ways to maintain and rehabilitate the nation's vast deteriorating public works infrastructure.

3. Further development of microcomputer technology and extension of its applications.

4. Development of technology to further increase agricultural productivity to cope with growing world population and hunger.

5. Design of structures that are more resistant to earthquakes, storms, and other ravages of nature.

6. Development of better ways to manage the disposal of hazardous wastes, including the radioactive wastes that accompany the production of nuclear power.

7. Exploration of interplanetary space and discovery of applications of space research to military and peaceful uses.

REFERENCES

1. GREGORY, MALCOLM S., *History and Development of Engineering*, Longman Group Limited, London, 1971.

2. FINCH, JAMES KIP, *The Story of Engineering*, Anchor Books, Doubleday and Company, Inc., Garden City, NY, 1960.

3. DE CAMP, L. SPRAGUE, *The Ancient Engineers*, Doubleday and Company, Inc., Garden City, NY, 1963.

4. FINCH, J. KIP, "Master Builders of Mesopotamia," *Civil Engineering*, American Society of Civil Engineers, New York, April, 1957.

5. HATHAWAY, GAIL A., "Dams—Their Effect on Some Ancient Civilizations," *Civil Engineering*, American Society of Civil Engineers, New York, January 1958.

6. UPTON, NEIL, *An Illustrated History of Civil Engineering*, William Heinemann, Ltd., London, 1975.

7. BEAKLEY, GEORGE C., AND H. W. LEACH, *Engineering: An Introduction to a Creative Profession*, 4th Edition, Macmillan Publishing Company, New York, 1982.

8. WHITE, J. E. MANCHIP, *Ancient Egypt: Its Culture and History*, Dover Publications, Inc., New York, 1970.

9. FINCH, J. K., "The Greek Architekton—Part 1," *Civil Engineering*, American Society of Civil Engineers, New York, May 1957.

10. FINCH, J. K., "The Greek Architekton—Part 2," *Civil Engineering*, American Society of Civil Engineers, New York, June 1957.

11. PAYNE, ROBERT, *Ancient Rome,* American Heritage Press, New York, 1970.

12. FINCH, J. K., "Roman Builders of the Republic—Part 1," *Civil Engineering,* American Society of Civil Engineers, New York, August 1957.

13. FINCH, J. K., "The Architectus of the Roman Empire—Part 2," *Civil Engineering,* American Society of Civil Engineers, New York, November 1957.

14. GRUN, BERNARD, *The Timetables of History,* A Touchtone Book, Simon and Schuster, New York, 1982.

15. SMITH, RALPH J., BLAINE R. BUTLER, AND WILLIAM K. LEBOLD, *Engineering as a Career,* 4th Edition, McGraw-Hill Book Company, New York, 1983.

16. LOBLEY, DOUGLAS, *Ships Through the Ages,* Octopus Books Limited, London, 1972.

17. JENSEN, OLIVER, *The American Heritage History of Railroads in America,* American Heritage Publishing Company, Inc., New York, 1975.

18. WRIGHT, PAUL H., NORMAN ASHFORD, AND ROBERT STAMMER, JR., *Transportation Engineering: Planning and Design,* John Wiley & Sons, Inc., New York, 1998.

19. *Transportation in America,* 17th Edition, Eno Transportation Foundation, Inc., Washington, DC, 1999.

20. "Milestones in U.S. Civil Engineering," *Civil Engineering,* American Society of Civil Engineers, New York, October 1977.

21. *Statistical Abstract of the United States 2000,* 120th Edition, U.S. Department of Commerce, Bureau of the Census, 2000.

EXERCISES

1.1 Prepare a report on the contributions of the Chinese to the development of engineering.

1.2 In your opinion, what is the single most significant contribution that engineers have made for the betterment of mankind? Prepare a brief report supporting your opinion.

1.3 Prepare a chart depicting significant developments in science and engineering by major civilizations as a function of time.

1.4 Make a scaled drawing of the Pyramid of Cheops. Estimate the quantity of stone required for that pyramid. Express your answer in cubic yards, cubic meters, and in metric tons.

1.5 List the most significant scientific or engineering achievements since A.D. 1300.

1.6 What are the principal reasons for the meager advancement in technology during the Middle Ages?

1.7 Write a short biography on one of the following scientists or engineers:
    a. Appius Claudius.
    b. Leonardo da Vinci.
    c. Galileo.
    d. Sir Isaac Newton.
    e. Thomas A. Edison.

1.8 Prepare a report on the development of sources of power since the dawn of civilization to the present time. Discuss the significance of these developments on people's physical and material well-being.

An Exemplary Engineering Achievement

The 800-mile Alaska Pipeline carries vital oil under and over some of the most hostile terrain in the world. The 48-inch-diameter steel line burrows through mountains, across rivers and lakes, and over permanently frozen ground on stilts. (Courtesy of the American Council of Engineering Companies.)

CHAPTER TWO

DEFINITION OF ENGINEERING

2.1 ENGINEERING

The Accreditation Board for Engineering and Technology (ABET) defines engineering as "the profession in which a knowledge of the mathematical and natural sciences gained by study, experience, and practice is applied with judgment to develop ways to utilize, economically, the materials and forces of nature for the benefit of mankind." (1)

Embodied in that definition are certain fundamental elements that describe the essence of engineering. Engineering is a profession. Like law, medicine, architecture, teaching, and the ministry, it aspires to high standards of conduct and recognizes responsibilities to clients, peers, and to society as a whole. It is based on a special body of knowledge, and its members attain professional status through well-defined avenues of education and training.

Engineering is based on a knowledge of mathematical and natural sciences.

Both the engineer and scientist are thoroughly educated in the mathematical and natural sciences, but the scientist primarily uses this knowledge to acquire new knowledge, whereas the engineer applies the knowledge to design and develop usable devices, structures and processes. In other words, the scientist seeks to know, the engineer aims to do. (2)

In the words of Theodore von Kármán (3): "Scientists explore what is; engineers create what had not been."

Glegg (4) contrasted the function of scientists and engineers as follows:

21

It seems fashionable to glamorize the position of the scientist and to imply that no other occupation is so rewarding in human, if not material, values. I do not think that this is true for several reasons. For instance, the engineer has the much wider horizon of possibilities. A scientist is lucky if he makes one real creative addition to human knowledge in his whole life, and may never do so.

An engineer has, by comparison, almost limitless opportunities. He can, and frequently does, create dozens of original designs and has the satisfaction of seeing them become working realities. He is a creative artist in a sense never known by the pure scientist. An engineer can make something. He creates by arranging in patterns the discoveries of science past and present, patterns designed to fit the ever more intricate world of industry. His material is profuse, his problems fascinating, and everything hinges on personal ability.

Engineering is viewed as an art as well as a science. It is perceived to embody a system of principles, methods, and skills that cannot be learned simply by study. It must be learned, at least in part, by experience and professional practice.

The engineer's knowledge must be tempered with professional judgment. Solutions to engineering problems must satisfy conflicting requirements, and the preferred optimum solution does not always result from a clear-cut application of scientific principles or formulas. The engineer must weigh conflicting constraints and make judgments based on knowledge and experience, seeking a best or optimum solution.

In seeking answers to problems, engineers utilize the materials and forces of nature. There is an almost unlimited list of materials, both natural and manufactured, that engineers can utilize to fashion their designs. They select appropriate materials on the basis of availability, cost, and physical properties (weight, strength, durability, elasticity, and so forth).

The engineer can access a much smaller list of sources of energy: petroleum, coal, gas, nuclear fission, hydroelectric power, sunlight, and wind. These sources vary widely in availability, cost, safety, and technological complexity.

Engineers recognize that the earth's supply of materials and energy is not limitless, and they must be concerned not only with utilization of these resources but also with their conservation. This involves recycling and reuse of existing materials, rehabilitation instead of replacement of old facilities, and the creative substitution of an abundant material for one that is in scarce supply. It also involves seeking solutions that are energy efficient and exploring for new sources of energy to replace those that are being depleted.

Engineers seek solutions that are economical. This implies that the benefits of their solutions must exceed the costs. It further means that they must exercise care in the management of money, time, materials, and other resources.

A. M. Wellington (5) emphasized this point in 1887 with this whimsical definition of engineering:

It would be well if engineering were less generally thought of ... as the art of constructing. In a certain important sense it is the art of not constructing ... of doing that well with one dollar which any bungler can do with two after a fashion.

Up until the late 1960s, economics was the principal constraint on the planning and building of engineering works. There was little concern about harmful environmental effects that accompanied the construction of airports, highways, buildings, and other facilities. A dramatic turnabout in public and official concern about the environmental impact of technological achievements culminated in the passage of the National Environmental Policy Act of 1969. This legislation requires that an environmental impact statement be prepared for federally funded projects that might cause environmental harm. Its passage reflected greater awareness of the need for engineers to weigh the negative effects of their projects as well as the benefits. Engineering must be practiced with appropriate awareness and concern for the possible harmful impacts of technology on people and the environment.

Ultimately, all of the engineer's work must benefit mankind. Recognition of this fact is demonstrated by the enactment of professional engineering registration laws in the various states for the purpose: "to safeguard life, health and property, and to promote the public welfare." Engineers must objectively evaluate their designs to insure that the positive effects exceed any adverse effects and that, on balance, their solutions are for the public benefit.

2.2 ENGINEERING SUPPORT PERSONNEL

Although it is possible for engineers to work alone, more commonly they work with a group of support personnel. The engineer and the support personnel comprise the engineering team, and the roles of each specialty group are often described in terms of an occupational spectrum. This spectrum includes the engineer, engineering technologists, engineering technicians, and craftsmen, arranged vertically as Table 2.1 illustrates.

At the top of the spectrum is the engineer who serves as innovator, designer, decision maker, and leader of the engineering team. Next is the engineering technologist, who assists the engineer in the planning, construction, and operation of engineering facilities. Typical activities for technologists include technical sales, construction supervision, routine product development, and coordination of work force, equipment, and materials. The engineering technologist's post-secondary education consists of a four-year program of study culminating in a Bachelor of Engineering Technology degree. The educational emphasis of the technologist's program of study is less theoretical and less mathematical than that of an engineer, but is more hardware and process oriented (6).

Engineering technicians are specialists in methodology devoted to the accomplishment of practical objectives. Typical activities of technicians

TABLE 2.1   *The Engineering Team*

Specialist	Typical Activities
Engineer	Conceptual design
	Research
	Project planning
	Product innovation
	System development
	Supervision of technologists, technicians, and craftsmen
Technologist	Routine product development
	Construction supervision
	Technical sales
	Hardware design and development
	Coordination of work force, materials, and equipment
	Supervision of technicians and craftsmen
Technician	Drafting
	Estimating
	Field inspections
	Data collection
	Surveying
	Technical writing
Craftsman	Uses hand and power tools to service, maintain, and operate machines or products useful to the engineering team

include drafting, surveying, estimating, collecting data, and performing field inspections on construction projects. Technicians normally have been trained in a two-year program in engineering technology leading to an associate degree.

Craftsmen are skilled workers who produce the materials and products or facilities specified by the design. Such specialists include electricians, carpenters, welders, machinists, and model builders. Craftsmen normally acquire their skills by on-the-job training; their education typically does not extend beyond high school.

It should be noted that the role of the engineering technologist in the occupational spectrum is not well defined. That occupation emerged in the early 1970s as two-year educational programs for technicians were expanded to four-year programs leading to a baccalaureate degree. Although the educational distinction between technologists and technicians is clear, the functions often overlap. The functional differences between technologists and engineers are likewise blurred. Kemper (7) explains:

> Technologists are supposed to work in that part of the engineering spectrum which lies between the engineer and the technician, in the routine aspects of product development, manufacturing planning, construction supervision, or technical sales. However, as is often the case, individual

*human talents may prove to be more important than the intentions of edu-
cational programs, and it has been observed that many persons educated
as technologists have actually emerged in industry functioning as engineers. Since their educations bear strong resemblances to those of engineers, such a development should not be especially surprising.*

ENGINEERING FIELDS OF SPECIALIZATION

Engineering is a diverse profession. It is composed of several major branches
or fields of specialization and dozens of minor branches. Engineers have created these branches in response to an ever-widening base of technological
knowledge. In the following paragraphs, some of the more prominent branches
of engineering are characterized. These are taken up in general order of
decreasing size of the discipline. It should be remembered that there is considerable overlap among the various specialties. It is not uncommon for an
engineer to practice more than one specialty within a major branch during the
course of his or her career.

2.3   ELECTRICAL ENGINEERING

The largest of all engineering branches, electrical engineering is concerned
with electrical devices, currents, and systems. Electrical engineers work with
equipment ranging from heavy power generators to tiny computer chips. Their
work contributes to almost every sector of society: electrical appliances for
homes, electronic displays for business, lasers for industry, and satellite systems for government and businesses.

Electrical engineers usually work in one of six specialty areas:

1. Power generation and transmission.
2. Electronics.
3. Communications systems.
4. Instrumentation and measurement.
5. Automatic controls.
6. Computers.

Electrical engineers are responsible for the generation, transmission, and
distribution of electric power. They locate hydroelectric, steam, diesel engine,
and nuclear power plants, and specify the engines, generators, and auxiliary
equipment for these plants. These engineers have contributed to the development of electric-generating stations in the United States that have a capacity of
about 700 million kilowatts and generate over 3 trillion kilowatt-hours of
power annually.

One of the most vibrant specialties in electrical engineering is the field of electronics. Generally speaking, this field deals with the emission, behavior, and effects of electrons. Electronics engineers design efficient circuits using a variety of electric elements that can produce, amplify, detect, or rectify electrical signals.

Electronics has applications in communications, power, transportation, medicine, and many other fields. With the advent of transistors, semiconductor diodes, integrated circuits, and lasers, electronic technology has changed dramatically in recent years. These and other advances provide even greater opportunities for rewarding work for electrical engineers in the field of electronics.

Electrical engineers have made and continue to make significant contributions to the field of communications. They use their knowledge of wave propagation, electromagnetic theory, and electronic principles to design radio, telephone, television, and satellite communication systems. Approximately 7 percent of electrical engineers work in the communications specialty.

Another small but important specialty area in electrical engineering is instrumentation and measurement. Engineers in this specialty are concerned with the use of electronics to make measurements needed for research, development, and operation. They have devised electronic instruments to measure a wide variety of properties and quantities such as temperature, speed, pressure, and flow rate. These instruments have broad applications in business and industry and contribute in many ways to public health and safety.

Increasingly, electronic engineers are employing the concept of feedback control to automatic operations and processes. Such systems compare a measured quantity (e.g., temperature, pressure, etc.) to a desired standard and automatically make appropriate adjustments to the mechanism or system to minimize any difference between the measured and the desired quantity or property.

Electrical engineers apply electrical and mechanical principles to design and construct electronic computers. They perform research in computer circuitry, develop new methods of data processing and storage, and seek new ways to apply computers to various types of data-processing problems.

As Table 2.2 illustrates, computer engineering has grown to be one of the largest branches in engineering. It is discussed more fully in the following section.

2.4   COMPUTER ENGINEERING (8)

Computer engineering is the field of engineering responsible for the design and implementation of digital systems and the integration of computer technology into an increasing number of systems and applications. It is a relatively new and rapidly growing engineering discipline with extraordinary challenges and opportunities. Since the invention of the transistor in 1947, technological advances in computer engineering have been astounding. Today, it is possible to integrate more than 100 million transistors in a single integrated circuit chip. At the same time, the switching speed of transistors has increased more than 10,000 fold, and it is now possible to design chips that operate at more than one billion operations per second. This rapid improvement in computer technology has challenged computer engineers: (1) to invent hardware and software design, and the tools to develop these integrated circuit chips and (2) to imagine, design, and verify systems containing these chips.

Rapid advances in computer technology, resulting in ever smaller, less costly, high-performance computers, have resulted in a vast number of applications containing embedded computers as elements. These range from highly complex communications systems to biomedical imaging devices, sophisticated consumer products, and household appliances.

BIOENGINEERING

Bioengineering is an interdisciplinary field that applies engineering principles to the study of biological processes. The purpose of bioengineering research is to develop new and better physical and mathematical concepts and techniques that address problems in medicine and biology. Bioengineering is being applied to a wide variety of problems, including the design and development of new medical devices such as assistive devices for people with spinal cord injuries and sensory aids for people with poor vision. Recent bioengineering research has included the development of ultrasonic and magnetic resonance instrumentation, which produce better imaging for medical diagnoses and treatment (9).

2.5   MECHANICAL ENGINEERING

One of the oldest and broadest areas of engineering activity, mechanical engineering, is concerned with machinery, power, and manufacturing or production methods. Mechanical engineers design and manufacture machine tools—the machines that make machines—and machinery and equipment for all branches of industry. For example, they design turbines; printing presses; earth-moving machinery; food processors; air conditioning and refrigeration systems; artificial hearts and limbs; and engines for aircraft, diesel locomotives, automobiles and trucks, and public transportation vehicles. Their machines move and lift loads, transport people and goods, and produce energy and convert it to other forms.

In the power specialty, mechanical engineers are involved in the design, production, and operation of hydraulic turbines for driving electric generators and of boilers, engines, turbines, and pumps for the development of steam power. They design and operate power plants and concern themselves with the economical combustion of fuels, the conversion of heat energy into mechanical power, and the use of that power to perform useful work.

In heating, ventilation, and air conditioning, mechanical engineers provide controlled conditions of temperature and humidity in homes, offices, commercial buildings, and industrial plants. They develop equipment and systems needed for the refrigeration of foods and the operation of cold storage warehouses and ice manufacturing plants.

Mechanical engineers work closely with industrial engineers and managers in many fields of manufacturing, designing imaginative machinery and systems that yield great economies in production.

Mechanical engineers may also be found working in marine engineering, designing machinery for boats, naval vessels, and merchant ships; in the automotive industry designing and manufacturing automobiles, trucks, and buses; and in the aerospace industry working in the design of new aircraft and spacecraft.

Mechanical engineering is a broad field that deals with diverse engineering problems. Its members can often be found in interdisciplinary activities such as automation, computer technology, and microelectromechanical systems (MEMS).

MICROELECTROMECHANICAL SYSTEMS (MEMS)

MEMS is an emerging interdisciplinary discipline that involves electrical engineering, mechanical engineering, and in some cases, bioengineering. MEMS stands for microelectromechanical systems. MEMS are physically small systems that have both electrical and mechanical components. Examples of such devices include inkjet-printer cartridges, accelerometers that deploy automobile airbags, and miniature robots. These systems typically have sensors that, because of their small physical size, can measure the environment without significantly modifying it. Examples of microsensors include devices that can measure pressure, acceleration, strain, temperature, vibration, proximity, sound, and many others. MEMS devices commonly include microactuators which interact with their environment. Microactuators are useful because the amount of work they perform on the environment is small; they can therefore be very precise. MEMS can be placed in small spaces, such as inside automobile engines, small appliances, and living organisms, to measure and affect their environment (10).

2.6 CIVIL ENGINEERING

Civil engineering affects many of our daily activities: the buildings we live in and work in, the transportation facilities we use, the water we drink, and the drainage and sewerage systems that are necessary to our health and well-being (see Figure 2.1). Civil engineers:

• Measure and map the earth's surface.

- Design and supervise the construction of bridges, tunnels, large buildings, dams, and coastal structures.
- Plan, lay out, construct, and maintain railroads, highways, and airports.
- Devise systems for the control and efficient flow of traffic.
- Plan and build river regulation and flood control projects.
- Provide plants and systems for water supply and sewage and refuse disposal.

Civil is a very broad branch of engineering, and it includes at least seven major specialized areas of practice:

1. Structural engineering.
2. Construction engineering and management.
3. Transportation engineering.
4. Geotechnical engineering.
5. Hydraulic and water resources engineering.
6. Environmental engineering.
7. Geodetic engineering.

The largest specialty within civil engineering, structural engineering, is concerned with the design of large buildings, bridges, tanks, towers, dams, and other large structures. These engineers design and select appropriate structural

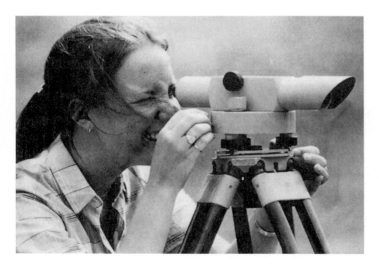

Figure 2.1 *Geodetic engineering, a branch of civil engineering, involves measuring and mapping the earth's surface. (Courtesy of Institute Communications and Public Affairs, Georgia Institute of Technology.)*

components (e.g., beams, columns, and slabs) and systems to provide adequate strength, stability, and durability.

A large fraction of civil engineers work in the construction industry, building the facilities that other engineers and architects design. The task of construction engineers is to utilize and manage the resources of construction (the vehicles, equipment, machines, materials, and skilled workers) to produce with timeliness and efficiency the structure or facility envisioned by the designer.

Transportation engineers are concerned with the planning and layout of highways, airports, harbors and ports, and mass transportation systems. They plan and design transportation terminals and devise and operate systems for the control of vehicular traffic.

Geotechnical engineers are concerned with the structural behavior of soil and rock. They analyze earth support systems and design foundations, earth walls, and highway and airport pavements.

Hydraulic and water resources engineers are concerned with the flow of water through ditches, conduits, canals, dams, and estuaries. They use their special knowledge of fluid mechanics to design dams, irrigation systems, municipal water works, and drainage and erosion control systems.

Environmental engineers are concerned with solid waste management, air and water pollution, and control of pesticides and radiological hazards. They design and oversee the operation of water treatment and sewage treatment plants and measure and monitor pollutants in the air, on land, and in lakes and streams.

Geodetic engineers measure and map the earth's surface. They locate precisely property and building lines and survey the locations, elevations, and alignment of engineering projects.

Civil engineers work with construction companies, manufacturing companies, power companies, and with consulting engineering firms. Many opportunities for civil engineering employment exist in city, county, and state engineering departments and in the various agencies of the federal government.

2.7   CHEMICAL ENGINEERING

Chemical engineering involves the application of chemistry, physics, and engineering to the design and operation of plants for the production of materials that undergo chemical changes during their manufacture (*11*). Such materials include various chemicals, such as paints, lubricants, fertilizers, pharmaceuticals and cosmetics, petroleum products, foods, metals, plastics, ceramics, and glass.

In these and other industries, chemical engineers are responsible for creating systems for producing large quantities of materials that chemists make in small quantities in the laboratory. Chemical engineers select appropriate processes and arrange them in proper sequence to produce the desired product. These include:

1.   Heat transfer processes.
2.   Mass transfer processes such as absorption, humidification, and drying.

3. Processes that involve mechanical action such as mixing, crushing, grinding, sizing, and filtering.

4. Processes that involve chemical reaction, including chlorination, polymerization, oxidation, and reduction (*6*).

Chemical engineers are in demand in practically all types of manufacturing. Looking to the future, a vigorous and expanding demand for chemical engineers is expected as manufacturers continue to develop new products in response to people's pursuit of better health and a higher standard of living. Chemical engineers can also be expected to play a major role in finding solutions to some of mankind's most challenging problems, for example, environmental pollution, depletion of energy supplies, and world overpopulation and hunger.

2.8   INDUSTRIAL ENGINEERING

Industrial engineers are concerned with the design, improvement, and installation of integrated systems of people, materials, and energy in the production of either goods or services (*7, 12*). They engineer processes and systems that improve quality and productivity (*13*). They are primarily interested in problems that involve economy in the use of money, materials, time, human effort, and energy (*11*). They are more concerned with the "big picture" of industrial management and production than with the detailed development of processes (*3*).

Most of the activities of industrial engineers fall into one of four categories:

- Those related to plant layout.
- Those designed to increase worker productivity.
- Those designed to control the quality of products.
- Those designed to reduce and control costs.

Plant layout involves determining the floor space needed for each production component—workers, equipment, and materials handling and storage—and arranging and sequencing the various operations to insure a safe, smooth, and efficient operation.

Industrial engineers perform time and motion studies of workers, set standards of work performance, and propose new and improved work methods to increase productivity. They employ quality control techniques to reduce waste and customer complaints. They use statistical procedures to establish reasonable tolerances in quality and develop procedures for making routine checks of product quality. In all of their work, industrial engineers must carefully monitor costs of production and seek ways to reduce costs without compromising product quality.

Although most industrial engineers are employed by manufacturing industries, they may also be found working in other settings such as in hospitals; airlines; railroads; retail businesses; and municipal, state, and federal government agencies.

2.9   AEROSPACE ENGINEERING

Aerospace engineering is concerned with all aspects of vehicular flight at all speeds and altitudes. It covers all phases of research, design, and development in this broad area that includes hovercraft designed to operate a few feet above land and water, helicopters that hover and maneuver in all directions, a variety of conventional airplanes, and complex spacecraft for orbiting the earth and exploring the solar system. The term *aeronautical engineering* is used to refer to the engineering of atmospheric flight, while *astronautical engineering* deals with space flight.

Aerospace engineers commonly work in one of several specialty areas such as aerodynamics, structural design, propulsion systems, and guidance and control.

Aerodynamics involves the efficient design of external surfaces of aerospace vehicles. Aerodynamics engineers supervise the performance of wind tunnel tests; measure and predict the forces of lift and drag; and develop and test theories of flight performance, stability, and control.

In aerospace engineering, structural designers seek to design and build aircraft systems that can be operated economically. This usually translates into maximizing the vehicle strength-to-weight ratio. They also study the response of aircraft structures to mechanical vibrations and other dynamic forces and design structures capable of withstanding these forces.

Aerospace engineers develop and refine propulsion systems for aircraft and spacecraft. The thrust for all of the many propulsion systems for aerospace craft is produced by accelerating a fluid rearward. In the case of the turbojet, burning fuel produces hot gas that is expanded further by a jet nozzle, providing the thrust. In other systems such as helicopters and small, low-speed aircraft, the propulsion is provided by a propeller driven by an engine that develops its power by compressing, burning, and expanding its fuel.

In the guidance and control specialty, engineers develop instruments for conventional aircraft that provide information directly to a pilot or automatically navigate, maneuver, or control the aircraft.

These specialists also develop systems that guide and control the trajectories of missiles. Such systems track the missile by radar or on-board equipment, compute and communicate the necessary corrections, and correct precisely the direction and velocity by vernier rockets (6).

Aerospace engineering offers one of the most exciting and challenging fields of activity for those who choose engineering as a career.

2.10   MATERIALS ENGINEERING

The term *materials engineering* refers in a general way to a group of engineering specialties that are concerned with the development, production, fabrication, and use of materials in specific technologies. Some of these specialties are:

Metallurgical engineering, which is concerned with the production of metals from ores and the development of metallic alloys.

Mining engineering, which encompasses the exploration, location, development, and operation of mines for extracting coal, metallic ores such as copper and zinc, and other minerals.

Petroleum engineering, which is concerned with the exploration, extraction, storage, and transportation of crude petroleum and natural gas.

Plastics engineering, which involves the formulation, manufacture, and applications of materials (e.g., polymers) that permanently deform under stress.

Ceramic engineering, which deals with products manufactured or used at high temperatures (above 1000°F) and the physical and chemical processes used in their manufacture.

Population growth, industrialization, and depletion of the world's natural resources should contribute to a strong and sustained future demand for materials engineers.

2.11   OTHER BRANCHES OF ENGINEERING

In the preceding paragraphs, some of the more prominent branches of engineering have been described. There are many more engineering specialties, but space limitations preclude a detailed description of these disciplines. Brief descriptions of some of these specialties follow.

- *Architectural engineers* work closely with architects to plan, design, and build large structures.

- *Oceanographic engineers* work with scientists to explore and study the oceans and to develop ways to utilize them for human benefit.

- *Operations researchers and systems engineers* apply advanced mathematical and computer-based techniques such as linear programming, queuing theory, and simulation to quantitatively predict the behavior of large systems.

- *Nuclear engineers* apply scientific and engineering principles to the design, development, and use of nuclear power systems.

- *Textile engineers* are concerned with the planning, design, and operation of manufacturing plants in the textiles industry.

- *Agricultural engineers* apply engineering principles, machines, materials, and energy to the production and processing of food products.

Table 2.2 shows the numbers of engineers employed in the various fields of engineering. Table 2.3 gives the percentages of employed engineers by sector of employment for six major engineering branches.

TABLE 2.2   *Employed Engineers by Field, 1998*

Field	Employment
Aerospace engineers	53,035
Chemical engineers	48,363
Civil engineers	195,028
Computer engineers	299,308
Electrical/Electronic engineers	356,954
Industrial engineers	126,303
Materials engineers	19,654
Mechanical engineers	219,654
Mining engineers	4,444
Nuclear engineers	11,694
Petroleum engineers	12,061
All other engineers	414,611

Source: *Engineers,* Vol. 6, No. 1, Engineering Workforce Commission of the American Association of Engineering Societies, Washington, DC, Spring, 2000.

TABLE 2.3   *Percentages of Employed Engineers by Major Field and Sector of Employment*

Sector of Employment	Aeronautical/ Astronautical	Chemical	Civil	Electrical/ Electronic	Industrial	Mechanical
Industry	63.3	74.0	48.9	69.6	76.7	75.8
Self-employed	11.1	12.7	14.4	12.2	11.5	11.4
Educational institutions	3.5	5.0	3.0	4.9	3.6	3.9
Nonprofit organizations	2.4	1.7	0.5	1.5	1.7	1.1
Federal government	14.7	4.6	9.3	9.3	4.6	6.1
Military	4.3	0.3	1.3	0.9	0.3	0.4
State/local/ other government	0.4	1.3	22.1	1.1	1.4	0.9
Other	0.3	0.4	0.5	0.5	0.2	0.4
Total	100.0	100.0	100.0	100.0	100.0	100.0

Source: *U.S. Scientists and Engineers: 1988*, Surveys of Science Resources Series, Selected Statistical Tables, National Science Foundation, Washington, DC.

2.12   FUNCTIONS OF ENGINEERING

Within a given engineering field of specialization, there is a wide range of functions or activities in which engineers may be involved (*8*). Engineers can be involved in some combination of these functions, and, conceivably, could perform all of them over the course of a career. These functions include: research, development, design, production, construction, operations, sales, and management.

1. *Research* involves seeking new knowledge or a better understanding of the significance and relationship of facts already known.
2. *Development* involves making the discoveries and results of research available in the form of useful products, methods, or processes.
3. *Design* is the process of converting concepts and information into detailed plans and specifications from which a finished product or facility can be manufactured or constructed.
4. *Production* is the industrial process by which products or articles are manufactured from raw materials.
5. *Construction* is the process of translating designs and materials into structures and facilities such as buildings, highways, and power and communication facilities.
6. *Operations* in engineering means the application of engineering principles or the performance of practical work. In manufacturing, operations involve procuring supplies, maintaining plant, and directing personnel. Engineers are prominently involved in the operations of utility companies, railroads, communications companies, and traffic control systems for large cities.
7. *Sales* in technological industries often requires the services of trained engineers to recommend the machines, tools, parts, or services to best serve the customers' needs.
8. *Management* positions in many industries are occupied by engineers. They are responsible for the solution of problems of policy, finance, organization, public relations, and sales. They also have the responsibility for the selection and supervision of personnel and the coordination of research, development, production, and all other departments.

Table 2.4 shows the percentages of employed engineers by primary work activity for six major fields of engineering.

CAREER PATHS FOR ENGINEERS (14)

There are at least seven career options for graduating engineering students:

1. The corporate ladder.
2. The independent entrepreneur.
3. The military.
4. Engineering and social service abroad.
5. The professor-engineer.

TABLE 2.4 *Percentages of Employed Engineers by Major Field and Primary Work Activity*

Primary Work Activity	Aeronautical/ Astronautical	Chemical	Civil	Electrical/ Electronic	Industrial	Mechanical
Basic research	1.6	1.0	0.3	0.8	0.2	0.6
Applied research	7.7	4.9	1.8	4.5	0.8	3.2
Development	37.1	28.7	13.2	37.9	17.9	39.0
Management of research and development	17.5	12.3	3.2	13.3	5.9	10.4
Other management/ administration	9.0	21.7	33.6	14.6	28.2	19.8
Teaching	2.7	2.3	1.9	2.5	2.6	1.9
Consulting	2.6	4.9	17.0	4.0	5.1	4.5
Production/ inspection	10.8	16.4	21.9	15.3	27.3	14.9
Reporting, statistical work, computing	5.8	3.5	4.4	4.2	7.6	2.8
Sales	1.4	3.4	1.4	1.9	3.4	2.2
Other	3.8	0.9	1.3	1.0	1.0	0.7
Total	100.0	100.0	100.0	100.0	100.0	100.0

Source: U.S. Scientists and Engineers: 1988, Surveys of Science Resources Series, Selected Statistical Tables, National Science Foundation, Washington, DC.

6.   Graduate work outside of engineering.

7.   A mix of two or more of the first six options.

The author has drawn freely from Reference 14 in describing these career paths for engineers.

2.13   THE CORPORATE LADDER

The great majority of engineers are employed by private industrial or business organizations (see Table 2.3). Most of the jobs in engineering are with large corporations. Engineers who work for large companies typically have many career options. The possibilities include the practice of "hands-on" engineering, proposal writing, marketing of engineering services, and upper echelon management.

The immense breadth of corporate activity minimizes the career damage that might result from working in an inappropriate job. The engineer, for example, who finds that by the age of thirty he is bored with the laboratory can quietly move laterally, if he is inherently qualified, into management or sales. No other option available to the graduating engineers offers quite this degree of flexibility and potential for substantial, even radical, career change.

Furthermore, because of the depth and variety of corporate resources, it is possible for the exceptionally promising engineer to climb the corporate ladder while simultaneously working toward post-baccalaureate degrees. Many progressive companies are willing to provide formal university training for young engineers after they have demonstrated their competence and dedication to the firm. Other companies have developed contractual relationships with universities by which employees may take regular courses for university credit in the evenings or during time-off periods during the day. In addition, many corporations perform a broad and ongoing educational function by offering in-house training courses taught by the company's technical staff.

The young engineer achieving his or her baccalaureate degree must realize that there is truly no such thing as "business" and no such genetic entity as "the corporation." Companies, even companies producing and marketing highly similar products, differ as much or more than individual human beings differ.

Some companies project a relatively conservative image. They tend to promote their employees primarily on the basis of longevity with the firm, and they are more concerned with what the employee has learned in the company than with what he or she has learned in school.

To other companies, experience is not a crucial factor, because they are developing new products and new technologies at such a pace that long-term experience can have little value. State-of-the-art knowledge and the ability to apply it imaginatively are more important. In contrast to the experience-based company, such knowledge-based firms often are in a state of constant evolution, generating for their employees a great deal of excitement, as well as many ulcers.

It should be remembered that companies also differ in relatively minor but often personally crucial ways. In one company, the weekly cocktail party is an essential ingredient in the corporate continuum; in another, the public consumption of anything stronger than steam beer is frowned upon. In one company, social groups may be important; in another, outside activities, such as community service, are more valued. One company pays for spouses to go to conventions; another company sends nobody at all. Such wide variations in corporate personality, while confusing to the engineer evaluating the corporate ladder option, are indicative of one of the strengths of this career choice. There is, somewhere, a company for nearly everybody. No matter what your temperamental inclinations, no matter what your interests, no matter what your biases or prejudices, no matter what your preference in clothes and haircuts, there is at least one company—and usually many—where you will feel right at home and be able to work effectively. It is just a matter of finding it.

2.14   THE INDEPENDENT ENTREPRENEUR

Many graduating engineers prefer to work for themselves. Some become consultants, providing engineering services to individual clients and to public agencies. A good way to gain entrance into this activity is to work for three to five years in a corporation, a public agency, or for another, more experienced consultant. That experience will help to build the high level of individual responsibility that consulting engineering firms demand.

If the consulting route to individual entrepreneurship takes a modicum of courage and steadfast determination, then turning your knowledge and competence into capital, and launching a new company—perhaps even right out of college—takes a good deal more. Yet it is done, and done successfully, quite often. Becoming an independent is, without question, one of the most exciting possibilities the engineer has to contemplate. The ultimate goal is to be independent and autonomous, answering to no one but yourself and, of course, your clients.

2.15   EMPLOYMENT OPPORTUNITIES IN GOVERNMENT

Government employment for engineers is available in two ways: you can join the military or you can work as a civilian employee. Many believe that the superior alternative is to join one of the uniformed services such as the U.S. Navy's Civil Engineer Corps or the Army Corps of Engineers.

Because of the nature of the defense establishment, young engineers wearing the uniform have opportunities for immediate and intensive interfacing with ultra-high technologies and state-of-the-art equipment that generally are not present in even the most advanced regions of the private sector. Also, because of the nature of the military establishment, there is far less stress on age, experience, and seasoning than one often finds in the civilian corporation or company. Consequently, the just-out-of-college engineer can move upward and inward with a rapidity that is seldom seen in even the most progressive companies in the private sector.

Moreover, because the military goes about its job without reference to profit-and-loss statements, there is a marked inclination to send promising young engineer-officers back to the university campus for advanced degrees, both M.S. and Ph.D. Indeed, joining the Air Force, Navy, or Army and letting those organizations foot the bill for graduate education at front-rank schools is now a standard route for ambitious young engineers of limited means to follow.

Large numbers of civilian engineers are employed by agencies of federal, state, and local governments. The greatest opportunities for work in government exist for civil engineers.

Civilian engineering positions exist in numerous agencies of the federal government including the Federal Highway Administration, the Federal Aviation Administration, the U.S. Army Corps of Engineers, and the National Aeronautics and Space Administration (NASA), to name a few. Civilian engineers can be found performing research in harbor protection, designing and maintaining facilities on Air Force bases and in naval shipyards, and contributing to NASA's vast and exciting program to explore outer space.

At the state level, engineers are employed in large numbers by state highway agencies and may be found in agencies concerned with port operation, water resources management, and protection of the environment.

At the local level, engineers serve as directors of public works, manage water treatment plants, and oversee pollution control programs.

Engineering positions in government may provide satisfying and interesting work, with the added benefits of secure employment with liberal holidays and vacations and attractive programs of health and retirement.

2.16   ENGINEERING AND SOCIAL SERVICES ABROAD

The service impulse, the urge to improve the quality of life of those less fortunate than ourselves, has special relevance for the engineer. There is profound, bitter irony in the fact that in the Golden Age of Technology, uncounted millions of people nevertheless exist in ignorance and squalor, standing all their brief lives in the shadow of pestilence and death, going to bed hungry and hopeless day after barren day and year after barren year.

The problem is both technological and cultural. Since World War II we have learned the hard way that no technology can be simply picked up and used by a culture that is not already pervasively technological. Moreover, to abruptly dump quantities of hardware on any culture that has been basically rural and agricultural for tens of thousands of years is to invite disaster—instead of strengthening the culture, we destroy it.

Hence the problem of technological transfer is perhaps the most urgent one facing an uneasy world today. It requires sensitivity beyond measure to devise techniques for grafting urgently needed technologies upon ancient cultures in such a way that the culture retains its social, economic, and religious validity, and ethnic integrity. This is the job for the engineer whose command of his or her specialty is balanced by sensitivity, humor, patience, empathy, great social imagination, and a love of people in all the incredibly immense variety of their values, attitudes, and lifestyles.

However, certain cautions are in order. Ancient cultures frequently move at a pace far slower than most Americans are accustomed to; the result, for an American, can be an intense sense of frustration. Moreover, in most countries of the Third World, it is next to impossible to depoliticize the engineering job—there is no such thing as "pure" engineering, and the engineer who is not willing to cope with the local politics of the region would be well advised to abandon this option altogether. Finally, the power of tradition and of traditional ways of doing things must never be underestimated. If the shift to the new and demonstrably more productive technology demands the abandonment of ancient patterns of thought, or centuries-old cultural habits, then it will not likely be accepted.

2.17   THE ENGINEERING PROFESSOR

The academic career option is essentially in two forms. Of the 280 or so departments, schools, or colleges of engineering in the nation, many are straightforwardly academic, campus-centered departments or colleges in just the sense that chemistry, or botany, or English at these same schools are academic departments. That is, the teaching task is primary and central. The engineering professors in these departments and colleges may and indeed generally do research leading to publication—like anyone else, they need to keep themselves on the leading edge of their specialty—but it is understood that whatever research projects they undertake must be fitted in around their classroom responsibilities. In other words, engineering professors at these mainline teaching institutions will generally carry a full teaching load, from 9 to 12 classroom hours per semester, and devote whatever time is left over, after lecturing, grading papers, and advising students, to their research.

In sharp contrast to such mainline, classroom-centered engineering departments and colleges are the institutions where research is awarded a place equal to and sometimes superior to classroom teaching. These are the institutions that pull in literally hundreds of millions of dollars every year in research funding, not only from governmental agencies, but also from the large corporate entities of the private sector as well. The engineering professors at these universities are as committed to teaching and excellence in the classroom as their colleagues at the teaching-oriented institutions, but it is believed that the researching being done may be of such urgency and significance that some relief from teaching responsibilities is often necessary.

Most engineer-professors who pursue their careers at research-oriented universities are extraordinarily aggressive and doggedly resourceful people, temperamentally comfortable in a situation where they frequently have to "wing it," not entirely sure where their next research dollar is coming from. This is not for everyone. Nevertheless, for those who are temperamentally suited to it, the dual life of teacher-scholar and funded researcher can be immensely rewarding, often in ways not available in any other option. Nowhere else can one find the freedom and autonomy for both teaching and research that are one of the traditional rewards of university life.

2.18   GRADUATE WORK OUTSIDE OF ENGINEERING

The person with a Bachelor of Science degree in engineering can move with great propriety from an undergraduate commitment to engineering into such fields as law, business, and medicine; this is a possibility that should never be overlooked by the undergraduate engineer assessing the possibilities of graduate work beyond the first degree. The engineer-lawyer whose client is an organization of farmers intent upon suing an upstream manufacturer for increasing the salinity of irrigation water will know the right questions to ask, will be able to spot fallacies and falsehoods in his opponent's defense, and will be able to deal with expert witnesses in a knowledgeable and authoritative way. Again, the business executive whose undergraduate work is in engineering will be able to approach the technical aspects of the design, testing, production, and marketing of any product with a confidence and authority that colleagues who studied only accounting and public relations in their undergraduate years will not possess. Finally, the medical doctor who can bring his engineering knowledge of relatively simple machines to bear on his study of that most complex of all machines, the human body, will be able to visualize biomedical hardware—pumps, valves, delivery systems—that usually stand well outside the conceptual boundaries of the more traditionally trained physician.

Indeed, the liberal and liberating effects of a rigorous course of study in undergraduate engineering are so pronounced, and so susceptible to generalization, that there is hardly a field of human endeavour into which the person with a B.S. in engineering cannot confidently move after graduation.

2.19   THE MULTIPLE-TRACK, VARIABLE CAREER

In one sense, of course, the above discussion of the six life-options facing most engineers achieving the baccalaureate degree is artificial and somewhat misleading, since it suggests that you must follow one option for life, to the exclusion of all the others. But this is not the case. Life is long, and the growth of the individual cannot be predicted in such a tidy manner. It is easy to imagine a career in which, for the first seven or eight years, you are a hands-on, laboratory-centered engineer immersed in research and development for a large corporation. With that experience under your belt, and some accumulated capital to go on, you abandon the corporate ladder and the big city, spending the next five or six years as an independent entrepreneur, running your own three-man consulting firm in a small town. Your reputation as a consultant grows with the years, however, and you find yourself occasionally abroad, serving as a technical advisor to foreign governments and corporations. You discover, a little to your surprise, that you have a taste for travel, a talent for languages, and a growing interest in foreign cultures, and so you finally accept a post offered by the government of one of the developing Third World nations. This in turn leads to American contacts at the embassy level that land you, after a decade or so, in the Pentagon as an advisor on military and economic aspects of your specialty. You round out your career with a return to the corporate ladder, only this time at the top: You accept a high-level managerial position with the very company you started with so many years ago. You retire finally from the position with honor and distinction—only to set up yet another consulting firm, this time solo, just to keep your hand in during the Golden Years. The moral of the story is that no one can predict the course his or her life will take, and it is a lot more fun if you do not try to do that.

INITIAL CAREER PROFILES

In an attempt to provide some ideas of what engineers do initially when they graduate with a bachelor's degree in engineering, Dr. David Irwin (*15*) contacted a number of graduates throughout the country who had been out of school less than 18 months and asked them to briefly describe their initial career paths. Their responses are summarized in the following paragraphs and are included with the permission of Dr. Irwin and the IEEE Press.[1]

2.20   CHEMICAL ENGINEERING GRADUATES

When Jerry graduated, he went to work for a paper mill in the southeastern part of the country. He is a process engineer. He works in a technical group comprised of six engineers. Their job is to get as much production as possible out of the mill. Projects are assigned individually, and he is responsible for his tasks. The company has only one mill, and therefore there is no travel associated with his job. He typically works 40 hours per week. Jerry likes his job and plans to stick with it. For recreation, he is an avid tennis player.

Monica is a process engineer with a large oil-refining company. She works with about a dozen other engineers, but is the only process engineer in the group. Her job is to ensure that the wastewater treatment facility meets the permit requirements for wastewater discharge. Most of her traveling is involved in taking continuing education courses. She typically works about 45 hours per week. She enjoys her work and plans to move around within the company to increase her experience. In her spare time, she likes to go to the beach.

Anthony graduated with a very high GPA. He came from a poor family but had excellent grades and was practically put through school on scholarships. He worked at summer jobs to supplement his income while going to school. His last summer job was with a major drug manufacturer, and he found that he really liked doing creative work. So he opted to go to graduate school and is currently attending one of the most prestigious universities in the country.

Harry is a sales engineer for a large chemical company that manufactures a large array of chemicals. He spends many hours on the road. Harry may spend as much as a month at a customer's location, running tests and trials in order to sell his product. He normally takes some technical support with him in the form of two other engineers. He typically works about 60 hours per week. He hopes to either move up in the management of his company or start his own business. In his spare time, he likes to play bridge.

Ginger graduated from the university with a high GPA. Although she planned to enter engineering practice, she had always had in the back of her mind that perhaps she would like to be a medical doctor; therefore, she decided that if she was ever going to try it, the best time would probably be right away. She entered a medical program in the Southwest and is doing very well. Although she misses engineering, she believes that she will be able, one day, to combine her knowledge of both areas in a viable career. She claims that she does not have a lot of spare time.

---

[1] © 1997 IEEE. Reprinted, with permission, from *On Becoming an Engineer* by J. David Irwin, IEEE Press, 445 Hoes Lane, Piscataway, NJ 08855-1331.

2.21   CIVIL ENGINEERING GRADUATES

Bridget graduated from the university with a very high GPA. She is an assistant project director with a state department of transportation (DOT). She is out on the job site (e.g., a bridge construction project), in a hard hat and boots from 7 A.M. to 4 P.M. It is her job to supervise the state workers on-site and the other construction companies that work for the DOT. She is personally responsible for the construction to be done correctly. She travels a lot locally and typically covers the entire county in which she lives. She normally works 40 hours per week and is paid for any overtime. In her spare time, she has been involved in judging science fair projects in the local school system, and she likes to swim. Her plans for the future involve going to graduate school.

George's title is that of civil engineer. His company is a small engineering firm with about 150 people (25 percent of whom are engineers) that does engineering work in the electrical, architectural, and mechanical areas. George's specialty is the design of wastewater distribution systems. He normally works in a team on big projects and if the project is primarily one of a wastewater nature, he will act as the project leader. If the project is small, then he will work alone. He travels on average about two days per month and works about 50 hours per week. His future plans involve going back to school to get an M.B.A. He is an avid golfer and consistently shoots in the high 70s.

Amy is project engineer with a civil and environmental engineering consulting firm. She is involved in what she calls "hard-core design." She designs wastewater treatment facilities and is also concerned with the environmental impact statements for landfills and storm water systems. The company has about 150 employees, and on small jobs she typically works with one other engineer. Her job involves both office and field work. A lot of her office work involves computer modeling for water transmission systems. The amount of traveling she does depends totally on the project and, in some cases, can involve quite a bit. She typically works about 50 hours per week. She loves her work and plans to stay with it. She does, however, want to get her Professional Engineer's license and move up to project manager. In her spare time, she exercises a lot and participates in church activities. At the time of the contact, she was planning a wedding and was totally immersed in that.

As Charlie went through his undergraduate program, he decided, based on some of his course work, that he wanted to work in the environmental engineering area. The school that he attended did not have a program in environmental engineering at the undergraduate level, so he decided to pursue a master's program in that area. He is currently about halfway through the program at a major university, working as a graduate teaching assistant. He is enjoying his studies and his teaching. He is paid a modest stipend to teach, but it is sufficient for his needs. He is looking forward to graduating in about a year and entering the workforce in the environmental area.

Clifford works for a small company (about 100 employees) that sells mixtures for concrete. He is in technical sales and is a lone ranger in that he works by himself. He does have some service people who back him up on occasions when their help is needed. He travels anywhere from 2000 to 3000 miles per month within the state where he lives. In his normal routine, he works about 55 hours per week. Clifford's goal is to have a business of his own. In his spare time, he likes to hunt, fish, and play tennis.

2.22   ELECTRICAL ENGINEERING GRADUATES

Lisa used the cooperative education program to get through school. Although she did her co-op work with a government contractor, when she graduated from school, she went to work for a major electric utility. She liked her co-op work and believes that it gave her a good idea of what to expect when she began working full-time in the real world. She designs the control systems, which employ programmable logic controllers, for the generation of steam in fossil-fuel power plants. She normally works by herself but has a support group that works with her on certain projects. She does the design in the office and then the installation is, of course, done in the plants. She will typically travel four to five days per month. She plans to get as much experience as possible in the design and instrumentation area and is currently not thinking beyond that point. In her spare time, she enjoys camping and traveling.

Joe was a co-op student while in school and maintained a high GPA. His co-op assignment was with a local telephone company. His father is a physician and could have easily paid for Joe's education, but did not do so because he believed that Joe would get more out of school if he worked his way through. During his senior year, Joe took an elective course in image processing and became fascinated with the subject. He decided that he would like to go to graduate school in that area. He was interested in applying image processing to medicine, with techniques such as magnetic resonance imaging (MRI). Joe is now a graduate research assistant at a major university, working with a professor whose research is in the image processing area. When he has a break in his schoolwork in the winter, he loves to snow ski and can do so with ease. In the summer, he likes to fish.

When Ian graduated from the university, he went to work with a friend of his father's. He has known the man most of his life. He is in the technical sales area and works as a manufacturer's representative. Ian covers an area of approximately a 200-mile radius, including two relatively large cities. He typically works with electronic measurement equipment and goes to customers in his area to demonstrate it. He does a lot of traveling and typically works about 55 hours per week. He enjoys hunting and fishing in his spare time and hopes to learn enough in his work to start his own business.

Sam's education in the area of electrical engineering was unusual from the very beginning. His father had a small law firm in a relatively unpopulated Midwestern area. His father wanted Sam to enter the law firm and eventually take it over when his father retired. Sam was interested in doing just that. So why did Sam go into electrical engineering if he was planning on a career in law? The answer is simply that his father had told him that he would need an undergraduate degree in some area before he could enter law school, and he felt that a degree in electrical engineering would teach him to think critically and analyze problems in a systematic manner. So Sam is now in law school at a different university and planning on joining his father upon graduation.

Fran's title is that of engineer, and she works for an engineering firm that derives the majority of its business from government contracts. She is involved in the design of infrared weapon systems and in her work uses a wide variety of software programs. She typically works by herself; however, because of her co-op experience gained while going through school, she also heads up a group that is involved in training other people in the company. Her traveling is confined to attending continuing education courses that keep her abreast of new technology in her field, and this traveling averages no more than one or two days per month. There are times when she will work 70 hours per week (that includes 13 hours per day on the weekend) while she is involved in supervising other contractors who work through her company for the government. She has just had a baby and is interested in obtaining an aerobic instructor's certificate. If she can get this certificate, she can teach aerobics after working hours, and the place where she would teach has a day care center where she can leave her child. In the future, she would like to pursue a master's degree in electrical engineering.

2.23   MECHANICAL ENGINEERING GRADUATES

Juan works for a mechanical contracting firm, and his title is that of engineer. The firm is small and does about $15 million worth of business per year. Juan estimates that his time is divided as follows: 70 percent of the time he is involved in estimating the cost of a job (i.e., bid specification), 10 percent of his time is spent in purchasing and making sure that equipment arrives at the job site on time, 10 percent of his time is spent in design, and the remaining 10 percent is spent in the CAD area with shop drawings. He normally works by himself, and on large jobs he is the key person responsible for all the air distribution and duct work. He enjoys what he does and feels that he is exposed to a wide range of design firms from all over the country. He does very little traveling and typically works about 50 hours per week. He plans to get his Professional Engineer's license and hopes to one day be a partner in the firm. For recreation, he likes to play tennis.

Teresa is called a general engineer and works with one of the U.S. government laboratories that does research on wood for paper products. She is involved in testing and analyzing the mechanical properties of paper, specifically its coefficient of friction. Her work impacts paper manufacturers and the printing industry. The laboratory has about 300 people, and she works in a group of about 10 people that moves from product to product to solve various problems. She typically works under one of the more senior engineers and normally works about a 40-hour week. She does very little traveling in her job, but what traveling she does is confined to continuing education courses and conferences. Her job is a fixed-time contract and will end after a three-year period. She wants to move to a position where she can do work in heating, ventilating, and air conditioning. At present, she is taking a correspondence course in preparation for taking the Fundamentals of Engineering exam; later, she would like to obtain a Professional Engineer's license. In her spare time, she is involved in all types of recreational activities.

Adrienne is a boiler performance engineer with a utility company. She travels throughout the company's service area testing boilers in power plants to make sure that they meet the clean air requirements. She is one member of a team of four engineers that attempts to balance efficiency and emission control. The engineering department of the company has hundreds of engineers, and there are groups such as the one that she is in whose jobs include testing turbines. Depending on the type of job in which she is involved, she may be the lead engineer or she may act in a support capacity, She does a lot of traveling. She is away from home, on average, about three months out of the year. It takes about three to four weeks to do a test, and therefore she is gone for this period. However, she is home on the weekends. Adrienne typically works about 40 hours per week unless they are very busy, in which case she may work 50 to 60 hours per week. She enjoys what she is doing and plans to stick with it, learning all that she can about the business. She is an outdoors-type person and enjoys playing basketball. At the moment, she is planning a wedding, and that activity is taking up most of her time.

Ryan works with a small engineering firm that has about 30 employees. The company is owned by a much larger company that does environmental engineering work. Ryan is involved in abatement and remediation work. He oversees the removal of such things as asbestos, PCBs (polychlorinated biphenyls), heavy metals, and aromatic hydrocarbons. Although he works in a team and reports to a project supervisor, he is responsible for his part of the project. In his work, he follows the job and relocates wherever the job is; that is, when he finishes one job, he moves to another. He normally works about 50 to 55 hours per week. At present, he has no plans for the future. He likes what he is doing and feels that he is too young to worry about planning too far ahead. He likes the outdoors and spends most of his spare time hunting and fishing.

Brad worked his way through school as a diesel mechanic. He worked for a very large trucking firm that had hundreds of tractors and trailers. When he received his degree, he was made the director of maintenance for the firm. As such, he is responsible for keeping all the rigs running. He also works very hard to control maintenance costs and keep all the electronics on the trucks in working order, and is the individual who is responsible for matching the most efficient tractor to trailer when purchasing new equipment. In addition, he is the person they call if there is an accident and diesel fuel is spilled. He supervises about 70 technicians who work in a number of depots over a multistate area. He typically makes about one trip per month in his supervisory position and attends professional meetings that deal with the trucking industry. He normally works about 45 to 50 hours per week, unless there is a diesel fuel spill somewhere in the country. He has passed the FE exam and is currently working toward his Professional Engineer's license. He plays golf with customers, and in his spare time he is a member of a softball league.

2.24   BIOMEDICAL ENGINEERING GRADUATES

When Paul was in high school, he thought that he might like to be a medical doctor. So he asked some of the physicians in his hometown if he could go with them while they visited with some of their patients. They were happy to accommodate his wishes, and, as a result, Paul decided to pursue a career as an orthopedic surgeon. During a visit to the university he planned to attend, he found that they had a program in biomedical engineering. He entered the program and took his elective courses in biomechanics. He is now in medical school pursuing a program in orthopedic biomechanics. He loves his studies, but has little or no time for anything else.

Curtis had always been interested in medicine, but did not want to practice as a medical doctor. He learned that the university had a program in biomedical engineering, and so he entered that program with the hope that he would be able to work for a drug company. When he graduated, he accepted a job with a large drug manufacturer and is currently involved in the development of delivery systems for genetically engineered drugs and screening tests that determine the applicability of this type of drug therapy. He enjoys his work and normally works a little more than 40 hours per week. His passions are skiing and backpacking, and he does these things every chance he gets.

2.25   COMPUTER ENGINEERING GRADUATES

Because Eileen's father was a computer systems programmer, she had been exposed to computers for a long time prior to entering the university. She decided that she wanted to pursue a similar career, and therefore she entered a program in computer engineering. While in school, she was much more interested in software than hardware and, as a result, when she graduated, she took a job with a major defense contractor as a software engineer. She does programming in a real-time environment for a weapon system under development for the military. She normally works about 40 hours per week unless there is a design review, in which case she may work overtime in preparation for her presentation. She enjoys playing golf in her spare time.

Keith was a little older than most students when he entered a program in computer engineering. He joined the Navy upon graduation from high school and worked as a radio operator. He then went to work for a major electronics manufacturer as a commercial electronics technician. When he graduated from the university, he went to work for a government contractor. He is involved in the development of a Windows-based automated testing system that controls complex communications test equipment and shipboard radio equipment. He has been able to replace some outdated equipment with some of the modern technology that is capable of efficiently handling the task with cheaper, more reliable equipment. His work schedule typically requires about 40 to 50 hours per week. He enjoys water sports and owns a small sailboat that he uses every chance he gets.

2.26 ENVIRONMENTAL ENGINEERING GRADUATES

Tim's family was always concerned about environmental issues, and he guesses that it was this influence that guided him toward a career in environmental engineering. When he graduated from the university, he went to work for a consulting firm that specializes in municipal wastewater treatment. He was paired with an experienced engineer involved in the design and construction of a new wastewater treatment system. In this capacity, he works with both the laboratory technicians to determine the characteristics of the wastewater and the state to obtain a discharge permit. He is also part of a team that must decide what types of processes must be linked together to achieve the level of treatment desired at the cheapest cost. His work schedule is approximately 45 hours per week, sometimes longer when he is in the field. Tim is really into backpacking and does it every chance he gets.

When Sheila entered the university, she was not really sure what curriculum she would follow. However, one of her girlfriends was going into environmental engineering, and so Sheila thought she would look at that curriculum closely as a possible career path. After talking to some of the professors in that area, she decided to enter that program. When she graduated, she took a job with a state agency that is involved in permitting activities for industrial and municipal wastewater treatment systems. Sheila calibrates a waste load allocation model of a receiving stream in order to set discharge limits for a proposed wastewater treatment system. She rarely works overtime, loves her job, and spends her free time exercising and working as an aerobics instructor.

2.27 INDUSTRIAL ENGINEERING GRADUATES

Melanie's father was an industrial engineer, and he had convinced her that this would be a good career path for her. After graduation, she went to work for a large semiconductor company on the West Coast. She works in a team that is designing the layout of a manufacturing process. They are concerned with efficiency and the control of production and materials. Melanie is personally responsible for the ergonomic aspects of the jobs and must ensure that each job is safe and that any risk of injury is removed. She enjoys her job and typically works about 40 to 50 hours per week. In her spare time, she likes to play tennis and has joined a health club where she can play and meet other people with similar interests.

When Allen graduated from the university, he joined a company that manufactures snack foods. He is on a one-year training assignment as a production supervisor. In this capacity, he is responsible for all aspects of the production line, including dealing with personnel problems, scheduling the materials, and maintenance. He will soon complete this assignment and looks forward to going into some engineering function with the company. Although Allen works a 40-hour shift, his work normally extends far beyond this time due to problems that invariably arise. When he has time to do so, Allen is an avid bicycle-racing enthusiast.

REFERENCES

1. *1985 Annual Report*. Accreditation Board for Engineering and Technology, New York (1986).

2. EIDE, A. R., R. D. JENISON, L. H. MASHAW, AND L. L. NORTHUP, *Engineering Fundamentals and Problem Solving*, McGraw-Hill Book Company, New York, 1979. Quotation reproduced with permission of McGraw-Hill. Reprinted with permission of the McGraw-Hill Book Company.

3. BEAKLEY, GEORGE C., AND H. W. LEACH, *Engineering: An Introduction to a Creative Profession*, Macmillan Publishing Company, New York, 1982.

4. GLEGG, GORDON L., *The Design of Design*, Cambridge University Press, London, 1969.

5. WELLINGTON, ARTHUR MELLEN, *The Economic Theory of the Location of Railways*, 6th Edition, corrected, John Wiley & Sons, Inc., New York, 1887.

6. SMITH, RALPH J., BLAINE R. BUTLER, AND WILLIAM K. LEBOLD, *Engineering as a Career*, 4th Edition, McGraw-Hill Book Company, New York, 1983.

7. KEMPER, JOHN DUSTIN, *Engineers and Their Profession*, Holt Rinehart and Winston, 1975, 1967, CBS College Publications, 1982.

8. *Computer Engineering*, Georgia Institute of Technology, Atlanta, GA, 2000.

9. *Bioengineering*, School of Electrical and Computer Engineering, Georgia Institute of Technology, Atlanta, GA, 2000.

10. *Tutorial Information about MEMS*, University of Wisconsin, www.mems.engr.wisc.edu/what, 2001.

11. DUDERSTADT, JAMES J., GLENN F. KNOLL, AND GEORGE S. SPRINGER, *Principles of Engineering*, John Wiley & Sons, Inc., New York, 1982.

12. RED, W. EDWARD, *Engineeering: The Career and the Profession*, Brooks/Cole Engineering Division, Monterey, CA, 1982.

13. *The True Champions of Change: Choosing a Career in Industrial Engineering*, www.iienet.org, Institute of Industrial Engineers, Atlanta, GA, 2001.

14. *Bachelor's/Master's/Doctor's: Is Graduate Study in Engineering for You?*, Colorado State University, Fort Collins, CO, 1982.

15. IRWIN, J. DAVID, *On Becoming an Engineer*, IEEE Press, The Institute of Electrical and Electronic Engineers, Inc., New York, 1997.

An Exemplary Engineering Achievement

The St. Lawrence Seaway Project tapped several hydroelectric opportunities. Long Sault Dam controls water passing through the Robert Moses Power Station. (Courtesy of the American Council of Engineering Companies.)

CHAPTER THREE

THE ENGINEER AS A PROFESSIONAL

This chapter describes the characteristics and responsibilities of professional engineers and the legal framework for the regulation of the practice of engineering through registration and licensing. It describes the purpose and importance of professional engineering societies and the codes of ethics developed by these organizations to protect the integrity of the engineering profession. The chapter includes several case studies to illustrate the application of ethical principles to the practice of engineering.

3.1 ENGINEERING AS A PROFESSION

Engineering is a profession in which the knowledge of mathematics and the natural sciences is applied with discretion and judgment in order to use economically the materials and forces of nature for the benefit of people.

It differs from other learned professions in a number of ways: in the type of service provided, in the training requirements for its practitioners, in the diversity of its leadership, and in the lack of uniformity and rigidity in its registration laws.

Engineers are concerned with the creation of structures, devices, and systems for human use. In contrast to other professionals, engineers tend to create machines, structures, processes, and the like for the use of groups of people rather than for an individual. They seldom deal directly with the users of their works or beneficiaries of their services, while other professionals (e.g., attorneys, physicians, psychologists, and dentists) commonly do so.

Although some form of engineering was practiced in ancient times, engineering is a relatively young profession that has not yet reached maturity. It has developed more slowly and has less rigid laws governing entrance and practice than have a number of other professions.

Engineers can practice their profession with an undergraduate degree, but graduate study leading to a master's degree is being recognized increasingly as an integral part of engineering education. In contrast, students aspiring to be lawyers usually take a three-year program of study in law school beyond an undergraduate degree. Students training for the medical profession typically graduate with a baccalaureate degree, then are given at least four years of medical training and internship in medical school. More years of training may be required in the physician's chosen specialty. Similarly, dentists, clinical psychologists, and architects require matriculation beyond the baccalaureate degree.

The Accreditation Board for Engineering and Technology (ABET) has defined engineering as "the profession in which a knowledge of the mathematical and natural sciences gained by study, experience, and practice is applied with judgment to develop ways to utilize, economically, the materials and forces of nature for the benefit of mankind"(1). The engineer's knowledge comes not only from study, but also from experience and practice. This knowledge must be applied with discretion and judgment. These vital qualities that form the *art* of engineering must be fashioned and honed by association with seasoned professionals and by a period of engineering practice.

As new technologies have emerged, engineering has splintered into a large number of specialties, and no single professional organization speaks with authority for all engineers. For a number of other professions, a strong and authoritative association has been formed to speak for its members, lobby for desirable legislation, guard the interests, and promote the image and integrity of the profession. For example, the American Medical Association (AMA) and the American Bar Association (ABA) serve in this role for the medical and legal professions, respectively.

At the urging of the AMA, ABA, and similar professional groups, many professions are governed by uniform state registration laws requiring universal registration of practitioners. The registration laws for engineering registration are not uniform throughout the various states, and many of these laws exempt engineer employees of public agencies, employees of manufacturing companies, and other groups from registration. As a result, only about 30 percent of the practicing engineers in the United States are registered professional engineers.

Although it differs significantly from other professions in several respects, engineering possesses those attributes that characterize a profession, namely (2):

1. It satisfies an indispensible and beneficial need.
2. It requires the exercise of discretion and judgment and is not subject to standardization.
3. It involves a type of activity that is conducted on a high intellectual plane based on knowledge and skills not commonly possessed by the general public.

4. It has group consciousness for the promotion of knowledge and professional ideals and for rendering social services.
5. It has a legal status and requires well-formulated standards of admission.

Herbert Hoover, the thirty-first president of the United States and a mining engineer, comparing engineering with other professions, made the following whimsical observations:

> *The great liability of the engineer compared to men of other professions is that his works are out in the open where all can see them. His acts, step by step, are in hard substance. He cannot bury his mistakes in the grave like the doctors. He cannot argue them into thin air or blame the judge like the lawyers. He cannot, like the architect, cover his failures with trees and vines. He cannot, like the politicians, screen his shortcomings by blaming his opponents and hope that the people will forget. The engineer simply cannot deny that he did it. If his works do not work, he is damned. That is the phantasmagoria that haunts his nights and dogs his days. He comes from the job at the end of the day resolved to calculate it again. He wakes in the morning. All day he shivers at the thought of the bugs which will inevitably appear to jolt its smooth consummation.*
>
> *On the other hand, unlike the doctor, his is not a life among the weak. Unlike the soldier, destruction is not his purpose. Unlike the lawyer, quarrels are not his daily bread. To the engineer falls the job of clothing the bare bones of science with life, comfort, and hope. (3)*

3.2   CHARACTERISTICS AND RESPONSIBILITIES OF PROFESSIONAL ENGINEERS

Professional engineers are expected to possess education, knowledge, and skills in an engineering specialty that exceed those of the general public. They must be willing to stay abreast of discoveries and technological changes by participation in professional meetings and continuing education. They must also possess a willingness to advance professional knowledge, ideals, and practice and to share their knowledge with their peers. Professional engineers must have a sense of responsibility and service to society and to their employers and clients, and they must act honorably in their dealings with others. They must be willing to follow established codes of ethics for their profession and to guard their professional integrity and ideals and those of their profession.

3.3   IDEALS AND OBLIGATIONS OF PROFESSIONAL ENGINEERS

The ideals and obligations of engineering as a profession have been embodied in solemn statements of intention prepared by engineering societies. Members of the National Society of Professional Engineers subscribe to this Creed (4):

As a Professional Engineer, I dedicate my professional knowledge and skill to the advancement and betterment of human welfare.
I pledge:
    To give the utmost of performance;
    To participate in none but honest enterprise;
    To live and work according to the laws of man and the highest standards of professional conduct;
    To place service before profit, the honor and standing of the profession before personal advantage, and the public welfare above all other considerations.
In humility and with need for Divine Guidance, I make this pledge.

The Ethics Committee of the Engineers' Council for Professional Development (5) prepared the following statement describing the faith of the engineer:

I AM AN ENGINEER. In my profession I take deep pride, but without vainglory; to it I owe solemn obligations that I am eager to fulfill.

As an Engineer, I will participate in none but honest enterprise. To him that has engaged my services, as employer or client, I will give the utmost of performance and fidelity.

When needed, my skill and knowledge shall be given without reservation for the public good. From special capacity springs the obligation to use it well in the service to humanity; and I accept the challenge that this implies.

Jealous of the high repute of my calling, I will strive to protect the interests and the good name of any engineer that I know to be deserving; but I will not shrink, should duty dictate, from disclosing the truth regarding anyone that, by unscrupulous act, has shown himself unworthy of the profession.

Since the Age of Stone, human progress has been conditioned by the genius of my professional forebears. By them have been rendered usable to mankind Nature's vast resources of material and energy. By them have been vitalized and turned to practical account the principles of science and the revelations of technology. Except for this heritage of accumulated experience, my efforts would be feeble. I dedicate myself to the dissemination of engineering knowledge, and especially to the instruction of younger members of my profession in all its arts and traditions.

To my fellows I pledge, in the same full measure I ask of them, integrity and fair dealing, tolerance and respect, and devotion to the standards and the dignity of our profession; with the consciousness, always, that our special expertness carries with it the obligation to serve humanity with complete sincerity.

Engineering graduates of Canadian universities participate in a ceremony of the Ritual of the Calling of an Engineer. The idea of the calling of an engineer to the profession dates back to 1922, when engineering professor H. E. T. Haultain suggested the development of an oath or creed to which young graduates in engineering could subscribe, something in the form of the Hippocratic oath in the medical profession. Professor Haultain recruited author Rudyard Kipling to help craft a suitably dignified ceremony. Kipling agreed and suggested a ceremony called the Ritual of the Calling of an Engineer. He outlined the purpose of the Ritual as follows:

> *The Ritual of the Calling of an Engineer has been instituted with the simple end of directing the young engineer towards a consciousness of his profession and its significance and indicating to the older engineer his responsibilities in receiving, welcoming and supporting the young engineers in their beginnings. (6)*

Kipling wrote the Obligation that is used in the Ritual ceremony, which gives men and women the opportunity to obligate themselves to the standards of ethics and diligent practice that is felt to be required of those in the engineering profession. Engineers who participate in the Ritual receive a symbolic iron ring, which they wear on the fifth finger of the working hand to remind them of their professional and ethical responsibilities.

Since the first ceremony in 1925, more than 212,000 engineers have been obligated at more than 1665 ceremonies organized across Canada. An Order of the Engineer has been established in the United States, which conducts ring ceremonies at which U.S. engineer candidates formally accept the Obligation of an Engineer (7).

3.4   PROFESSIONAL REGISTRATION

The registration of engineers in the United States was instituted by the state of Wyoming in 1907 to protect the public from incompetent individuals claiming to be engineers (8). This occurred during a period of extensive land and water resources development, and the legislation was intended to stop the abuses in land surveys and irrigation systems. By 1950, all 50 states and the five jurisdictions (the District of Columbia, Puerto Rico, the Canal Zone, Guam, and the Virgin Islands) had legislation for the practice of engineering and/or land surveying. These laws stem from the police powers of a state, which are based on the constitutional mandate to safeguard life, health, and property, and to promote the general welfare.

There are now approximately 670,000 professional engineering registrations in the United States. Since it is possible to be registered in more than one state, this represents an estimated 402,000 registered individuals of the 1.76 million engineers now practicing.

The registration laws are administered by independent registration boards in the states and jurisdictions, each operating within the framework of its own laws. Although there are statutory differences and variations among the boards in procedures and policies, a great deal of progress has been made in promoting uniform standards. This progress is attributable in large part to the efforts of an umbrella organization known as The National Council of Examiners for Engineering and Surveyors.

The boards of registration typically have five to seven members who are appointed by the governor, usually based on the recommendation of state professional engineering societies. In some of the states, one or more public members or consumers serve on the board.

These boards are primarily responsible for evaluating the education and experience of applicants for registration, administering an examination to those applicants who meet the minimum requirements, and granting registration to those who successfully complete the examination. In most states, a four-year engineering education is required plus four years of experience as a prerequisite. A common pattern for registration is the requirement that the applicant:

1. Graduate in an engineering curriculum of not less than four years.

2. Acquire not less than four years' experience in engineering work of a character satisfactory to the Board.

3. Pass a written examination.

The examination consists of two parts: (1) The Fundamentals of Engineering, and (2) The Principles and Practice of Engineering. The first part consists of an eight-hour test on mathematics, physics, chemistry, and other basic and engineering sciences to determine whether the candidate possesses minimum technical knowledge. Most states permit the applicant to take the first part of the examination at, or just prior to, the time of graduation. Graduates who pass this part of the examination are qualified as Intern-Engineers or Engineers-in-Training.

The second part of the examination, which also requires eight hours, covers the principles and practices of engineering. It is taken after the applicant has passed Part 1 and has had the minimum required experience subsequent to graduation.

State registration laws may provide more than one career path to engineering registration. Some state laws permit registration of candidates with a four-year or two-year degree in Engineering Technology provided they possess eight or more years of satisfactory engineering experience. Other laws provide for registration on the basis of apprenticeship. Under this arrangement, a candidate qualifies to take the registration examination on many years of practical experience with little or no acceptable engineering education.

In addition to evaluating candidates for registration, the board of registration establishes and enforces rules of professional conduct and/or a code of ethics. The board investigates alleged violations of the registration law and the rules of professional conduct. In this connection, the board may be given power to subpoena witnesses and compel their attendance at a hearing and to produce books, papers, documents, and other materials relevant to an investigation.

Typically, a board may take one of three actions against a registrant who violates the registration statutes or rules of professional conduct:

1. It may issue a reprimand.

2. It may suspend the registrant's license for a specified time.

3. It may permanently revoke the registrant's license.

3.5 PROFESSIONAL ORGANIZATIONS

Nearly 200 engineering societies or related groups presently exist to serve the technical and professional needs of the engineering profession. Professional engineering organizations publish educational journals and provide a forum for professional interaction by means of meetings and conferences. Many engineering organizations publish handbooks, training manuals, and other engineering monographs, sponsor seminars, and provide other continuing education opportunities for their members. They are usually organized on a local and national basis and sponsor local meetings as well as national meetings that appeal to all or a large segment of their membership.

The most prominent of the professional engineering organizations are five of the oldest and largest groups known as the "founder societies":

1. American Society of Civil Engineers (ASCE).
2. The Institute of Electrical and Electronics Engineers (IEEE).
3. American Society of Mechanical Engineers (ASME).
4. American Institute of Chemical Engineers (AIChE).
5. American Institute of Mining, Metallurgical, and Petroleum Engineers (AIME).

The founder societies have a combined membership of more than 500,000, including an undetermined number of duplicate memberships. The founding date and headquarters address of the founder societies and other prominent engineering organizations are given in Table 3.1.

Figure 3.1 *Engineering societies provide opportunities for engineers to discuss common professional goals and aspirations. (Courtesy of the Society of Women Engineers, Oakland, California.)*

Figure 3.2   *Engineers share information on technological advancements by preparing and distributing technical papers at professional meetings. (Courtesy of the Society of Women Engineers, Oakland, California.)*

Special mention should be made of several of the organizations listed in Table 3.1. The oldest engineering society in the United States is the American Society of Civil Engineers; the largest is the Institute of Electrical and Electronics Engineers. The National Society of Professional Engineers (NSPE) promotes the profession of engineering as a vital social and economic influence in the United States. With headquarters in Washington, DC, NSPE maintains a direct interest in legislation that affects the engineering profession.

As the name suggests, the American Society for Engineering Education (ASEE) is primarily concerned with the education and training of engineers. To a large extent, its members are college and university professors, department heads, deans, and administrators.

The American Association of Engineering Societies (AAES) was formed in 1980 to provide a central voice for the engineering profession as a whole, when such representation is appropriate, and help develop public policy regarding the engineering profession. The AAES is an "umbrella" type of organization— a federation of engineering societies in which the societies rather than individuals hold membership. Member societies are given voting strength in AAES in proportion to their numbers of members. An important component of AAES, the Engineering Manpower Commission, conducts studies of the demand, salaries, and efficient utilization of engineers and technicians.

TABLE 3.1 *Professional Engineering Organizations*

American Academy of Environmental Engineers
Founded in 1913.
130 Holiday Court, Suite 100,
Annapolis, MD 21401.
Internet: www.enviro-engrs.org

American Congress on Surveying and Mapping
Founded in 1941.
6 Montgomery Village Avenue, Suite 403,
Gaithersburg, MD 20879.
Internet: www.survmap.org

American Institute of Aeronautics and Astronautics
Founded in 1963 from the consolidation of the American Rocket Society and the Institute of Aerospace Science.
1801 Alexander Bell Dr., Suite 500,
Reston, VA 20191.
Internet: www.aiaa.org

American Institute of Chemical Engineers
Founded in 1908.
Three Park Avenue,
New York, NY 10016-5901.
Internet: www.aiche.org

American Nuclear Society
Founded in 1954.
555 North Kensington Ave.,
LaGrange Park, IL 60525.
Internet: www.ans.org

American Society of Agricultural Engineers
Founded in 1907.
2950 Niles Road,
St. Joseph, MI 49085-9659.
Internet: www.asae.org

American Society of Civil Engineers
Founded in 1852.
1801 Alexander Bell Dr.,
Reston, VA 20191-4400.
Internet: www.asce.org

American Society for Engineering Education
Founded in 1893.
1818 N Street, NW,
Washington, DC 20036.
Internet: www.asee.org

American Society of Heating, Refrigerating and Air-Conditioning Engineers
Founded in 1959 from the consolidation of the American Society of Heating and Air-Conditioning Engineers and the American Society of Refrigeration Engineers.
1791 Tullie Circle NE,
Atlanta, GA 30329.
Internet: www.ashrae.org

The American Society of Mechanical Engineers
Founded in 1880.
Three Park Avenue,
New York, NY 10016.
Internet: www.asme.org

Institute of Industrial Engineers
Founded in 1880.
25 Technology Park,
Atlanta, Norcross, GA 30092.
Internet: www.iienet.org

The Institute of Electrical and Electronic Engineers
Founded in 1884.
1828 L Street, NW, Suite 1202,
Washington, DC 20036.
Internet: www.ieeeusa.org

The Minerals, Metals and Materials Society
Founded in 1959.
184 Thorn Hill Road,
Warrendale, PA 15086.
Internet: www.tms.org

National Council of Examiners for Engineering and Surveying
Founded in 1920.
P. O. Box 1686,
280 Seneca Creek Road,
Clemson, SC 29633.
Internet: www.ncees.org

National Institute of Ceramic Engineers
Founded in 1938.
P. O. Box 6136,
Westerville, OH 43086-6136.
Internet: www.acers.org

(continues)

TABLE 3.1   *Professional Engineering Organizations (continued)*

National Society of Professional Engineers	Society for Mining, Metallurgy, and Exploration
Founded in 1934.	Founded in 1959.
1420 King Street,	P. O. Box 625002,
Alexandria, VA 22314-2794.	Littleton, CO 80162-5002.
Internet: www.nspe.org	Internet: www.smenet.org
Society of Automotive Engineers	**Society of Naval Architects and Marine Engineers**
Founded in 1905.	Founded in 1893.
400 Commonwealth Drive,	601 Pavonia Avenue,
Warrendale, PA 15096-0001.	Jersey City, NJ 07306.
Internet: www.sae.org	
	Society of Petroleum Engineers
Society of Manufacturing Engineers	Founded in 1959.
Founded in 1932.	P. O. Box 833836,
One SME Drive, Dearborn, MI 48121.	Richardson, TX 75083-3836.
Internet: www.sme.org	Internet: www.spe.org

Source: U.S. Department of Labor, Bureau of Labor Statistics, www.bls.gov, 2001.

In 1932, an organization called the Engineering Council for Professional Development (ECPD) was formed to represent the profession in matters related to the development, maintenance, and improvement of quality engineering education. The major thrust of this organization has been on the accreditation of educational programs in engineering and in engineering technology. The organization has provided leadership for the development of accreditation criteria and, with volunteer professionals, the certification of programs of study in various institutions of higher learning. In 1980, the ECPD changed its name to the Accreditation Board for Engineering and Technology (ABET) and transferred four of the nonaccreditation activities (guidance, ethics, student development, and development of young engineers) to appropriate committees of AAES.

3.6   ENGINEERING ETHICS

Ethics is the study of the morality of human actions. It is the science of determining values in human conduct and of deciding what ought to be done in different circumstances and situations. Engineering ethics represents the attempts of professional engineers to define proper courses of action in their dealings with each other, with their clients and employees, and with the general public.

The problem of engineering ethics, as well as those of other professions, begins with the fact that the professional possesses specialized knowledge that is superior to that possessed by clients, employers, or the general public. With this knowledge, a responsible and honest engineer can be a very useful member of society. An irresponsible or corrupt engineer can weaken the confidence of the public in the engineering profession and even become a dangerous member of society (*9*).

It is ironic that as a discipline or area of focused inquiry, engineering ethics is still young, much younger, for example, than medical ethics or legal ethics. Engineering is the largest of the learned professions, and it affects all of us in most aspects of our lives. The works of engineering confront us practically everywhere we turn our eyes and every time we do something. The decisions of physicians and attorneys usually affect one person at a time; the judgment of a design engineer can influence hundreds of lives at once (*10*).

3.7 MORAL FOUNDATIONS OF ENGINEERING ETHICS

Engineering ethics involves the study of moral issues and decisions. It seeks answers to questions about conduct and behavior that is morally correct. It is appropriate therefore that we examine some of the foundations of moral development.

Kohlberg (*10, 11*) suggests that an individual may reason and approach moral decisions from three main levels of moral cognitive development. The most primitive he calls the *Preconventional Level*, in which proper conduct is regarded as what directly benefits oneself. This is the level of development of most young children. At this level, individuals are motivated primarily by an unquestioning submission to power, by a desire to avoid punishment, or by a desire to satisfy their own needs.

At the next level of moral development, termed the *Conventional Level*, the individual accepts the norms of one's family, group, or society as the standard of morality. At this level, individuals are motivated by the desire to please others and to conform to the expectations of the social unit rather than upon their self interest. Here an act is deemed to be morally right when it is approved by convention or law and wrong when it violates group customs or laws.

According to Kohlberg, the highest level of moral development is the *Postconventional Level*, at which an individual is motivated by what is morally reasonable for its own sake without regard to self-interest or to social conventions. Such individuals are *morally autonomous* because they think for themselves and do not respond to ulterior motives or assume that group customs are always right.

It is helpful to examine further the moral underpinnings of ethical behavior. What makes certain actions morally right and others morally wrong? Martin and Schinzinger (*10*) describe four types of moral theories that help to answer this question:

1. **Utilitarianism.** This theory considers the good and bad consequences of an action and seeks to maximize *utility*, defined as the overall balance of good over bad consequences. Our actions ought always to produce the most utility, considering everyone affected by those actions.

2. **Duty ethics.** This theory maintains that there are duties which ought to be performed even though performing them may not always produce the most good: to be fair, to be honest, etc.

3. **Rights ethics.**   Under this theory, an action is morally right if it does not violate the rights of other people.

4. **Virtue ethics.**   This theory regards an action right if it supports good character traits (virtues) and wrong if it manifests bad character traits (vices).

Martin and Schinzinger (*10*) describe the application of these theories by the following illustration. An influential County Executive in Maryland had the authority to award contracts for public works projects to engineering firms. In exercising that authority, he participated in a lucrative kickback scheme. Two consulting engineers were given special consideration in receiving contracts for public-works projects so long as they made secret payments to the County Executive of 5 percent of their fees. Why was it wrong for the engineers to make secret payments to the executive in return for preferential award of contracts?

> *One answer is that more bad than good resulted. Other engineering firms were harmed by not having a chance to obtain the contracts they may have been best qualified to receive. The system also removed the potential benefits of healthy competition among a wider range of firms, benefits such as lower costs and better products for the public. Equally significant, discovery of the scheme led to a loss of trust in public officials, a trust important for the well-functioning of government. And the perpetrators themselves eventually suffered greatly. . . .*
>
> *A different answer to what was wrong in engaging in the kickback scheme would have us focus directly on the actions involved, rather than their consequences. The actions were intended to keep outsiders deceived about what was going on. They were also inherently unfair to other people who were denied equality of opportunity to bid for the contracts. Hence the actions, irrespective of their actual or probable consequences, violated at least two basic principles of duty: "Avoid deceiving others" and "Be fair". . . .*
>
> *Yet another answer to why it was wrong to participate in the kickback scheme is that it violated the rights of other people. A shared understanding exists that there will be equality of opportunity in seeking public contracts and that elected officials will grant contracts based on merit, not bribes. Against this background, qualified persons or firms acquire a right to unbiased consideration of their contract proposals, and these rights were violated by the kickback scheme. It might also be argued that the public's rights to the benefits of fair competition were violated as well . . .*
>
> *A very different answer to why it was wrong to enter into the kickback scheme makes reference to virtues and vices, that is, to good and bad traits of character. [The County Executive] displayed unfairness, dishonesty, and greed—that is the kind of person he showed himself to be. [The engineers] displayed moral weakness, deceptiveness, dishonesty, and perhaps cowardice in the face of temptation. Morally better people would have manifested virtues such as courage, honesty, fairness, and conscientiousness. (10)* (Reproduced with permission of McGraw-Hill.)

In his book *The Civilized Engineer*, Florman (*12*) enlarges on this theme. He writes:

> *I propose that the essence of engineering ethics be recognized as something different and apart from white-hat heroics. There is no single word adequate to define this "something", but conscientiousness is fairly close to what I have in mind. . . . I [have] noted that engineers are accustomed to having their fellow citizens rely upon them. As a consequence, if engineers do their jobs well they are being more than competent; in serving their fellow humans, and in serving them well, they are being good. Reliability is a virtue. Therefore, the conscientious, effective engineer is a virtuous engineer.*
>
> *If we relate engineering ethics to the protection of the public interest, then clearly diligence is more moral than conventional "morality". A kindly, generous, well-intentioned, even saintly engineer may still be an inept engineer, that is, a "bad" engineer whose work does not serve the public well. Engineering ethics is not the same as conventional ethics. In technical work, competence is more good than "goodness". . . .*
>
> *Other words come to mind: dedication, energy, self-discipline, caution, alertness, awareness—and, most of all, as I have suggested, conscientiousness. The greatest threats to moral engineering are carelessness, sloppiness, laziness, and lack of concentration. An engineer may start out honest and high-minded but become immoral by falling prey to one or more of these sins. On the other hand, an engineer who starts out by being conscientious must end up by being honest, since competent engineering, excellent engineering, is in its very nature the pursuit of truth.* (*12*)

3.8   THE FRAMEWORK OF ENGINEERING ETHICS

The engineer's primary responsibility is to place the safety of the public above all else. He or she must be sensitive to and strive to avoid the potential for harm, but, given a choice, should opt for doing good (*13*). While engineers are constantly challenged to create solutions to problems within given cost and time frames, they must do so without jeopardizing the safety of the users of the technology.

The engineer is a knowledge expert specially trained to design and evaluate the performance characteristics of technology within his or her area of expertise. One component of his or her knowledge is theoretically derived. It comes from formal training and education, library research, or possibly through mathematical derivation. Another knowledge component is empirical. It comes from experience, recordkeeping, or experimental testing or use. A competent engineer understands that his or her knowledge about a problem is sometimes incomplete. As Figure 3.3 illustrates, there may be known missing knowledge and unknown missing knowledge. A competent engineer will acknowledge his or her limitations about a technology.

■ Empirically Tested Knowledge

■ Theoretically Derived Knowledge

□ Known Missing Knowledge

□ Unknown Missing Knowledge

Figure 3.3 *Knowledge base available to solve an engineering problem with one engineer's contribution. (Source: Adapted from Reference 11.)*

Engineers commonly work for an organization and may serve as a part of an engineering team. In this way, organizational competence comes from the combined competence of the members of the team. (See Figure 3.4.) It is possible, of course, for gaps to occur because of insufficient resources, time, or effort to have been expended, or the problem may require knowledge beyond the competence of the team. If the gaps are known by at least one member of the engineering team, the team fails to meet the requirement of organizational competence.

3.9   CODES OF ENGINEERING ETHICS

Engineers have attempted to establish rules or standards of conduct in the form of codes of ethics. These codes not only protect the public, but also build and preserve the integrity and reputation of the profession. There is no single code of ethics for all engineering societies. However, there is considerable agreement among engineers as to what constitutes ethical behavior, and there is a great deal of similarity among the various ethical codes. The *Code of Ethics for Engineers* (*14*) published by the National Society of Professional Engineers (NSPE), is reprinted in the following paragraphs by permission of NSPE. The NSPE *Code of Ethics* consists of a preamble, six fundamental canons or authoritative rules, five rules of practice, and nine professional obligations. This document comprises basic rules of professional behavior suitable for all engineering specialties. Since ethical decisions are sometimes difficult and equivocable, more detailed guidelines have been prepared by several engineering organizations.

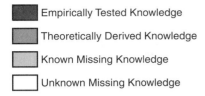

Empirically Tested Knowledge

Theoretically Derived Knowledge

Known Missing Knowledge

Unknown Missing Knowledge

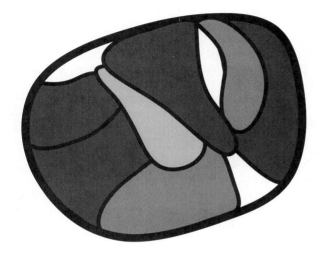

Figure 3.4   *Organizational competence in which several engineers contribute specialized knowledge for the problem's solution.* (Source: *Adapted from Reference 11.*)

Code of Ethics for Engineers: July 1996–Present

Preamble

Engineering is an important and learned profession. As members of this profession, engineers are expected to exhibit the highest standards of honesty and integrity. Engineering has a direct and vital impact on the quality of life for all people. Accordingly, the services provided by engineers require honesty, impartiality, fairness and equity, and must be dedicated to the protection of the public health, safety, and welfare. Engineers must perform under a standard of professional behavior that requires adherence to the highest principles of ethical conduct.

I.   Fundamental Canons

Engineers, in the fulfillment of their professional duties, shall:
1.   Hold paramount the safety, health and welfare of the public.
2.   Perform services only in areas of their competence.
3.   Issue public statements only in an objective and truthful manner.
4.   Act for each employer or client as faithful agents or trustees.
5.   Avoid deceptive acts.
6.   Conduct themselves honorably, responsibly, ethically, and lawfully so as to enhance the honor, reputation, and usefulness of the profession.

II.   Rules of Practice

1. Engineers shall hold paramount the safety, health, and welfare of the public.
   a. If engineers' judgment is overruled under circumstances that endanger life or property, they shall notify their employer or client and such other authority as may be appropriate.
   b. Engineers shall approve only those engineering documents that are in conformity with applicable standards.
   c. Engineers shall not reveal facts, data or information without the prior consent of the client or employer except as authorized or required by law or this Code.
   d. Engineers shall not permit the use of their name or associate in business ventures with any person or firm that they believe is engaged in fraudulent or dishonest enterprise.
   e. Engineers having knowledge of any alleged violation of this Code shall report thereon to appropriate professional bodies and, when relevant, also to public authorities, and cooperate with the proper authorities in furnishing such information or assistance as may be required.

2. Engineers shall perform services only in the areas of their competence.
   a. Engineers shall undertake assignments only when qualified by education or experience in the specific technical fields involved.
   b. Engineers shall not affix their signatures to any plans or documents dealing with subject matter in which they lack competence, nor to any plan or document not prepared under their direction and control.
   c. Engineers may accept assignments and assume responsibility for coordination of an entire project and sign and seal the engineering documents for the entire project, provided that each technical segment is signed and sealed only by the qualified engineers who prepared the segment.

3. Engineers shall issue public statements only in an objective and truthful manner.
   a. Engineers shall be objective and truthful in professional reports, statements, or testimony. They shall include all relevant and pertinent information in such reports, statements, or testimony, which should bear the date indicating when it was current.
   b. Engineers may express publicly technical opinions that are founded upon knowledge of the facts and competence in the subject matter.
   c. Engineers shall issue no statements, criticisms, or arguments on technical matters that are inspired or paid for by interested parties, unless they have prefaced their comments by explicitly identifying the interested parties on whose behalf they are speaking, and by revealing the existence of any interest the engineers may have in the matters.

4. Engineers shall act for each employer or client as faithful agents or trustees.
   a. Engineers shall disclose all known or potential conflicts of interest that could influence or appear to influence their judgment or the quality of their services.
   b. Engineers shall not accept compensation, financial or otherwise, from more than one party for services on the same project, or for services pertaining to the same project, unless the circumstances are fully disclosed and agreed to by all interested parties.

    c. Engineers shall not solicit or accept financial or other valuable consideration, directly or indirectly, from outside agents in connection with the work for which they are responsible.

    d. Engineers in public service as members, advisors, or employees of a governmental or quasi-governmental body or department shall not participate in decisions with respect to services solicited or provided by them or their organizations in private or public engineering practice.

    e. Engineers shall not solicit or accept a contract from a governmental body on which a principal or officer of their organization serves as a member.

5. Engineers shall avoid deceptive acts.

    a. Engineers shall not falsify their qualifications or permit misrepresentation of their or their associates' qualifications. They shall not misrepresent or exaggerate their responsibility in or for the subject matter of prior assignments. Brochures or other presentations incident to the solicitation of employment shall not misrepresent pertinent facts concerning employers, employees, associates, joint venturers, or past accomplishments.

    b. Engineers shall not offer, give, solicit, or receive, either directly or indirectly, any contribution to influence the award of a contract by public authority, or which may be reasonably construed by the public as having the effect or intent of influencing the awarding of a contract. They shall not offer any gift or other valuable consideration in order to secure work. They shall not pay a commission, percentage, or brokerage fee in order to secure work, except to a bona fide employee or bona fide established commercial or marketing agencies retained by them.

III. Professional Obligations

1. Engineers shall be guided in all their relations by the highest standards of honesty and integrity.

    a. Engineers shall acknowledge their errors and shall not distort or alter the facts.

    b. Engineers shall advise their clients or employers when they believe a project will not be successful.

    c. Engineers shall not accept outside employment to the detriment of their regular work or interest. Before accepting any outside engineering employment, they will notify their employers.

    d. Engineers shall not attempt to attract an engineer from another employer by false or misleading pretenses.

    e. Engineers shall not actively participate in strikes, picket lines, or other collective coercive action.

    f. Engineers shall not promote their own interest at the expense of the dignity and integrity of the profession.

2. Engineers shall at all times strive to serve the public interest.

    a. Engineers shall seek opportunities to participate in civic affairs; career guidance for youths; and work for the advancement of the safety, health and well-being of their community.

    b. Engineers shall not complete, sign, or seal plans and/or specifications that are not in conformity with applicable engineering standards. If the client or employer insists on such unprofessional conduct, they shall notify the proper authorities and withdraw from further service on the project.

    c. Engineers shall endeavor to extend public knowledge and appreciation of engineering and its achievements.

3. Engineers shall avoid all conduct or practice that deceives the public.

    a. Engineers shall avoid the use of statements containing a material misrepresentation of fact or omitting a material fact.

    b. Consistent with the foregoing, Engineers may advertise for recruitment of personnel.

    c. Consistent with the foregoing, Engineers may prepare articles for the lay or technical press, but such articles shall not imply credit to the author for work performed by others.

4. Engineers shall not disclose, without consent, confidential information concerning the business affairs or technical processes of any present or former client or employer, or public body on which they serve.

    a. Engineers shall not, without the consent of all interested parties, promote or arrange for new employment or practice in connection with a specific project for which the Engineer has gained particular and specialized knowledge.

    b. Engineers shall not, without the consent of all interested parties, participate in or represent an adversary interest in connection with a specific project or proceeding in which the Engineer has gained particular specialized knowledge on behalf of a former client or employer.

5. Engineers shall not be influenced in their professional duties by conflicting interests.

    a. Engineers shall not accept financial or other considerations, including free engineering designs, from material or equipment suppliers for specifying their product.

    b. Engineers shall not accept commissions or allowances, directly or indirectly, from contractors or other parties dealing with clients or employers of the Engineer in connection with work for which the Engineer is responsible.

6. Engineers shall not attempt to obtain employment or advancement or professional engagements by untruthfully criticizing other engineers, or by other improper or questionable methods.

    a. Engineers shall not request, propose, or accept a commission on a contingent basis under circumstances in which their judgment may be compromised.

    b. Engineers in salaried positions shall accept part-time engineering work only to the extent consistent with policies of the employer and in accordance with ethical considerations.

    c. Engineers shall not, without consent, use equipment, supplies, laboratory, or office facilities of an employer to carry on outside private practice.

7. Engineers shall not attempt to injure, maliciously or falsely, directly or indirectly, the professional reputation, prospects, practice, or employment of other engineers. Engineers who believe others are guilty of unethical or illegal practice shall present such information to the proper authority for action.

    a. Engineers in private practice shall not review the work of another engineer for the same client, except with the knowledge of such engineer, or unless the connection of such engineer with the work has been terminated.

    b. Engineers in governmental, industrial, or educational employ are entitled to review and evaluate the work of other engineers when so required by their employment duties.

    c. Engineers in sales or industrial employ are entitled to make engineering comparisons of represented products with products of other suppliers.

8. Engineers shall accept personal responsibility for their professional activities, provided, however, that Engineers may seek indemnification for services arising out of their practice for other than gross negligence, where the Engineer's interests cannot otherwise be protected.

    a. Engineers shall conform with state registration laws in the practice of engineering.

    b. Engineers shall not use association with a nonengineer, a corporation, or partnership as a "cloak" for unethical acts.

9. Engineers shall give credit for engineering work to those to whom credit is due, and will recognize the proprietary interests of others.

    a. Engineers shall, whenever possible, name the person or persons who may be individually responsible for designs, inventions, writings, or other accomplishments.

    b. Engineers using designs supplied by a client recognize that the designs remain the property of the client and may not be duplicated by the Engineer for others without express permission.

    c. Engineers, before undertaking work for others in connection with which the Engineer may make improvements, plans, designs, inventions, or other records that may justify copyrights or patents, should enter into a positive agreement regarding ownership.

    d. Engineers' designs, data, records, and notes referring exclusively to an employer's work are the employer's property. Employer should indemnify the Engineer for use of the information for any purpose other than the original purpose.

As Revised July 1996

3.10   CASE STUDIES IN ENGINEERING ETHICS

Twelve case studies have been incorporated into this chapter to illustrate the application of codes of ethics and guidelines to common problems that face professional engineers. The first six examples were adapted from *Ethical Problems in Engineering* by Alger, Christensen, and Olmsted (9) and are used with the permission of the publisher. The remaining six examples are reproduced from Reference 15 and constitute opinions from the Board of Ethical Review, National Society of Professional Engineers. The NSPE Board of Ethical Review, typically comprised of seven professional engineers, considers ethical cases involving either real or hypothetical matters submitted to it from NSPE members, other engineers, students, and the public. In regard to the question of application of the NSPE *Code of Ethics* to engineering organizations (e.g., corporations, partnerships, sole-proprietorships, government agencies, university engineering departments, etc.), the specific business form or type should not negate nor detract from the conformance of individuals to the NSPE *Code of Ethics.* The NSPE *Code of Ethics* deals with professional services, which states that services must be performed by real persons. Real persons in turn establish and implement policies within business structures. These opinions are for educational purposes only and are reprinted with the permission of the National Society of Professional Engineers.

Case 1   KICKBACK TO PUBLIC OFFICIALS

At the urging of the Mayor, the City Council approved the concept of building another runway and expanding the terminal building at Municipal Airport. Hearing of the proposed work, the principals of Warren[1] and Associates, a local engineering firm, submitted to the Mayor a letter of interest in furnishing engineering services. The following week, the President of the firm received a telephone call from the Mayor's Executive Assistant, and arrangements were made for a meeting at City Hall. At that meeting, attended by the President of the firm and the Airport Engineer, the Assistant informed the engineers that in order to obtain work from the city a contribution would be required, and the amount of the contribution was specified. The engineers thanked the Assistant for his time and departed. The following day, after consulting with her partners, the President of the firm withdrew from the project. Six weeks later, the Mayor's Public Information Director issued a press release announcing an agreement with Transport Engineers, Inc., a firm from another state, to provide engineering services.   ■

DISCUSSION

Many situations that engineers deal with are complex, and it is not always obvious that an act is ethical or unethical. This case, however, involves a clear-cut and unequivocal application of Canons 5 and 6 of the *Code of Ethics.* Had the engineer made the political contribution in order to secure engineering work, it would have clearly been unethical and almost certainly illegal.

Unfortunately, the events described here are more common than professional engineers would like to believe. Professional societies should adopt a militant attitude toward kickbacks and bribes to public officials and publicly condemn any known instances of such practices. No reputable engineer should accept work under such conditions.

Case 2   PLANS SIGNED BY OUTSIDE ENGINEER

A small steel fabricator having engineering graduates on its payroll prepared the plans for the roof truss of a local building. The city inspector refused to

---

[1] This and all other names used in these cases are fictitious.

accept the plans because they were not signed by a registered engineer. The steel company carried the plans to a local consulting engineer and asked that he certify and place his seal and signature on the plans. The engineer, after satisfying himself that the design and plans were adequate and economical, agreed to certify the plans but insisted on receiving the same fee as if he had prepared the plans.

Was such a procedure ethical? Was the engineer unreasonable in demanding such a fee? Should the owner be expected to pay the additional cost involved or should the steel fabricator be expected to pay the engineer for his services?

■

DISCUSSION

From the standpoint of the engineer, this procedure was ethical. There is an ethical question with respect to the fabricator, who would have willingly passed off an uncertified set of plans for a truss had he not been prevented from doing so by an alert city inspector.

It would have been unethical for the engineer to seal the design without checking the adequacy and economics of the truss design. Therefore, the engineer was not unreasonable in requiring the same fee he would have received had he been completely responsible for the design of the truss.

Case 3   ADVERTISING OF ENGINEERING SERVICES

The following two-column classified advertisement was published in a business magazine sponsored by the city Chamber of Commerce:

Consulting Engineers, Inc. *555-1212*		
SOUND LOW-COST STRUCTURES BEGIN WITH GOOD DESIGN	*Building Design *Appraisals *Cost Estimates *We may be able to save you future worries and needless expense through proper design and supervision of construction.*	*Soil Investigations *Safe Floor Loads *Vibration Control

QUESTION

Does this advertisement conform to ethical practices with respect to the advertising of professional services?

■

DISCUSSION

While advertising of engineering services is not unethical *per se*, it is required that advertisements be dignified, free of ostentation, and contain no laudatory expression. The statement, "We may be able to save you future worries and needless expense through proper design and supervision of construction" is boastful and implies that the firm can render a professional service not available from others. The use of the word "proper" also gives an impression of discrediting other engineers. The advertisement fails to meet the requirements to be circumspect, discreet, and dignified; this therefore does not conform to ethical practice.

Case 4   FAILURE TO GIVE CREDIT TO OTHERS

Two researchers, M. Smith and F. Jones, are working independently on a problem. After a great deal of laboratory work, Researcher Smith writes a report explaining his results. In his report, however, he is unable to correlate his data into a simple pattern.

Researcher Jones approaches the problem from a more theoretical viewpoint and discovers that Smith's data can be described by a well-known classical formula. She reports her findings to Smith in an informal discussion.

A few months later, Smith publishes a paper explaining all of his data through the use of the formula suggested by Jones, but he fails to acknowledge the contribution. Should he have done so? Was he right in his position that since it was only a well-established formula that was suggested, no acknowledgment was needed?　　　　　　　　　　　　　　　　　　　　　　　　　■

DISCUSSION

NSPE's *Code of Ethics*, *Professional Obligations*, paragraph 9a, states: "Engineers shall give proper credit for engineering work to those to whom credit is due, and recognize the proprietary interests of others. Whenever possible, they shall name the person or persons who may be responsible for designs, inventions, writings, and other accomplishments." In failing to recognize Jones' contribution, it appears that Researcher Smith violated this guideline.

Giving credit to a predecessor or one who makes a contribution never hurts and is advisable. Doing so does not take anything away from the report, and it is a credit to the person reporting. Professional engineers should be careful not to injure the professional reputation, prospects, practice, or employment of another engineer and should treat other engineers with honor and respect.

Case 5   RECTIFICATION OF AN ERROR

Paul Jackson, a professional structural engineer, was asked to investigate an existing structure, now supporting two identical condensers, to determine the advisability of adding a third condenser to the structure. The structure had been designed two years earlier by a group of engineers under Jackson's supervision. Jackson did not review the original design, but he was responsible for the group under his supervision.

In checking the design, Jackson discovers that the original placement of reinforcing steel did not provide adequately for earthquake loading. The inadequacy, although real, is probably not too significant. The structure has been in service for two years without incident, but there has not been an earthquake in that time.

Jackson must choose from three courses:

1. Should he say nothing about the inadequacy and simply report that the structure is not capable of carrying the proposed new load?
2. Should he work out a system of reinforcement for the structure that would both rectify the original inadequacy and provide for support of the new load in a single package?
3. Should he admit to the original error and suggest to the owner that repairs be made against the possibility of damage if an earthquake should occur? ∎

DISCUSSION

In this case, the engineer should disclose the original error to his client. Jackson did not perform his responsibility of reviewing and approving the original design, although he was paid to do so. Ethically, therefore, the responsibility is still his, since it had never been discharged. Jackson must now bring the whole matter into the open for consideration of the owner and take appropriate action to correct the problem. He should not proceed independently and secretly on any of the proposals mentioned.

Case 6   STICKING TO A GRADUATE'S COMMITMENT

Three months before graduation, electrical engineering student Laura Anderson accepts an offer of employment from one firm and subsequently is invited in by another firm for an interview. The travel distance to the second firm is considerable, and it has offered to pay the expenses incident to the trip. What action should be taken by the student? ∎

DISCUSSION

In this case, Miss Anderson has accepted a job and with it has accepted certain obligations. She cannot ethically accept employment with the second firm unless she is released by the first firm. She may visit the second firm and accept its expense money provided she informs the second firm that she is committed to the first firm and cannot accept employment there unless the first firm consents. If the second firm is willing to interview her and to pay her expenses under these conditions, she may take the trip. A more dignified procedure unquestionably is to decline the invitation to a second firm or to inform the first firm that she would like to visit the second firm and to see what they have to offer, although she acknowledges that her primary obligation is to the first firm.

Case 7   USE OF ENGINEERING TITLE BY NONENGINEERS

ENGCO, an engineering firm, distributes a brochure that, along with the usual information, contains a listing of key personnel. Some are licensed professional engineers; others are not. In some instances, key personnel who do not hold an engineering degree and may in fact be high school graduates only, are given such titles in the brochure as "Engineer," "Design Engineer," etc. This practice has arisen from federal agency engineering contracts that refer to inspection personnel as "Engineers." ENGCO is concerned that the company brochure may be conveying a misrepresentation, implying that there are more engineers on its staff than is the true situation.

QUESTION

Is it ethical for ENGCO to refer to its nondegreed personnel as "engineers"? ■

REFERENCES

Sections I.3, I.5, II.3, II.5, II.5a.

DISCUSSION

Although the industry and governmental agencies sometimes use the term indiscriminently, we in the profession must not. Most states even have it in their law (licensing act) how and when "engineer" can be used, usually requiring a college degree and/or meeting licensing requirements.

An engineering firm's brochure is a sales tool and should describe accurately the academic qualifications of its employees. People reading and relying on the information in an engineering brochure would assume the title "engineer" means one educated or registered as such. The use of the term for high school graduates is a gross misrepresentation of the firm's qualifications and essentially falsifying them. If the engineering personnel have passed the state requirements for licensing, they may use the term regardless of their formal education.

CONCLUSION

It is not ethical for ENGCO to refer to its nondegreed, nonregistered personnel as "engineers."

Case 8   GIFTS TO FOREIGN OFFICIALS

Engineer A is a consulting engineer who does work in the United States and abroad. Engineer A is contacted by the government of Country A and asked to submit a proposal on a major water project being constructed in Country A. As part of the project, Engineer A is encouraged to associate with and retain Engineer B, a local engineer in Country A, with whom Engineer A has worked in the past on private projects in Country A. One of the acceptable "customs" in Country A is for consultants such as engineers to give substantial gifts to public officials in connection with the awarding of public works contracts. Engineer A recognizes that the giving of such gifts may be a violation of U.S. law—although they may not technically be a violation of the law in Country A. Engineer B proposes to Engineer A that if the project is awarded to Engineer A's firm, Engineer B will handle "business arrangements" in Country A and that Engineer A be involved in overall management of the project as well as all technical matters.

QUESTION

Would it be ethical for Engineer A to proceed with the project under these circumstances?

REFERENCES

I.5, II.1.d.

DISCUSSION

With the increase in international engineering practice as a result of the North America Free Trade Agreement (NAFTA) and the General Agreement on Trade in Services (GATS), engineers are being exposed to differing design selection methods. These practices are in many cases quite similar to the practices used in the United States and elsewhere; however, in some cases, particularly in the developing world and in some cultures, there are sometimes different methods of selection. Some of these methods involve a design selection process which is more deliberative, more subjective, and more personal than the methods employed in the United States. Engineers need to be sensitive to these differences, practicing in a manner that is consistent with the ethical principles of the U.S. engineering community, and at the same time being respectful of the differing cultural traditions and expectations that manifest themselves in other societies. Engineers must not take actions that bring dishonor on other engineers, and this is equally true when engineers are practicing in the international arena (see NSPE *Code of Ethics*, Section II.1.d.).

Engineers must always follow their ethical compass on matters of this type, and there can be no doubt that as a matter of general principle, engineers must be consistent in their ethical conduct regardless of where it is the engineer is rendering professional services. While certain conduct may be acceptable or even the generally accepted rule in other cultures, such conduct does not necessarily become acceptable for engineers who adhere to a code of ethics containing proscriptions in these areas. While engineers must be careful not to pass judgment on a particular matter, engineers who are faced with this type of ethical quandary should make every attempt to carefully, delicately, and diplomatically sidestep the matter in order to remove any appearance of an ethical conflict.

Turning to the facts of the case, it is clear that Engineer A is being asked to participate in a project under circumstances that may involve a violation of U.S. law as well as the NSPE *Code of Ethics*. While being respectful of all of the parties involved in this matter, Engineer A should diplomatically indicate that while Engineer A would be interested in participating in the project in question and offering the professional service, under the described arrangement, it would be illegal and unethical for Engineer A to participate in the project and that while Engineer A would be willing to consider an alternative arrangement under circumstances that were consistent with U.S. law and engineering ethics, the present arrangement would not be acceptable.

CONCLUSION

It would not be ethical for Engineer A to proceed with the project under the circumstances. ∎

Case 9   PROMOTIONAL REFERENCE TO WORK AND CLIENTS OF PREVIOUS EMPLOYERS

Engineer A is the principal in a new engineering firm that has been in existence for approximately 18 months. All of the engineers in the firm have come from other engineering firms. Engineer A develops a firm promotional brochure that contains the following: (1) a "list of clients" implying those companies on the list are clients of the firm and (2) a "list of projects of the firm" implying the projects were performed by the new firm. In fact, the client list is actually those companies for whom the firm's engineers have performed work with their former firms, and not with the new firm. Similarly, the project list is a series of projects performed by the firm's engineers for their former firms.

QUESTION

Was it ethical for Engineer A to produce a promotional brochure for his new firm that contains (1) a "list of clients" implying those on the list are current clients of the firm and (2) a "list of projects" implying the projects were performed by the new firm?   ■

REFERENCES

Sections II.3a, II.5a, III.3a.

DISCUSSION

It is clear that these situations frequently are delicate and sometimes difficult, particularly where long-established business relationships exist between engineering firms, engineers, and their clients. Obviously, no engineer or engineering firm "owns" a relationship with a client, as clients are free to determine for themselves which engineer or engineering firm is appropriate for their present and future needs and requirements.

Under the facts, we are deeply troubled by the manner in which Engineer A undertook to promote his new engineering firm because we believe there was a clear effort on the part of Engineer A to engage in misleading and deceptive acts. To imply that certain companies are the "clients" of the new firm and to imply and take credit for projects that were performed in an entirely different context by other engineering firms is wholly improper. We cannot identify any context in which Engineer A could have accurately used the term "client" to describe the new firm's relationship with the companies listed on the brochure. A "client" implies some past or present business relationship between an engineer, the engineer's firm, and a company. To use the term "client" to refer to a relationship that existed between an engineer when he was employed in an entirely different context is misleading, deceptive, and a violation of the NSPE *Code of Ethics*. We cannot think of any clarification that could have been included in such a brochure that would have made the reference to "client" less misleading or deceptive (see Code Sections II.3.a., II.5.a., III.3.a.).

Similarly and for the same reasons, the reference to the "projects of the firm" is misleading, deceptive, and a violation of the NSPE *Code of Ethics*. Had the promotional brochure contained a clarification specifically stating that the projects identified were performed by current employees of the new firm when they were employed by the named firms, and depending upon all of the facts and circumstances, the Board may have reached a different result.

CONCLUSION

It was not ethical for Engineer A to produce a promotional brochure for his new firm that contained (1) a "list of clients" implying those on the list are current clients of the firm and (2) a "list of projects" implying the projects were performed by the new firm.   ■

Case 10   ENGINEERING RESEARCH—CLIENT CHANGES TO REPORT

Engineer A is a research professor at a major engineering college. He performs important research in connection with certain new technologies in the field of transportation. As part of his work, the university has received a number of grants from major corporations and the federal government. As the principal investigator, Engineer A collaborates with several other research professors at the university as well as graduate students. In addition, he routinely meets with representatives of government agencies and private funding groups and reports on the status of his research, and publishes the results in professional journals and at technical conferences. Engineer A has a long-standing relationship with the university and is a tenured professor. He has received multiple honors and awards for his services. Engineer A highly values his reputation as a professor and researcher.

Engineer A meets with the major commercial sponsor of his transportation research and presents the results of his research in a paper, including charts, graphs, and other illustrative material. The commercial sponsor clearly has a significant interest in the research report and its conclusions, and, subsequently, the commercial sponsor makes certain changes in the research report bearing Engineer A's name without his knowledge and approval. The changes include altering report text, altering tables, and removing figures.

Engineer A seeks assistance concerning the appropriate course of action.

QUESTIONS

1. Would Engineer A be ethical in taking action against the sponsor?
2. Was the sponsor ethical in altering Engineer A's report?   ■

REFERENCES

Fundamental Canon 4, Sections II.1.d, II.2.b, II.3.a,b,c, III.2.b,c, III.3.a.

DISCUSSION

There are several aspects of this case that need to be discussed in order to evaluate appropriate courses of action and ethical implications. There are questions which need to be answered before reaching an opinion in this case. Did the changes improve the report quality? Did the changes modify or change the results inappropriately? Did the changes make the report more readable or make it more confusing? Was the report published by the sponsor or just used in-house? In considering this case, some assumptions need to be made.

One could argue that if the "changed" report is to be used specifically and only by the sponsor in their internal decision-making process and if the "certain changes" made by the sponsor did not change the actual conclusions of the engineer's report, there might appear to be ethical implications on the part of the sponsor. The sponsor paid for the research and it is theirs to use as they see fit as long as they do not modify the results to serve a purpose not intended by the research engineer. However, the Board of Ethical Review (BER) believes that the report remains the responsibility of the author and should not be changed. The sponsor could ethically write another report using the information from Engineer A's report with appropriate reference to Engineer A's report. Code Section II.2.b. requires that the engineer's name not be affixed to any document not prepared under his or her direction and control.

If the "changed" report is to be published by the sponsor or if the "certain changes" made by the sponsor did change the actual conclusions of the engineer's report, there again appear to be ethical questions on the part of the sponsor. The sponsor paid for the research and it is theirs to use but not in a way that modifies the results to serve a purpose not intended by the research engineer. The sponsor is obligated to notify the engineer of the changes and seek his permission before making the changes. Under these circumstances, the engineer should at a minimum request the removal of his name from the changed report and if not granted, never accept a research project from that sponsor and at a maximum, take the sponsor to court. Of course, several actions between these extremes are possible and should be explored.

Referring to II.3.a. of the *Code of Ethics*, an engineer shall be objective and truthful in reports and shall include all relevant and pertinent information in such reports. Furthermore, Section II.1.d. states that an engineer must not permit the use of his or her name in business ventures with any person that they have reason to believe is engaging in fraudulent or dishonest business or professional practice. Fundamental Canon 4 of the *Code of Ethics* states that the engineer shall act in professional matters for each employer or client as a faithful agent or trustee. Assuming that the sponsor involved in this case was an engineer, he should also be aware of and adhere to the profession's ethics code.

CONCLUSIONS

1. Engineer A would be ethical in taking action against the sponsor.
2. The sponsor in this case did not act ethically toward Engineer A.   ∎

Case 11   USE OF CD-ROM FOR HIGHWAY DESIGN

Engineer A, a chemical engineer with no facilities design and construction experience, receives a solicitation in the mail with the following information:

> *Engineers today cannot afford to pass up a single job that comes by— including construction projects that may be new or unfamiliar.*
>
> *Now—thanks to a revolutionary new CD-ROM—specifying, designing, and costing out any construction project is as easy as pointing and clicking your mouse—no matter your design experience. For instance, never designed a highway before? No problem. Just point to the* Highways *window and click.*
>
> *Simply sign and return this letter today and you'll be among the first engineers to see how this full-featured interactive library of standard design can help you work faster than ever and increase your firm's profits.*

Engineer A orders the CD-ROM and begins to offer facilities design and construction services.

QUESTION

Was it ethical for Engineer A to offer facilities design and construction services under the facts presented?   ∎

REFERENCES

Sections II.2, II.2.a,b,c, III.2.b.

DISCUSSION

The issue of whether an engineer possesses the appropriate level of competence to perform specified services is one of most basic professional and ethical issues faced by practitioners (See Code Section II.2.a.). NSPE has been supportive of the concept that a qualified individual engineer, regardless of his or her particular area of technical discipline, should be licensed as a "professional engineer". However, this position should not be understood to suggest that all engineers are free to practice without restriction in any and all areas within the practice of engineering. Instead, all engineers are implored to exercise careful professional judgment and discretion and practice solely within his or her area(s) of competency.

It is clear that Engineer A, a chemical engineer, has no apparent substantive background or experience in the area of facilities design and construction. A CD-ROM that permits virtually anyone to "specify, design, and cost out" a project clearly is not an appropriate basis upon which an individual can obtain professional competency to perform facilities design and construction services.

An individual seeking to obtain an acceptable level of competency in the basic elements of facilities design and construction (e.g., civil, structural, mechanical, electrical engineering) should seek and be able to demonstrate appropriate engineering and related education and experience. Relying on a "how to" CD-ROM appears to show a general disregard for the fundamental role that professional engineers play in protecting the public health and safety, and minimizes the high level of knowledge and expertise necessary to perform these critical responsibilities. Professional engineering cannot be reduced to an activity whereby practitioners rely upon computers and technical information instead of time-tested professional experience and engineering judgment.

In a sense, the direct mail product described under the facts is not unlike mail order certifications offered by so-called diploma mills whereby individuals "self-certify" their competency based upon a perfunctory review process that rarely involves comprehensive study, examination, or practice. By ordering and using the CD-ROM, Engineer A in a sense was "self-certifying" his competency to perform facilities design and construction services without obtaining the substantive education, experience, and qualifications to perform those services in a competent and professional manner. The Board considers such activities completely contrary to the basic ethical principles established in the *Code of Ethics*.

In closing, the Board's decision should not be understood as a wholesale rejection of the use of computers, CD-ROMs, and other technological advances. Rather, it is the Board's position that technology has an important place in the practice of engineering, but it must never be a replacement or a substitute for engineering judgment.

CONCLUSION

It was not ethical for Engineer A to offer facilities design and construction services under the facts presented.   ∎

Case 12   PROVIDING REFERRAL FEES TO A CONTRACTOR

Engineer A receives the following letter from a contractor:

> *Dear Engineer A:*
>
> *If you have not already heard of us, please allow me to introduce myself. I am Contractor X, owner of X Construction Company.*
>
> *We are a medium-sized general contractor firm with twenty years' experience. One of my company's strengths is our ability to interpret a blueprint or drawing and properly execute the construction of the project as it was conceived.*
>
> *This year I would like to associate my company with an engineering firm that we can refer clients to and receive clients from. I understand that there is a necessary ethical distance that must be maintained between an engineer and a contractor. I also know that it is not unethical for an engineer to provide their clients with a list of a few qualified contractors.*

As an incentive to include my company on such list or as a referral to your clients, I am prepared to offer you a flat $500 plus 3% of the total contract price, as a finder's fee/commission for every contract I sign as a result of your referral.

Once a client has called for an estimate of proposal, we work directly with them. I will in no way use your good name or any association with your firm as a sales tool.

All I ask is for is the opportunity for my firm's proposal to be included in the client's decision-making process.

We both work from different ends of the same field. It is possible for our firms to establish an arm's length relationship, it can be very beneficial to both of us.

We are fully licensed, insured, registered with the Better Business Bureau and can provide a long list of satisfied clients.

Please call or write if you would like to discuss this further and take full advantage of this new season which is just underway.

Sincerely yours,
Contractor X

QUESTION

Is it ethical for Engineer A to associate with Contractor X and the X Construction Company under the circumstances being proposed in this situation?   ■

REFERENCES

Sections II.4.a,c, II.5.b, III.5.b.

DISCUSSION

It is essential that an engineer maintain an "arm's length" relationship with contractors, vendors, etc. having, or potentially having, contractual arrangements with the engineer's employer or client.

Two primary issues are involved in the case before the Board: (1) Engineer A making referrals to his clients and (2) receiving a commission for making referrals to his clients and others. Engineer A's referral to his clients is a definite conflict of interest due to receiving a commission for doing so. Contractor X makes no suggestion that Engineer A disclose to his client his conflict of interest as required by Section II.4.a. of the *Code*. In addition, Section II.4.c. prohibits the receiving of commission or other valuables from a contractor. Contractor X's proposal will be a violation of this Section. While Section II.5.b. addresses political contributions, a broad interpretation of the Section would indicate that an engineer receiving contributions (commissions) or other valuable considerations would also be a violation of the *Code*.

CONCLUSION

It would not be ethical for Engineer A to associate with Contractor X and the X Construction Company under the circumstances being proposed in this situation.

■

REFERENCES

1. *1991 ABET Accreditation Yearbook*, Accreditation Board for Engineering and Technology, New York, 1992.

2. *Annual Report*, 1945, Engineers Council for Professional Development, New York, 1945.

3. *Memoirs of Herbert Hoover, Vol. 1: Years of Adventure*, Macmillan Publishing Company, 1951.

4. *The Engineer's Creed*, National Society of Professional Engineers, Washington, DC, adopted June 1954. Reprinted by permission of the National Society of Professional Engineers.

5. *Faith of an Engineer*, prepared by the Ethics Committee, Engineers Council for Professional Development, New York.

6. JESWIET, J., *Information Relevant to the Iron Ring Ceremony*, www.conn .me.queensu.ca/dept/jj-ring.htm, 2001.

7. MEYER, ALVIN H., *Order of the Engineer*, Office of Student Affairs, University of Texas, www.engr.utexas.edu/sao/order.htm, 2001.

8. *History: The Birth of Registration*, National Council of Examiners for Engineering and Surveying, Seneca, SC, 1991.

9. ALGER, PHILIP L., N. A. CHRISTENSEN, AND STERLING P. OLMSTED, *Ethical Problems in Engineering*, John Wiley & Sons, New York, 1965.

10. MARTIN, MIKE W. AND ROLAND SCHINZINGER, *Ethics in Engineering*, 2nd Edition, McGraw-Hill Book Company, New York, 1989.

11. KOHLBERG, LAWRENCE, *The Philosophy of Moral Development*, Vol. 1, Harper and Row, New York, 1971.

12. FLORMAN, SAMUEL C., *The Civilized Engineer*, St. Martin's Press, New York, 1987.

13. PINKUS, ROSA LYNN B., LARRY J. SHUMAN, NORMAN P. HUMMON, AND HARVEY WOLFE, *Engineering Ethics,* Cambridge University Press, Cambridge, UK, 1997.

14. *Code of Ethics for Engineers, July 1996–Present,* National Society of Professional Engineers, Alexandria, VA, revised July 1996.

15. *Opinions of the Board of Ethical Review*, Vol. 8, National Society of Professional Engineers, Alexandria, VA, 1999.

EXERCISES

3.1 Prepare a "family tree" diagram illustrating the evolution of the engineering profession and the beginning of the various engineering specialties. Indicate approximate dates each of the branches of engineering began as an identifiable discipline.

3.2 Write an essay describing the feasibility of allowing engineering technologists and technicians to become registered professional engineers. Discuss the problems associated with such a policy and comment on desirable safeguards to insure that such individuals are competent and trustworthy as engineers.

3.3 Explain possible reasons why only approximately one-third of practicing engineers are registered professionals. List the branches of engineering and career paths for which engineering registration is most needful.

3.4 Discuss the ethical considerations involved in the following situations:

  a. A consulting structural engineer is retained as an expert witness by an attorney in litigation resulting from the collapse of a gymnasium roof. She finds the failure of the roof to be the result of inadequate design by another professional engineer. What are the ethical responsibilities of the expert witness to the designer?

  b. A consulting engineer is asked by a plaintiff's attorney to reconstruct the events leading to an automobile crash. He finds that the crash is explained solely by negligence of the plaintiff rather than the defendant. He so advises the attorney. Subsequently, he is asked to serve as an expert witness for the defendant in the same litigation. What should be his response?

  c. The vice president of a consulting engineering firm serves as a member of the municipal water pollution board. Engineer Abel, who is not associated with either the firm or the board, learns that the consulting firm has accepted a contract for engineering services from the board, constituting an apparent violation of ethics. What should Abel do?

  d. As an employee of a county's public works department, a young engineer has the responsibility of checking and approving engineering plans for subdivision streets. During a holiday season, the engineer receives a gift valued at $50 from a consulting firm that designs subdivision streets and regularly submits plans to the engineer for approval. What should be the engineer's response?

  e. A professional engineer working full-time for a consulting firm is offered a part-time position with another firm. This would involve weekend work only that would not interfere with the engineer's responsibilities to the original consulting firm. What are the engineer's ethical responsibilities?

3.5 The County Executive described in Section 3.7 later became an official in the federal government. Identify this individual, and write a report on the consequences of his actions. If necessary, consult Reference 10.

3.6 Write an essay about ethical considerations regarding bidding for engineering services. May engineers bid ethically for engineering services? May they refuse to do so? Are clients required to seek bids for engineering services? What, if any, registration board rules exist in your state that prohibit competitive bidding for engineering services? What does the Federal Sherman Act have to say about competitive bidding for engineering services? If necessary, consult Reference 12.

An Exemplary Engineering Achievement

Solar power heats the Wilton, Maine, wastewater treatment plant and, coupled with heat generated by biochemical reactions, completes the treatment process. (Courtesy of the Council of Engineering Companies.)

CHAPTER FOUR

LEARNING AND CREATIVE THOUGHT

4.1 INTRODUCTION

This chapter, which deals with creativity and the learning process, could be the most important chapter in this book. Here we offer practical suggestions on how to be a successful student, how to study, how to learn more efficiently, and how to approach and deal successfully with quizzes and examinations. We briefly describe the learning process and how we receive and remember information. We conclude the chapter with a treatment of the creative process and explore ways to develop and nurture creativity in engineering.

To the casual reader, some of the following material may seem shallow or obvious. However, to many beginning university students to whom this book is addressed, this material is not self-evident. This chapter is intended to help such a student approach his or her academic and professional career with purpose and confidence.

4.2 THE SUCCESSFUL ENGINEERING STUDENT

Not all of the students who enter engineering programs of study succeed. Some are unable to cope with the rigors of academic life and withdraw, voluntarily or involuntarily, from school. Others struggle, fail to adjust to the demands of an academic life, and do not perform to the level of their capabilities.

The educational system is designed to produce successful students. Most universities admit only those students whose high school grades and standardized test scores predict that they can achieve academic success. The faculty and staff of colleges and universities want their students to succeed—to learn, to

Figure 4.1   *Increasing numbers of women are preparing for careers in engineering. (Courtesy of Institute Communications and Public Affairs, Georgia Institute of Technology.)*

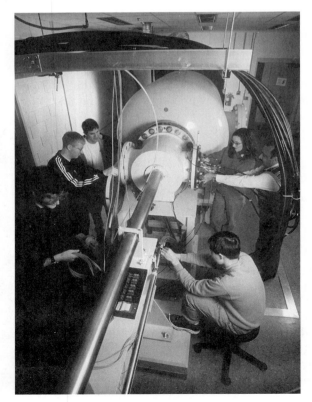

Figure 4.2   *Engineering students must spend a great deal of time in the laboratory. (Courtesy of Institute Communications and Public Affairs, Georgia Institute of Technology.)*

pass their quizzes and examinations, and ultimately to graduate. To this end, most institutions of higher learning make available a number of facilities and services to foster and enrich the learning process and to make it more enjoyable.

The successful student quickly learns to take advantage of the library, computer center, laboratories, and other campus facilities. He or she becomes aware of the many services designed to aid the learning and growing process. Such services include: tutoring, counseling and career planning, physical education and recreation, cultural presentations, health services, financial aid, housing, veteran's affairs, and others. The beginning student should realize that such services are provided for his or her benefit and should not hesitate to make appropriate use of them.

However strong the faculty's desire for a student to succeed and however extensive the university support system, it is the student who determines his or her success or failure. The pursuit of academic success requires motivation and dedication to the task. It requires the exercise of uncommon self-control during a time when adjustments to a new living environment are required and conflicting choices and demands on one's time must be faced.

4.3   THE ENGINEERING CURRICULUM

The Accreditation Board for Engineering and Technology (ABET) lists the following minimum accreditation requirements for a baccalaureate degree in engineering:

> One year of an appropriate combination of mathematics and basic sciences
>
> One and one-half years of engineering topics
>
> One-half year of humanities and social sciences[1]

Studies in mathematics must be beyond trigonometry and must include differential and integral calculus and differential equations. ABET encourages additional mathematics work in one or more subjects of probability and statistics, linear algebra, numerical analysis, and advanced calculus.

Studies in basic sciences must include both general chemistry and calculus-based general physics with at least a two-semester sequence in either area. Additional work in life sciences, earth sciences, advanced chemistry, or physics may be used to satisfy the basic science requirement.

The basic sciences serve as the foundation of an engineering education. On this foundation, a sequence of courses referred to as engineering sciences is added. These courses include solid and fluid mechanics, thermodynamics, electrical and

---

[1] Beginning with the 2001–2002 accreditation cycle, instead of the humanities and social sciences requirement, ABET specifies the inclusion of a general education component that complements the technical content of the curriculum and is consistent with the program and institution objectives.

Figure 4.3   *The pursuit of academic success requires motivation and dedication to the task. (Courtesy of Institute Communications and Public Affairs, Georgia Institute of Technology.)*

electronic circuits, materials science, and computer science (not computer programming). Such courses are strongly rooted in basic science and mathematics, providing a bridge between these basic subjects and engineering design.

Typically, in the third and fourth year of an engineering education, course work in engineering is introduced. These are highly specialized courses intended to equip the student for practice in his or her chosen specialty.

ABET requires that each accredited program include a meaningful, major engineering design experience that is based on the knowledge and skills acquired in earlier course work and that includes engineering standards and realistic constraints such as economic factors, safety, reliability, ethics, and social and environmental impact.

Essential ingredients in any engineering program of study are the humanities and social sciences. Such courses include literature, philosophy, history, economics, psychology, and sociology. Courses in the humanities and social sciences help the student understand and appreciate the impacts of engineering works on society and the natural environment.

Engineering students usually acquire training in other specialized areas during their undergraduate studies, including ways to effectively communicate with their clients, fellow workers, and the public. Many engineering students take elective courses in accounting, management, statistics, and law

Beginning with the 2001–2002 accreditation cycle, ABET requires that engineering programs have in place detailed published educational objectives, a curriculum, and processes that assure the achievement of those objectives, including a system of evaluation and assessment. ABET requires that each engineering program demonstrate that their graduates have:

An ability to apply knowledge of mathematics, science, and engineering;

An ability to design and conduct experiments, as well as to analyze and interpret data;

An ability to design a system, component, or process to meet desired needs;

An ability to function on multidisciplinary teams;

An ability to identify, formulate, and solve engineering problems;

An understanding of professional and ethical responsibility; and

An ability to communicate effectively.

The broad education necessary to understand the impact of engineering solutions in a global and societal context includes:

A recognition of the need for and an ability to engage in life-long learning;

A knowledge of contemporary issues; and

An ability to use the techniques, skills, and modern engineering tools necessary for engineering practice.

Table 4.1 shows a typical freshman engineering curriculum. Such a curriculum does not tend to vary significantly among colleges and universities or engineering disciplines.

Table 4.2 gives an example of an engineering curriculum beyond the first year for students in civil engineering. Note that the curriculum described in Tables 4.1 and 4.2 adheres to the requirements of ABET. That curriculum is based on the semester system. Many universities operate on the quarter system, in which the academic year is divided into three periods of about 12 weeks duration. A quarter-based curriculum would, of course, be "packaged" differently but would be similar to one based on the semester system.

TABLE 4.1 *Typical Freshman Engineering Curriculum*

	Semester Hours Credit	
Freshman Year Courses	**1st Semester**	**2nd Semester**
MATH 1501—Calculus I	4	—
MATH 1502—Calculus II	—	4
CHEM 1211—General Chemistry	4	—
ENGL 1101—English Composition I	3	—
ENGL 1102—English Composition II	—	3
CS 1301—Computer Science I	3	—
Elective in History, Political Science, or International Affairs	3	—
ME/CEE 1770—Engineering Graphics	—	3
PHYS 2211—Physics I	—	4
HPS 1040/1061—Wellness	—	2
TOTAL SEMESTER HOURS	17	16

TABLE 4.2 *Example Curriculum for Students in Civil Engineering*

Sophomore Year Courses	Semester Hours Credit	
	1st Semester	2nd Semester
MATH 2401—Calculus III	4	—
PHYS 2212—Physics II	4	—
CEE 2000—Applications Probability/Statistics	1	—
CEE 2010—Computational Modeling	3	—
ISYE/MATH 3770—Introduction to Probability/Statistics	3	—
Humanities/Social Sciences Elective	3	3
MATH 2403—Differential Equations	—	4
BIOL 1510—Biological Principles	—	4
CEE 2020—Statics and Dynamics	—	3
ECON 2100—Economic Analysis	—	3
TOTAL SEMESTER HOURS	18	17

Junior Year Courses	Semester Hours Credit	
	1st Semester	2nd Semester
CEE 3000—CE Systems	3	—
CEE 3020—CE Materials	3	—
CEE 3030—Strength of Materials	3	—
EAS 2601—Earth Processes	4	—
ME 3322 or CHE 2100—Thermodynamics or Chemical Processes	3	—
CEE 3010—Geomatics	—	3
CEE 3040—Fluid Mechanics	—	3
CEE 3050—Structural Analysis	—	3
PST 3109—Ethics	—	3
Engineering Elective	—	3
TOTAL SEMESTER HOURS	16	15

Senior Year Courses	Semester Hours Credit	
	1st Semester	2nd Semester
CEE 4100—Construction Engineering	3	—
CEE 4200—Hydraulic Engineering	3	—
CEE 4300—Environmental Systems	3	—
CEE 4400—Geosystems Engineering	3	—
CEE Elective	3	3
Approved Elective	3	3
CEE 4600—Transportation Planning and Design	—	3
CP 4030—City and Technology	—	3
CEE Elective (Design)	—	3
TOTAL SEMESTER HOURS	18	15

4.4 CURRICULUM PLANNING AND MANAGEMENT

Although engineering students usually follow a more rigid curriculum than students in other disciplines, they must make a number of decisions relative to the sequencing of courses and the selection of free and technical electives. Proper planning and management of the curriculum will make the educational experience more pleasant and lessen the likelihood of delays in completing the program of study.

Beginning students should study the appropriate engineering curriculum. They should seek and take advantage of assistance offered by academic advisors and refer to course descriptions published in the institution's bulletin or catalog. Published course descriptions are often brief, and it may also be desirable to solicit advice from more advanced students and to refer to published student evaluations of courses and faculty. Table 4.3 shows examples of course descriptions from a university catalog; Table 4.4 gives typical descriptions from a student guide to courses and faculty.

Here are some suggestions for proper curriculum planning and management:

1. Ensure that all prerequisite courses have been completed before each course is scheduled.

2. Since all courses are not usually offered each term, schedule each course during a term when it is to be offered.

3. Giving appropriate consideration to nonacademic demands on your time, seek a balanced course workload.

4. Attempt to schedule an appropriate mix of required and elective courses.

5. Give thoughtful consideration to your choice of elective courses, choosing those that further your educational and professional goals.

TABLE 4.3   *Typical Engineering Course Descriptions from University Catalog*

MATH 1307. Calculus I

5-0-5. Prerequisite: Entrance algebra and trigonometry.

The derivative, derivatives of elementary functions, applications of derivatives. Credit is not allowed for both MATH 1307 and MATH 1712 except in Industrial Management programs.

Text: At the level of Thomas and Finney, *Calculus and Analytic Geometry.*

EE 3700. Elements of Electric Circuits and Instruments

3-0-3. Prerequisites: PHYS 2122 and MATH 2307.

For nonelectrical engineering students. Elements of electric and electronic circuits principally from a terminal characteristics viewpoint.

Text: Carlson and Gisser, *Electrical Engineering Concepts and Applications.*

TABLE 4.4   *Typical Descriptions from a Student Guide to Courses and Faculty*

MATH 1307. Calculus I

Almost all engineering majors receive their introduction to the University through these courses and, to say the least, they consistently rank as the most unpopular courses in the Institute. The courses introduce and develop the concept of differential calculus that makes up the basis of almost all engineering math.

Professor A _____ ranks well as a lecturer. His lectures are well organized and cover the material. They are from the book with an "occasional, beneficial divergence from the text." "A _____ has to one of the most personable instructors at this university. Friendly, jovial, always helpful and pleasant. Super patient, in and out of class."

A _____ gives only four tests during the quarter. These quizzes test "the extreme limits of your comprehension." As a result, the class average was rather low.

EE 3700. Elements of Electric Circuits and Instruments

Nicknamed "shocks for jocks" by EE professors and students, this course gives non-EE majors a chance to look at basic electronics. The course covers the same material as several EE major courses, including basic circuits, diodes, and transistors, but does it in less depth.

Professor B_____ presents "organized" lectures but seems to "lack clarity" and has a habit of "making mistakes on the board which he fails to correct." B_____ also seems to have trouble relating directly to students and "belittles them" when questioned. B_____ puts little emphasis on the book, making his lectures fairly important to attend.

B_____ grades two major tests, a final exam, homework, and weekly tests. He also allows students to drop a certain percentage of their grade. Grading of papers is "slow." The weekly tests are "representative of the material" while the major tests are a bit more difficult. Homework problems are "a good guide for the tests," and overall the course requires slightly more work than most three-hour courses, but this is due to the material, not the instructor.

4.5   ADAPTING TO THE COLLEGE CLASSROOM

Although most engineering professors are highly specialized and knowledgeable in their field, few have taken any courses in how to teach. The engineering professors who are effective teachers—and many are—were either naturally gifted or learned the skills of teaching on the job. Furthermore, college deans and department heads usually offer only the broadest of educational guidelines to the faculty.

Because of this hit-or-miss approach, students must cope with a highly varied cadre of instructors. Some take roll; some do not. Some assign much homework and require that it be turned in and graded; others do not. Instructors may be friendly or aloof; demanding or easy; skillful or inept; laid back or formal and businesslike. This, of course, makes the learning process more difficult and places additional demands on the student.

Beginning students must also cope with large classes. Some first-year classes may have enrollments of 100 or more. For this reason, instructors find it difficult to establish personal relationships with their students, who may consider the system too formal and impersonal.

THE LEARNING PROCESS

4.6   THE NATURE OF LEARNING (1)

Learning is a lifelong, continuous process. We experience many kinds of learning at various times and in many ways. One of the simplest and most basic forms of learning is known as *conditioning*. Conditioning is the acquisition of fairly specific patterns of behavior in the presence of well-defined stimuli.

Classical conditioning was discovered by Russian physiologist Ivan Pavlov, who found that dogs could be trained to salivate at the sound of a bell rung a few seconds before the dogs were fed. The reaction (salivation), he found, could be transferred to another stimulus (the sound of the bell) that would not normally produce this reaction.

A slightly different type of conditioning, known as *operant conditioning*, occurs when some desired voluntary behavior is rewarded or reinforced while undesired behavior is ignored or punished. American psychologist B. F. Skinner demonstrated operant conditioning in experiments with rats in the early 1930s. In his research, he placed a hungry rat in a small box outfitted with a bar which, when pushed, would release food pellets. He found that a rat could be quickly trained to press the bar in order to get the food.

Learning specialists recognize that human behavior may be strongly influenced by secondary reinforcers whose value is learned through association with other reinforcers. Money, for example, is a secondary reinforcer that, because of its association with food, clothing, and other primary reinforcers, is widely recognized as a powerful reward.

Today, psychologists recognize that learning is much more than behaving in a certain way. Much learning does not involve classical or operant conditioning. We learn not only through direct experiences (i.e., conditioning), but also by watching what happens to other people or by just being told about something. This is the nature of most of the learning that occurs in school. We learn vicariously from other people's experiences, and our learning may be influenced by symbolic reinforcers such as affection, compliments, and attention from others.

4.7   INFORMATION PROCESSING AND MEMORY (1)

We receive information from our various senses: sight, hearing, smell, touch, and taste. As Figure 4.4 illustrates, stimuli from these senses come into our sensory registers where it is retained for a few seconds. If nothing more happens to this raw information, it is forgotten. Generally, information from the

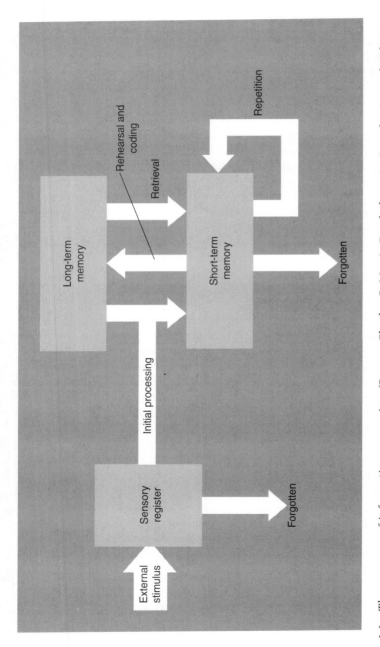

Figure 4.4 *The sequence of information processing. (Source: Charles G. Morris, Psychology: An Introduction, 4th Edition, Prentice-Hall, Inc., copyright 1982. Reprinted by permission of Pearson Education, Inc. Upper Saddle River, NJ 07458.)*

visual sensory register fades very quickly or is replaced or erased by new visual information. The auditory echo tends to last longer, typically for several seconds.

The raw data that enters the sensory register must be processed for meaning. Exactly how this occurs is not fully understood. One possibility is that we match incoming information to a set of templates stored in our long-term memory. Some specialists believe that we have approximate, rough prototypes stored in our long-term memory that help us to identify new information and give it meaning. Still others believe that we have *feature detectors* that allow us to process and understand new information.

We cannot, of course, be aware of all of the details that attack our senses. There is, it is believed, a filtering process at the entrance to the nervous system that can turn off or at least turn down unwanted signals without rejecting them entirely. In this way, we give attention to certain information by selecting which information is chosen for further processing. The information that we do not give attention to is discarded and lost. The selected information enters our short-term memory.

Our short-term memory is active, conscious, and temporary. It is capable of holding much less information than our sensory registers but for a slightly longer time. Learning specialists generally agree that the short-term memory can deal with no more than 9 or 10 items at a time. Typically, information in the short-term memory will disappear in 10 to 20 seconds unless it is repeated or rehearsed. A distraction or interference from other information can also cause us to lose information from the short-term memory.

Everything we know and need to think is stored in the long-term memory; there is no known limit to its capacity. There is reason to believe that long-term memory is divided into several stores of knowledge, some containing verbal information, some visual, and others with information on tastes, sounds, and smells.

How information is organized in our long-term memory is not fully understood. Psychologists often compare long-term memory to a book and its index or to a library and its card catalog. The more associations or indexes an item of information has, the easier it will be to remember. Material in long-term memory may be available but inaccessible. We can forget material in long-term memory because of interference from competing information, but this is believed to be caused by errors in retrieval rather than a loss of stored material.

4.8 DETERMINANTS OF EFFICIENT LEARNING

Educational psychologists report (*2*) that learning efficiency depends on at least three factors:

1. The material to be learned.
2. The psychological state of the learner.
3. Learning strategies.

Generally speaking, the more meaningful the material to be learned, the more easily it is learned. Material that can be related to what is already known is more likely to be remembered than meaningless facts. Teachers can make their subject material more meaningful by presenting new material in stages, making sure their students have learned one stage before introducing the next.

Studies have also shown that the novelty of the material can affect the learning process. The introduction of some novelty into the learning process is thought to increase attentiveness and learning efficiency. Students should not overlook the value of using new and innovative approaches to performing their homework assignments.

Although a moderate level of anxiety is believed to be beneficial to learning, extremely low or extremely high levels are detrimental to a student's success. The student who fears failure is more likely to perform poorly on examinations, as is one who is poorly motivated.

Although educational strategies differ from student to student, there are certain learning techniques that are widely viewed as effective. One of the most popular strategies is rehearsal. Generally, the more students practice, the better they perform. In preparing for examinations, many students find it helpful to organize the study material in different ways. Making lists, solving problems, preparing summaries, and writing answers to expected questions are some of the techniques that students have found to be helpful. Some students rehearse the study material aloud as well as writing it, involving the sense of hearing as well as that of sight.

4.9   PRACTICAL SUGGESTIONS FOR LEARNING

Here are some practical guidelines that are offered to help engineering students learn and improve their performance on homework and examinations.

1. Regularly attend classes and laboratory sessions. Professors tend to interpret poor class attendance as a lack of interest on the part of the student.

2. Find a quiet place to study. Early in the term, develop a regular routine that includes adequate times for class preparation.

3. Be alert in class. Listen attentively and demonstrate interest in class and in laboratory activities.

4. Record points of significance for the instructor's lecture. Think about the major points of emphasis. Too often, taking notes in class fits this definition: "The process by which the material in the professor's notebook gets into the student's notebook without passing through the mind of either."

5. Do not hesitate to seek clarification on matters that are not clear. Ask questions in class, and take advantage of offers of assistance during the professor's office hours.

6. Begin preparing for examinations on the first meeting of the class. Maintain the pace of the course. Avoid the need to "cram" on the night before an examination.

7. Approach your work with a positive mental attitude. Develop a habit of attending class, doing homework, and taking quizzes and examinations because you *want to,* not because you *have to.* Behavioral experts claim that such a change in attitude will almost certainly improve a student's performance.

8. In preparing for a difficult quiz or examination, visualize yourself taking the examination. Develop a mental picture of yourself confidently answering the questions, working the problems, and finishing on time. Think of yourself as someone who approaches examinations with confidence, and rehearse this mental image over and over again. Positive visualizations are helpful in overcoming the problem that many students have of "choking" on exams.

9. While continuing to devote sufficient time and effort to your work, find time to relax and rest. From time to time, take stock of your life, and be sure that you are not underemphasizing, overemphasizing, or omitting completely some part of your life. In other words, try to keep all of life's goals and aspirations in proper balance.

DIFFERENCES IN THE WAY PEOPLE THINK

We know from experience that there is great variability in the way people think and learn and approach problem solving. In the past two decades, researchers have shed some light on differences in the way we acquire and process information. Here we examine some of those differences.

4.10   THE FOUR-QUADRANT MODEL OF THINKING

While directing the management education program for the General Electric Company in the mid-1970s, Herrmann (3) developed a self-administered questionnaire designed to identify the learning styles of participants in training seminars. As he improved the instrument and gathered more data, he discovered that the overall data were not bimodal but seemed almost equally distributed in four clusters. Further research led him to develop a four-quadrant model of preferred modes of knowing and brain dominance. The model is a metaphor of what is now understood about the four specialized parts of the human brain.

Herrmann (3) and his associates have gathered data on more than 500,000 people and analyzed them in terms of the four-quadrant modes-of-knowing model. The model describes individuals in terms of dominance in one or more of the four quadrants (see Figure 4.5 and Table 4.5). On the basis of the completed survey instrument, scores are assigned on a scale of 0 to 100 for each of the four quadrants. The results can then be displayed graphically as Figure 4.6 illustrates.

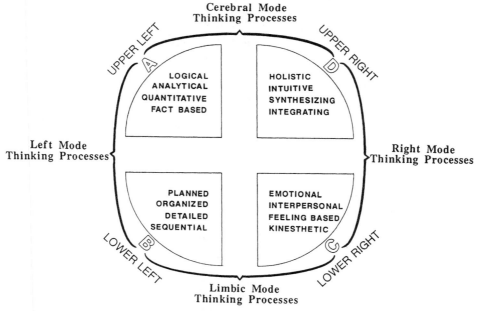

Figure 4.5   *The whole brain model as proposed by Herrmann (3).* (Source: *Ned Herrmann,* The Creative Brain, *Brain Books, Lake Lure, NC, 1990.)*

Herrmann's findings suggest that about 7 percent of people are single dominant, 60 percent are double dominant, 30 percent are triple dominant, and 3 percent are quadruple dominant. He has concluded that "individuals with different profiles tend to behave in specific predictable ways with regard to such things as time, creativity, dress, money, problem-solving and intuition." (*3*)

TABLE 4.5   *A General Description of Herrmann's Four-Quadrant Model of Thinking Modes*

Examples of Descriptors			
Left-Oriented Descriptors		**Right-Oriented Descriptors**	
Quadrant A	**Quadrant B**	**Quadrant C**	**Quadrant D**
Factual	Ordered	Musical	Artistic
Logical	Detailed	Spiritual	Holistic
Rational	Sequential	Talkative	Flexible
Theoretical	Controlled	Emotional	Imaginative
Mathematical	Conservative	Empathetic	Synthesizing

Source: Herrmann, Ned, *The Creative Brain*, Brain Books, Lake Lure, NC, 1990.

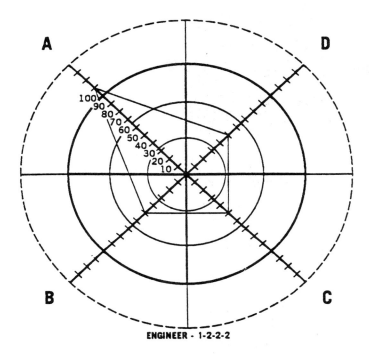

Figure 4.6 *An example of a profile chart for an engineer.*
(Source: *Ned Herrmann,* The Creative Brain, *Brain Books,
Lake Lure, NC, 1990.)*

4.11 HINDRANCES TO PROBLEM SOLVING

Engineering students should be aware of certain conditions of the mind that
can hinder effective problem solving. One such condition is known to psychologists as *fixation* or *mental set.* It involves the persistent application of an
inappropriate strategy to a problem because of previously acquired knowledge
or experience.

Martin Scheerer (4) published several illustrations to exemplify how insight
to a problem solution can be delayed or thwarted by fixation of an inappropriate solution. One example required that nine dots (Figure 4.7) be connected by
four straight lines without lifting the pencil from the paper. To solve this problem, one must extend the lines beyond the dots (see the solution, Figure 4.8).
Most people assume incorrectly that they may not do this and are not able to
solve the problem.

Another problem required that six matches (Figure 4.9) be assembled to
form four congruent equilateral triangles, each side of which is equal to the
length of the matches. This problem cannot be solved as long as one assumes
that the matches must be in one plane, as most people do. The solution, an
equilateral tetrahedron (Figure 4.10), becomes apparent as soon as one realizes
that the matches need not lie flat.

Luchins (5) demonstrated the tendency of people to cling to an inappropriate method of solution because of the fixation effect. In an experiment involving 2009 students, he asked each participant to measure out mentally a desired quantity of liquid using three jars of specified sizes. The set of problems is given in Table 4.6. All but one of the problems (number 8) could be solved in the following way: (a) fill Jar B, (b) pour off enough to fill Jar A, and (c) then pour off enough to fill Jar C twice. This method can be stated by the formula: $B - A - 2C$. This leaves the desired amount in Jar B.

Problems 6 and 7 are solvable by the formula but can also be solved by simpler ones: $A - C$ and $A + C$, respectively. The last two problems are similar in structure to the sixth and seventh problems and can also be solved by a simpler method. Problem 8 does not conform to the formula $B - A - 2C$ but can be solved by $A - C$.

Luchins found that 64 percent of the experimental group failed to solve problem 8, but only 5 percent of the control group failed that problem. Because problems 1 through 5 all call for the $B - A - 2C$ solution, 83 percent of the experimental group used it for problems 6 and 7 even though a simpler method existed. Only 0.6 percent of the control group used the more difficult formula.

Researchers have also found that a student's motivational level can affect his or her ability to solve problems. It is well known that students who are not highly motivated to study for a test are not likely to perform well on it. Curiously, the opposite experience is also possible. Students can be so hypermotivated to prepare for a test that it will interfere with their performance. A number of studies have shown that there is an optimal motivational level for efficient problem solving. That level tends to vary with the complexity of the problem. In general, the simpler the task, the greater the motivation required for optimal performance.

Figure 4.7 *Nine dots problem proposed by Scheerer (4).* *Connect all of the dots by four straight lines without lifting the pencil from the paper. The solution is shown in Figure 4.8.*

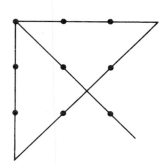

Figure 4.8 *The solution to nine dots problem. (Source: Reference 4.)*

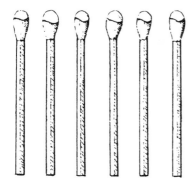

Figure 4.9 *Six matches problem proposed by Scheerer (4). Assemble six matches to form four congruent equilateral triangles, each side of which is equal to the length of the matches. The solution is shown in Figure 4.11.*

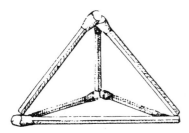

Figure 4.10 *The solution to six matches problem.* (Source: *Reference 4.*)

TABLE 4.6 *Problems Used by Luchins (4) to Illustrate Fixation Effect*

	Given Jars with These Capacities:			
Problem Number	*A*	*B*	*C*	Obtain
1	21	127	3	100
2	14	163	25	99
3	18	43	10	5
4	9	42	6	21
5	20	59	4	31
6	23	49	3	20
7	15	39	3	18
8	28	76	3	25
9	18	48	4	22
10	14	36	8	6

Source: A. S. Luchins, "Classroom Experiments on Mental Set," *American Journal of Psychology,* Vol. 59, 1946, pp. 295–298.

ON CREATIVITY

Engineering is a creative profession. Engineering students therefore need to make optimal use of their creative potential. Few people can hope to attain the creative genius of a Galileo, da Vinci, or Newton. However, all of us are creative, and we can learn to develop and use more efficiently our creative abilities. Socrates wrote: "That which is used strengthens and grows, while that which is not used withers and dies."

In the remaining sections of this chapter, we define creativity and describe the creative process. Then we list some of the obstacles to creative thinking and suggest ways to develop and improve creativity.

4.12   WHAT IS CREATIVITY?

Psychologists who have studied creativity define it in various ways. A general definition is: "Mental processes that lead to ideas, solutions, conceptualizations, theories, artistic forms or products that are unique and novel." Harmon (6) stated that the creative process is "any process by which something new is produced: an idea or object, a new form or arrangement of old elements." Arieti (7) expressed it in this way: "Human creativity uses what is already existing and available and changes it in unpredictable ways."

Smith (8) gave this definition: "Creativity is sinking down taps into our past experiences and putting these selected experiences into new patterns, new ideas, and new products."

The creative process involves inventive, artistic, and inspirational thought. It is characterized by originality and imagination.

Glegg (9) expressed the belief that the logical or rational must be the controlling element in the creative mind. He wrote: "The inventive and the artistic, the inspirational and the intuitive all have a place in the creative process, but the rational must hold the power of veto over them all."

Arieti (7) expressed a similar view:

> Creativity is not simply originality and unlimited freedom. There is much more to it than that. Creativity also imposes restrictions. While it uses methods other than those of ordinary thinking, it must not be in disagreement with ordinary thinking—or rather, it must be something that, sooner or later, ordinary thinking will understand, accept, and appreciate. Otherwise the result would be bizarre, not creative.

4.13   THE NATURE OF CREATIVITY

There are many types of creativity, and it exists in almost all realms of human existence. There is a special kind of creativity that is associated with profound and abstract concepts, the kind possessed by the Albert Einsteins and Sir Isaac Newtons of the world. Creativity for such gifted individuals often begins with almost childlike and primal questions such as "What is air and light?" "Why is fire hot?" and "Why does an apple fall to the earth?" From such basic questions have come some of the most brilliant, creative thought known to mankind.

Other types of creativity are associated with the artists and writers, who are said to be *inspired*, and whose genius largely seems to come from the subconscious. Still others possess a natural creativity which allows them to be great dancers, singers, musicians, or athletes.

The type of creativity that is most often associated with engineers and scientists is *applied* creativity which often involves taking sensory experiences and existing things and transforming them into theoretical knowledge or a new design or process. George Washington Carver, Madame Curie, and Thomas Edison are examples of people who functioned in this creative realm. Such people are inspired and imaginative, but their work is tempered with the practical and more controlled with logic and reason.

4.14   CHARACTERISTICS OF CREATIVE PEOPLE

What types of people are most likely to be creative? What are the developmental, cognitive, and personality hallmarks that set them apart from ordinary individuals? Such issues have been studied at length by psychologists and social scientists, and while their findings have not always been certain and consistent, they have revealed some interesting insights into the nature and characteristics of creative people. The following paragraphs, abstracted from Reference 10, briefly summarize some of these findings.

Researchers have reported that children who are raised in a diversified and stimulating home environment, who experience unusual situations, and who are exposed to a wide range of ideas are more likely to be creative adults. They have also reported that creative adults, while children, liked school and did well, developed excellent work habits, were voracious readers, and were happier with books than with people.

Investigators have identified four traits that are commonly associated with creative individuals: originality, verbal fluency, relatively high intelligence, and a good imagination. Creative people also tend to possess logical thinking skills, yet cope well with novelty and can avoid fixed ways of thinking. They show flexibility and skill in making decisions and possess an independence of judgment.

Some researchers have reported that creative individuals question accepted norms and assumptions and are alert to gaps in knowledge in their domain. They commonly have the ability to recognize "good" problems in their field and to apply themselves to solving these problems while ignoring others.

Creative people are open to new experiences and growth. They typically are perseverant, curious, and inquisitive. They usually are highly motivated and well focused and are willing to confront hostility and take intellectual risks. They prefer to set their own rules rather than follow those set by others. They are sometimes unconventional in behavior, withdrawn, reflective, and internally preoccupied.

4.15   THE CREATIVE PROCESS

The creative process begins with an observation of a need or problem. Next is a need to analyze the situation and gather as much data as possible. Then comes concentration—saturating the mind with all of the elements of the problem. At this point, the creative person engages in free thinking: searching for possible solutions, listening to suggestions, and letting the mind wander. Then it is important that the mind be open to all alternative solutions, including those that are divergent and unconventional. The mind is filled with the context of the problem, followed by a period of relaxation and thinking about something else. According to Glegg (9), "Concentration and then relaxation is the common pattern behind creative thinking."

Psychologists call this period of relaxing the mind *incubation.* It is widely recognized that incubation precedes the birth of a new idea—the *illumination.* Most of us at one time or another have experienced illumination, the sudden, spontaneous appearance of an answer to a problem during a time when the mind is seemingly engaged in other matters.

The final phase of the creative process may involve experimentation to test promising solutions. It involves the evaluation and verification of the creative idea or product.

To summarize, no single parameter can explain the creative process. In fact, the process often seems to an observer to be somewhat haphazard and without a definite pattern. Certain observable attributes are, however, frequently present:

1.   Recognition of the need or problem.
2.   A period of intense concentration.
3.   A period of relaxation or incubation.
4.   The illumination, when the solution suddenly and spontaneously appears.
5.   The evaluation or verification of the solution.

4.16   OVERCOMING OBSTACLES TO CREATIVE THINKING

How does one become a more creative thinker? To VanGundy (11), it is a matter of learning to use efficiently both hemispheres of the brain.

> Creative thinking requires the use of both thinking modes—only at different times during the thinking process. Specifically, the right brain helps us to avoid rigid, linear thinking so that we can concentrate on developing ideas, while the left brain helps us to evaluate these ideas and test them against reality. . . . Both brain hemispheres need to work in harmony if we are to produce creative solutions to our problems. (11)

VanGundy lists 30 obstacles to creative thinking which fall into five categories: perceptual, emotional, cultural, environmental, and intellectual/expressive. Examples of these obstacles are shown in Table 4.7.

TABLE 4.7   *Examples of Obstacles to Creative Thinking*

Category of Obstacle	Example
Perceptual	Imposing too many constraints on the problem
Emotional	Feeling overwhelmed by the problem
Intellectual/expressive	Use of rigid problem-solving strategies
Cultural	Overemphasis on reason and logic
Environmental	Lack of time and suitable study place

Source: Arthur B. VanGundy, *Training Your Creative Mind*, Prentice-Hall, Inc., Englewood Cliffs, NJ, 1982.

There are some specific actions and attitudes that can be employed to overcome obstacles to creative thinking, including (*11*):

1. Avoid placing unnecessary constraints on the problem being solved.
2. Search for different ways to view the problem, avoiding preconceived beliefs and stereotypical thinking.
3. Recognize that there are nonengineering solutions to many problems. Consider approaches that might be used by other disciplines.
4. Most creative thought involves putting experiences and thoughts into new patterns and arrangements. Look therefore for relationships that are remote and solutions that are unusual and nontraditional.
5. Divide complex problems into manageable parts and concentrate on solving one part at a time.
6. After periods of intensive concentration, allow time for incubation.
7. Be open for a variety of problem-solving strategies.

REFERENCES

1. MORRIS, CHARLES G., *Pyschology: An Introduction,* 4th Edition, Prentice-Hall, Inc., Englewood Cliffs, NJ, 1982.
2. BRAUN, JAY, DARWIN E. LINDER, AND ISAAC ASIMOV, *Psychology Today: An Introduction,* Random House, New York, 1979.
3. HERRMANN, NED, *The Creative Brain,* Brain Books, Lake Lure, NC, 1990.
4. SCHEERER, MARTIN, "Problem Solving," *Scientific American,* April 1963, pp. 118–128.
5. LUCHINS, A. S., "Classroom Experiments on Mental Set," *American Journal of Psychology,* Vol. 59, 1946, pp. 295–298.
6. HARMON, L. R., "Social and Technological Determiners of Creativity," The University of Utah Research Conference on *The Identification of Creative Scientific Talent,* Salt Lake City, University of Utah Press, 1956, quoted by Stuart E. Golann in *Creativity: Theory and Research,* Morton Bloomberg, ed., College and University Press, New University Press, New Haven, CT, 1973.

7. ARIETI, SYLVANO, *Creativity: The Magic Synthesis,* New York, Basic Books, Inc., 1976. (Quotations reprinted by permission of Harper Collins Publishers, Inc.)

8. SMITH, JAMES A., *Creativity: Its Nature and Nuture,* The J. Richard Street Lecture, School of Education, Syracuse University, Syracuse, NY, 1964.

9. GLEGG, GORDON L., *The Design of Design,* Cambridge University Press, London, 1969.

10. STERNBERG, ROBERT J., *The Nature of Creativity,* Cambridge University Press, Cambridge, UK, 1988.

11. VANGUNDY, ARTHUR B., *Training Your Creative Mind,* Prentice-Hall, Inc., Englewood Cliffs, NJ, 1982.

12. DUDERSTADT, JAMES J., GLENN F. KNOLL, AND GEORGE F. SPRINGER, *Principles of Engineering,* John Wiley & Sons, Inc., New York, 1982.

RECOMMENDED READING

Psychology Today: An Introduction, by JAY BRAUN, DARWIN E. LINDER, AND ISAAC ASIMOV, Chapter 11, Random House, New York, 1979.

Engineering: The Career and the Profession, by W. EDWARD RED, Chapter 4, Brooks/Cole Engineering Division, Monterey, CA, 1982.

EXERCISES

4.1 Study the curriculum that is published in your university catalog for your chosen engineering specialty. How does the curriculum measure up to the minimum accreditation requirements of the Accreditation Board for Engineering and Technology? (See Section 4.3.)

4.2 Prepare a flow diagram for your chosen curriculum that depicts the recommended sequencing and phasing of courses by quarter or semester. By arrows, show prerequisites for each course.

4.3 Prepare a list of ways in which a university professor could discourage engineering students from developing their creative potential.

4.4 For each of the following problems or situations, prepare a list of creative approaches or solutions.
   a. How to transport an army across a river.
   b. How to measure the height of a tall building with the aid of a barometer (*10*).
   c. How to transport sawdust down a mountain to a waste site 2000 feet away.
   d. How to reduce the number of bicycle thefts on a college campus.
   e. How to eliminate an unsafe pedestrian crossing.
   f. How to control rats in an impoverished area.
   g. How to eliminate litter on a college campus.
   h. How to control parking on a college campus.

4.5 Prepare a report on the research performed by Russian physiologist Ivan Pavlov on classical conditioning. Refer to Reference 1 or some other introductory textbook in psychology.

4.6 Prepare a report on the research work performed by American pyschlogist B. F. Skinner on operant conditioning. Discuss the relevance of Skinner's work to the development of good study habits.

An Exemplary Engineering Achievement

The Sturgeon Point water treatment plant, Erie County, New York, applies computer technology to the quest for drinkable water. (Courtesy of the American Council of Engineering Companies.)

CHAPTER FIVE

THE ENGINEERING APPROACH TO PROBLEM SOLVING

Unlike problems usually assigned to engineering students, real-world problems are often unstructured and open-ended. At times, not all of the required data are known or available. In other instances, it is necessary to sort through a plethora of information and identify which parts of it are needed to solve the problem under consideration.

Novice engineers are sometimes surprised to discover that a problem may not have a single categorical solution. Often, the objective is to select a preferred solution from among several alternatives. It may be necessary to weigh several conflicting consequences of an engineering action and then select the solution that best meets the needs and desires of an employer, a client, or the public.

THE NATURE OF ENGINEERING DESIGN

Engineering work often involves planning and analysis in the initial stages, but the essence of engineering problem solving is design. Engineering design is as varied as the engineering profession, and it is as broad as the problems facing humankind. An engineer's designs may be as small and intricate as a microchip for a computer system or as large and complex as a space shuttle. To perform engineering design is to conceive, imagine, devise, and plan a device, a structure, a process, or a system that will benefit people.

As a profession, engineering is relatively young. In earlier times, the design process was the domain of the craftsman, and the art and knowledge of design was passed from master craftsman to apprentice. Since the birth of engineering as a profession, the problems have grown exceedingly in complexity and diversity. At the same time, advancements in technology have greatly expanded the ability of engineers to improve the comfort and well-being of the people they serve.

With advancements in technological knowledge have come more formal institutions and procedures for the transfer of knowledge. Modern engineers must not only gain experience under the tutelage of other engineers but must also be educated in formal college- or university-level programs of study. Engineering design has become more varied and challenging, requiring a greater degree of specialization as well as a need for teamwork. It is not uncommon, therefore, for many large engineering projects to be carried out by dozens or even hundreds of engineering specialists.

Engineering Teams

Engineering teams may be used as simply a means of dividing up the workload. Similarly-trained engineers may be assigned specific design tasks by an engineering manager. In other instances, several engineers contribute specialized knowledge and provide organizational competence to the solution of a problem where the knowledge of any one engineer would be inadequate to solve it.

When complex problems are faced, it may be desirable to establish a nontraditional organizational structure in which team members have a dual reporting relationship to a functional manager or administrative supervisor as well as to a team leader. The design of an industrial plant, for example, may require the knowledge and skills of several types of engineers: industrial, chemical, civil, mechanical, and electrical. Members from each of the specialties could be assigned to a task force or a design team for the duration of the design process while reporting to a functional manager in their respective specialty as well as to the project engineer. Such design teams are often temporary and appointed for a specific purpose, then dissolved when the work is completed. (*1*)

THE ENGINEERING METHOD

The nature of problems that must be solved by engineers varies both between and among the various branches of engineering. Indeed, an individual engineer may face a variety of problems during the course of his or her daily work activities. Because of the variability of engineering designs, there is no definitive procedure or list of steps that will always fit the engineering problems at hand. However, engineers tend to deal with problems in a special way. Certainly, the engineering method of approaching and solving problems differs greatly from that of most other professionals.[1] Engineers are trained to think in analytical and objective terms and to approach problems methodically and systematically.

---

[1] It is, however, similar to the better-known "scientific method."

A number of engineering writers have set forth a list of steps or phases that comprise the "engineering design method." Typically, the list includes:

1. Identification of the problem.
2. Gathering needed information.
3. Searching for creative solutions.
4. Stepping from ideation to preliminary designs (including modeling).
5. Evaluation and selection of preferred solution.
6. Preparation of reports, plans, and specifications.
7. Implementation of the design.

As we describe these steps, it is important to keep in mind that in many instances, one or more of the steps may not appear. In other cases, it may be necessary to repeat the entire protocol several times in an attempt to converge on a desired solution. Let us now examine the various steps or phases of engineering design.

5.1 IDENTIFICATION OF THE PROBLEM

There is a tendency to think that this phase of the solution process is trivial and unimportant. Such is not the case. An incorrect or improper definition of the problem will cause the engineer to waste time and may lead to a solution that is inappropriate or incorrect. Pearson (*2*) states: "A problem properly defined is a problem partially solved. To state the problem correctly is a major step toward its solution."

It is important that the stated needs be real needs. A truly great design may be worthless if it duplicates other known designs or if it solves a problem that does not impact many people. If it is a product that is being designed, it may be difficult to predict the mass appeal and the resulting marketability of a proposed design. A preliminary market analysis will usually identify the prospective users and statistics about comparable devices or methods and volume of sales.

The needs to be satisfied should be broadly defined and distinguished from possible solutions. In this phase, care should be taken not to prejudice the solution by incorrectly defining the problem. Consider the following example.

For decades in the United States, deaths of drivers and passengers in motor vehicle crashes were considered to be one of the nation's most serious public health problems. Traffic safety specialists defined the problem in terms of *accident prevention* rather than *loss reduction*. They spoke in terms of a need to prevent accidents rather than a need to reduce losses from accidents. In so doing, they presupposed the problem solution and focused their attention exclusively on driver behavior. Predictably, their "solution" to the problem was driver education, traffic enforcement, and "Drive Safely" campaigns. They overlooked possible benefits from more crashworthy vehicles and a safer roadway environment.

To the extent possible, the problem should be defined in objective terms. Here is an example of a problem that is defined in objective terms.

Design an energy attenuation system that will control the energy of a crash of a 2500-pound car traveling 60 miles per hour at impact. The device should not be longer than 10 feet and should cost no more than $10,000 per unit. The deceleration should not exceed 6 gs (193 ft/s²).

Contrast this definition with the following situation:

Design an energy attenuation system that will control the energy of a car traveling at a fast speed at impact. The device should be short and inexpensive to build. The deceleration should not be harmful to the driver.

Finally, the problem should not be unnecessarily constrained. If too many constraints are placed on the problem, it may make its solution extremely difficult or even impossible. In fact, a careful examination of the example problem stated above in light of Newton's second law of mechanics shows that it is overconstrained. The device would need to be longer than 10 feet to meet the other conditions of the problem.

5.2   GATHERING NEEDED INFORMATION

Once the problem is identified and the needs properly defined, the engineer then begins to gather information and data needed to solve it. The type of information needed will, of course, depend on the nature of the problem to be solved. It could be physical measurements, maps, results of laboratory experiments, patents, results of opinion surveys, or any of a number of other types of information. This phase of the problem-solving process involves gathering and evaluating information that is already available. If the engineer is employed by a large corporation or a public agency, it will probably be desirable to search old files and interview other employees to see if others have undertaken similar work. Subsequently, it may be necessary to supplement this information by making additional measurements or conducting more laboratory experiments, opinion surveys, and the like.

In this phase of the process, engineers typically undertake a literature search to determine what others have learned about related problems. They may visit technical libraries and study textbooks, journal articles, and manufacturers' catalogs. Librarians can be very helpful in locating textbooks and journal references, and most libraries now have access to computer-aided searching services that are fast and relatively inexpensive. Some libraries also maintain manufacturers' catalogs reduced onto microfiche film with a subject index to help in locating already-manufactured components.

Finally, it is worthwhile to perform a patent search, especially if there is a patent library nearby. Most "mouse traps" never make it to market or to press; consequently, there are many great designs described in intricate legal detail, which can be found in the chronological listing of U.S. patents.

5.3   SEARCHING FOR CREATIVE SOLUTIONS

After completing the preparatory steps in the design process, the engineer is ready to begin identifying creative solutions. Actually, the development of new ideas, products, or devices may result from *creativity*, a subconscious effort, or from *innovation*, a conscious effort.

There are several operational techniques that may be used to help a group or individual to produce original ideas. These techniques are designed to enable the group or individual to overcome obstacles to creative thinking such as those described in Chapter 4.

Brainstorming

One of the most popular techniques for group problem solving is brainstorming. Typically, a brainstorming session consists of 6 to 12 people who spontaneously introduce ideas designed to solve a specific problem. In these sessions, all ideas are encouraged, including those that appear to be completely impractical. Efforts are made to generate as many ideas as possible. Participants are encouraged to combine or improve on ideas of others. Judgment and evaluation of the ideas are not permitted in the idea-producing session.

It is suggested that participants in brainstorming sessions be chosen from a diversity of backgrounds and that people with little direct experience with the problem be included. Brainstorming sessions usually last not longer than one hour. Ideas produced by a brainstorming session are recorded and evaluated at a later time by the brainstorming group or by another group or individual.

A form of the brainstorming technique can also be used by an individual. The individual follows the same rules used for a group session: combination of ideas, postponement of evaluation, and an emphasis on obtaining a large number of ideas. The individual brainstorming session need not take more than a few minutes. Again, the ideas are recorded and evaluated at a later time.

Checklists

One of the simplest ideas for generating new ideas is to make a checklist. The checklist encourages the user to examine various points, areas, and design possibilities. For example, suppose that you were attempting to improve a certain device. You might make a checklist that includes:

Ways the device could be put to other uses.

Ways the device could be modified.

Ways the device could be rearranged.

Ways the device could be magnified.

Ways the device could be lessened, and so on.

Attribute Listing

Another technique that can be used by individuals to produce original problem-solving ideas is attribute listing. With this technique, all of the major characteristics or attributes of a product, object, or idea are isolated and listed. Then, for each attribute, ideas are listed as to how each of the attributes could be changed. Every idea is listed, no matter how unrealistic or impractical. After all of the ideas have been listed, each of the various ideas is evaluated, bringing to light possible improvements that can be made in the design of the product or system.

Consider the following example of how the attribute listing technique could be used to improve the design of a telephone (3).

Attribute	Ideas
1. Color	Could be any color
	Could be transparent
	Could utilize designs such as plaid
	Could have a personalized design
2. Material	Could be metal
	Could be glass
	Could be wood
	Could be hard rubber
3. Dial	Could be 10-push-button design
	Could be a lever system
	Could use abacus-type system
	Could be push buttons arranged in a line
4. Handset and base	Make it square
	Make it round
	Make it oval
	Use higher base
	Use lower base
	Eliminate handset by using microphone and speaker

Forced Relationship Technique

Another group of operational techniques that individuals may use to generate ideas is known as forced relationship techniques (3). That is, such techniques force a relationship between two or more normally unrelated ideas or products to begin the idea-generating process. One such technique consists of selecting the fixed element in the forced relationship, that being the product or device that is to be designed or an idea related to the problem statement. Next, attention is focused on some other element, chosen randomly. Then a forced or unnatural relationship between the fixed element and the randomly chosen element is established. This forms the basis for a free-flowing list of associations from which hopefully new and original ideas will emerge.

For example, suppose that we are interested in designing a weed-cutting device. The device is the focused object. Suppose that we choose arbitrarily an automobile wheel as the other element. Some of the ideas that might occur based upon the characteristics of the automobile wheel include:

A round weed cutter.

A rubber weed cutter.

A weed cutter that rolls.

A weed cutter that has spokes.

A weed cutter that has pneumatic tires.

A weed cutter that has brakes.

A weed cutter that will not break, and so on.

Notice that we began this process by merely taking the characteristics of the wheel—roundness, rubber material, ability to roll, and so on—and applying them to the weed cutter. Other ideas may then develop based upon simple verbal relationships or similar-sounding words. For example, the word "brakes" led to the idea of a weed cutter that does not "break."

This technique takes little time. If the forced relationship being used does not seem to be profitable, one can simply select a new random element and repeat the process. As with other idea-generating techniques, many impractical, even foolish, ideas may be generated. Evaluation of these ideas should not be undertaken during the idea-generation stage.

Morphological Analysis

An operational technique for idea generation attributed to Fritz Zwicky (3) involves listing every conceivable theoretical solution. This technique consists of first defining the problem in terms of its dimensions or parameters and devising a model that enables one to visualize every possible solution. For a solution with only two parameters, the model takes the form of a large square divided into a group of smaller squares. The horizontal axis would show various possible choices for one parameter; the vertical axis would show possible choices for the other parameter. Such an arrangement allows the user to examine the combined effects of attributes of the variables.

For problems with more than two parameters, the model becomes a matrix with each parameter assigned to one axis of a rectangular array. This is best explained by an example.

Referring again to the design of a weed-cutting device, suppose that we wish to examine three attributes or variables: the type of power supply, the type of blade motion, and the type of material used in its construction. We list the possible methods of satisfying each attribute, for example:

Power: electric engine, gasoline engine, water pressure.

Blade action: rotary, reciprocating.

Material: steel, aluminum, plastic.

The combination of these conditions yields 18 possible solutions that may now be subjected to scrutiny and evaluation. Figure 5.1 graphically illustrates the various combinations that comprise possible solutions. Each of the small cubes represents one possible solution. For example, cube A represents a steel device with an electric engine and a rotary blade.

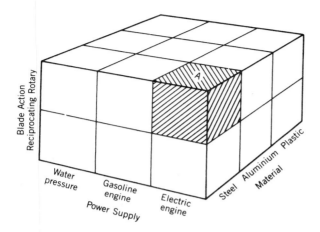

Figure 5.1 *An illustration of the morphological technique.*

5.4   STEPPING FROM IDEATION TO PRELIMINARY DESIGNS

The engineer is now ready to move from ideation to preliminary designs. This is the heart of the design process, and it is the phase that relies most on experience and engineering judgment. Here, unworkable ideas are discarded, and promising ideas are molded and modified to form workable plans and designs.

This step may require many decisions to be made about alternative layouts, configurations, materials, dimensions, and other specifications. Conceptual sketches may need to be drawn; preliminary plans may need to be prepared; and thought may need to be given to material specifications.

Preliminary designs may evolve through *analysis* or *synthesis*. *Analysis* involves the separation of a whole into constituents for individual study. *Synthesis* involves combining facts, principles, or laws into a whole idea that will accomplish some desired result or solve a problem.

In this phase, it is necessary to subject possible solution ideas to careful scrutiny. Possible solutions are carefully and critically examined and studied. There are many ways that this can be done. In certain instances, preliminary sketching of a device or casual analysis of a process will show that an idea is not worthy of further consideration. In other cases, a component may need to be examined by laboratory tests. In still other instances, a formal and comprehensive research program may need to be undertaken to examine the validity of a hypothesis or the efficacy of a proposed solution.

To facilitate the design process, engineers often rely on models. Duderstadt, et al. (4) defines a model as "any simplified description of an engineering system or process that can be used to aid in analysis or design." Engineers use a variety of models that may be tangible or intangible. In the broadest definition of the term, sketches and graphs (discussed in Chapter 6) can be thought of as types of models. In addition, three types of model are commonly used to facilitate the solution of engineering problems:

1. Analytical or mathematical models.
2. Simulation models.
3. Physical models.

Mathematical Models

A mathematical model consists of one equation or a group of equations that represents a physical system. For example, the following equation represents the wind pressure on a structure:

$$p = KV^2$$

where p = wind pressure expressed in pounds per square foot
K = a factor that depends principally on the shape of the structure
V = the wind velocity expressed in miles per hour

Many physical phenomena can be described by mathematical models. Such models may be based on scientific theories or laws that have stood the test of time. Others are empirically based, relying upon or derived from observations and experiments.

Generally speaking, mathematical models can describe only relatively simple physical phenomena. Mathematical models designed to describe complex phenomena tend to be so intractable as to be of little value.

Simulation Models

When studying complex systems, engineers often employ *computer simulation models.* Such a model may incorporate empirically based mathematical models as components of the total model. For example, Thomasson and Wright (5) used computer simulation to study traffic at a two-way stop controlled intersection. They first made empirical studies of driver behavior at the intersections and found that the phenomenon could be separated into several well-defined events:

1. The arrival of cars on the side and main streets.
2. Turning movement decision.
3. Acceptance or refusal of available gaps in the traffic on the main street.
4. Start time, the hesitation prior to moving into the intersection.
5. Service time, the time the intersection was occupied.

The description of these events was based in part on actual observations of drivers or on empirical mathematical models that had been reported by other researchers. For example, it was found that the time a vehicle occupies the intersection could be described by a normal probability distribution (see Figure 5.2). (A discussion of the normal probability distribution appears in Chapter 7.)

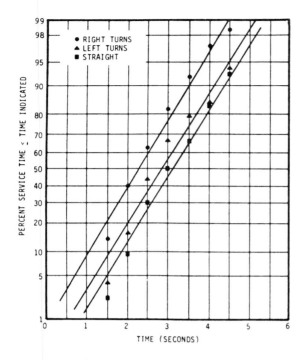

Figure 5.2 *The results of an empirical study used for a simulation model. The figure shows distributions of times that vehicles occupy an intersection.*

A computer program (or model) was then developed to describe the behavior of drivers that arrived at and passed through the intersection. Using a procedure described by the general flowchart shown as Figure 5.3, the researchers modeled traffic flow through the intersection and estimated delays to motorists under different conditions of traffic flow, as Figure 5.4 illustrates.

Physical Models

Physical models have long been used by engineers to gain a better understanding of complex phenomena. Such models probably constitute the oldest method of structural design. Physical models have also been used for many years in the fields of hydraulics, hydrodynamics, and aerodynamics.

Examples of studies made with physical models include:

1. Dispersion of pollutants throughout a lake.
2. Behavior of waves within a harbor. (See Figure 5.5.)
3. The underwater performance of submarines of different shapes.

Full-scale models are sometimes built, but they are often built to a smaller scale. Typical scales for physical models range from 1 : 4 to 1 : 48 (*6*).

Perhaps the greatest value of physical models is that they allow the engineer to study a device, structure, or system with little or no prior knowledge of its behavior or need to make simplifying assumptions.

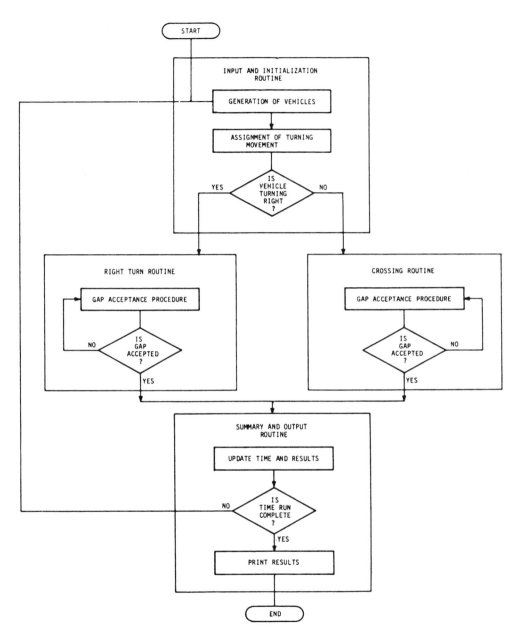

Figure 5.3 *A general flowchart for a simulation model.*

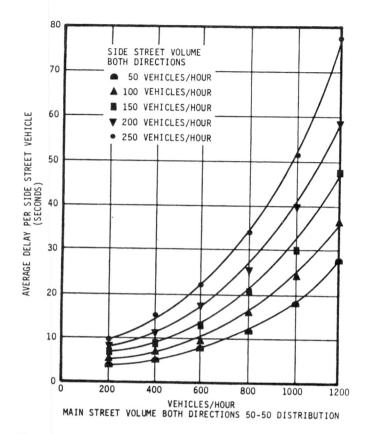

Figure 5.4 *Output from a computer simulation model. The figure shows the average times cars wait to cross a main street.*

An Example of Physical Models   Some of the most beneficial research with physical models has been accomplished with wind tunnels (see Figures 5.6 and 5.7). A brief description of wind tunnels, abstracted from Reference 6, is given in the following paragraphs.

Wind tunnels are based on a fundamental law of fluid dynamics, namely, that a body immersed in a moving fluid experiences the same forces as if the body were moving and the fluid stationary, assuming that the relative speed of the fluid and solid object is the same in both cases. This means, for example, that the conditions surrounding an airplane in flight can be replicated by holding the plane stationary and moving the air past it at a velocity comparable to flight speeds.

Advantages of wind tunnels over flight testing are economy, safety, and research versatility. A model airplane can be tested in a wind tunnel at a fraction of the cost of building and operating a full-scale prototype, and the airworthiness of new and experimental designs can be tested without risking a

Figure 5.5 *A physical model used to study the behavior of waves in a harbor. (Courtesy of the U.S. Army Corps of Engineers.)*

Figure 5.6 *Some of the most beneficial research with physical models has been accomplished with wind tunnels. Here a ram jet model is being studied in a 10 ft. × 10 ft. test section. (Courtesy of the National Aeronautics and Space Administration.)*

Figure 5.7 *This giant air passage houses a massive set of stationary guide vanes in one elbow of a wind tunnel which force the air to make a right angle smoothly. (Courtesy of the National Aeronautics and Space Administration.)*

pilot's life. Wind-tunnel testing can simulate flight under conditions more controlled and measurable than would be possible in a flight test. Even before the Wright brothers' first flight, the wind tunnel was the principal tool of the aeronautical engineer.

All wind tunnels have common features that circumscribe their characteristics and capabilities. All have a test section in which a model, component, or system can be fixed or suspended. The cross section may be round, oval, rectangular, or polygonal. Test sections may vary in width and height from a few inches up to 100 feet or more.

Wind tunnels may be either return or nonreturn. Nonreturn tunnels draw air from the atmosphere, pass it through a tube that includes a test section, and discharge it into the atmosphere. Such tunnels are simple and inexpensive to build but are inefficient and limited in the types of flow they can generate. Many sophisticated tunnels use a return-type circuit in which the same air is moved around a closed loop.

A major advantage of closed tunnels is that they can be pressurized, a technique that allows objects to be studied that are a fraction of the full scale. Comparability between conditions of wind-tunnel tests on models and conditions experienced by a full-scale aircraft in flight depends on a dimensionless mathematical quantity known as the Reynolds number (named for the nineteenth century British engineer Osborne Reynolds). The Reynolds number is a flow-similarity parameter that describes forces acting on a body in motion with respect to the fluid in which it is immersed. The number is directly proportional to the size of the body and the density and relative speed of the fluid, and inversely proportional to the viscosity of the fluid. Other things being equal, a model "moving" with respect to an airstream would have a smaller Reynolds number than a full-scale plane in flight. The easiest way to equalize the Reynolds numbers—and thus to obtain comparable flow conditions for the plane and the model—is to increase the speed or density of the airstream in which the model is immersed.

Almost all wind tunnels employ a complex array of balances and other measuring devices designed specifically for the purpose. Most closed-circuit tunnels use tunnel vanes to guide the airflow smoothly around the corners in the circuit. Most tunnels use complex arrays of settling chambers, screens, and throat contractions to smooth and straighten the airstream as it accelerates into the test section. A variety of model-support systems is used, depending on the configuration of the test object. Some tunnels use smoke to help visualize airflow. Some are rigged with special photographic devices that record shock waves produced at high speeds. Some tunnels are refrigerated to produce ice on the models like that encountered under certain flight conditions. In fact, wind tunnels have been designed to replicate nearly every condition encountered by airplanes in flight (*6*).

5.5   EVALUATION AND SELECTION OF PREFERRED SOLUTION

As the engineering design process evolves, the engineer may evaluate again and again alternate ways of solving the problem at hand. Typically, the engineer winnows the unpromising design choices, yielding a progressively smaller set of options. Feedback, modification, and evaluation may occur repetitively as the device or system evolves from concept to final design. Depending on the nature of the problem to be solved, evaluation may be based on any number of factors. If it involves a product, safety, cost, reliability, and consumer acceptability are often of paramount importance.

Perhaps the most straightforward way to evaluate a product is to develop a prototype and simply test it in operation. In some cases the prototype might not work due to one or more components of the design. The designer should try to identify all of the weak links of a prototype before accepting or discarding the design idea. Many great ideas have been discarded prematurely, and many working prototypes have failed to operate as expected when turned into a product. No idea should be evaluated solely on the basis of one prototype or one test.

There are many indirect methods for evaluating a proposed design. For example, wind-tunnel testing a scale model of an aircraft design can reveal good and bad features of the design at a small fraction of the cost and risk of a full-scale assembly. Alternatively, the aerodynamics of the new aircraft design can be evaluated using computer simulation of the expected flight conditions. The associated mathematical equations used in the computer simulation may not accurately account for some of the complicating factors such as the component interference and turbulence. However, the computer simulation can indicate approximate features of the design, which makes it easier to design the first scale model for wind-tunnel testing.

The optimization scheme can become very difficult when the design requires a human operator and a man-machine interface. This difficulty exists because no two human beings are the same. The basic anatomical and physiological differences between humans makes the human factors of the design difficult to quantify. One human user may find a design very acceptable and efficient, while another may consider it to be intolerable; therefore, the optimization of human factors becomes a matter of statistical comparisons. Hence, the user population must be identified and characterized before attempting to optimize any designs that involve human operators.

In addition to the routine judgments that engineers make about a device or system, more formal and structured evaluations are often needed. This is especially true of public works projects, which must be judged from the viewpoints of competing and often conflicting groups. Such evaluations have traditionally relied on economic analysis, but recent concerns with social and environmental impacts of public projects have produced much broader evaluation techniques. Let us now examine some of these formal evaluation techniques.

Economic Analysis

For at least 50 years, economic analyses have been used by engineers as a decision-making tool for the building of dams, bridges, highways, and other public works. Conceptually, such analyses attempt to compare the public benefits from such projects with the costs of providing them.

Economic studies may be used:

1. To determine the feasibility of a project.
2. To compare alternate designs.
3. To determine the priority of construction of a group of projects.
4. To evaluate specific features of design.

In economic analyses, it is important to recognize the time value of money. Because of the existence of interest, a quantity of money is worth more now than the prospect of receiving the same quantity at a later date. Therefore, in order to compare costs and benefits of an engineering project on a sound basis, they must be converted to equivalent values at some common date. This procedure, which is known as discounting, is accomplished by using a suitable interest rate in accordance with established economic principles. Such concepts are more fully described in textbooks on economic analysis and facility design (7, 8).

One approach is to compare benefits and costs on the basis of *present worth* or *present value*. For example, the present worth, P, of some future single payment, F, can be calculated by the following equation:

$$P = \frac{F}{(1 + i)^n} \tag{5.1}$$

where i = the interest rate or discount rate per period

n = the number of interest periods, usually years

Example 5.1

Suppose that a bridge is to be constructed over a river and that it will cost $385,000 to dismantle it at the end of its expected life of 40 years. Determine the present value of dismantling the bridge using an interest rate of 10 percent.

Solution   By Equation (5.1),

$$\text{present value, } P = \frac{\$385,000}{(1 + 0.10)^{40}} = \$8500$$

Economic equivalencies such as these are often illustrated in the following manner:

The present worth, P, of a series of uniform annual end-of-period payments, A, can be calculated by the following equation (7).

$$P_s = A\frac{(1 + i)^n - 1}{i(1 + i)^n} \tag{5.2}$$

Example 5.2

Suppose that it is estimated that the annual user benefits (in excess of any maintenance costs) of the bridge described in Example 5.1 are a uniform $94,500 per year. Determine the present value of these benefits assuming an interest rate of 10 percent and an analysis period (bridge life) of 40 years.

Solution   By Equation (5.2),

$$\text{present value, } P_s = \$94,500\frac{(1 + 0.1)^{40} - 1}{0.1(1 + 0.1)^{40}} = \$924,000$$

Economic analyses may be carried out by one of several methods. Two popular methods are the *net present value method* and the *benefit-cost ratio method.*

The net present value method involves reducing all benefits and costs to their present value in accordance with the principles previously described.

The net present value is defined as the difference between the present values of the benefits and the costs of the project.

Example 5.3

Suppose that the initial costs of building the bridge described in Examples 5.1 and 5.2 was $800,000. Determine by the net present value method whether the bridge is economically justified.

Solution   As previously calculated, the present value of the benefits is $924,000. The present value of the costs would be the sum of the initial cost and the present value of the dismantling cost or $800,000 + $8500 = $808,500. The difference between these amounts is $115,000. Since the benefits exceed the costs, the project is economically feasible.

The benefit-cost ratio method, as the term suggests, is simply the ratio of the benefits to the costs, each expressed as present values. A benefit-cost ratio greater than 1.0 would indicate that a project is economically justified. A value less than 1.0 indicates that it is not. In the previous example, the benefit-cost ratio is $924,000 divided by $808,500 or 1.14, again showing that the project is economically viable.

Other Evaluation Techniques

Over the past several years, there has been increasing awareness of the impact that engineering works may have on people and the environment. Such projects may cause families and businesses to be relocated and subject citizens to noise and water and air pollution. Many of these impacts cannot be simply reduced to a dollar amount. Techniques are available, however, to help the engineer, to some extent at least, quantify such impacts. These techniques generally involve ranking alternate projects on a scale based upon some predetermined criteria. The rankings may be made by a panel of experts or citizens or based on attitude surveys. This approach is illustrated by the following example, which was abstracted from Reference 9.

Suppose that a city considering a new mass transit system has established the following objectives for the system:

1. The system should provide economy.
2. There should be minimum disruption of individuals by relocation.
3. The system should provide a high level of comfort and convenience.
4. The central area should be highly accessible.
5. The system should be accessible to low-income areas.

The following criteria were selected to provide a measure of each objective:

1. Benefit-cost ratio.
2. Number of persons relocated.
3. Load factor on transit vehicles in peak hour.
4. Accessibility index of core areas.
5. Transit accessibility index to low-income traffic zones.

A panel of citizens and engineers then established the following ratios of relative importance for these objectives: 40 percent, 20 percent, 20 percent, 10 percent, and 10 percent. They then evaluated these objectives for each of three alternate projects, with the following results:

Evaluation Matrix:	Possible Effectiveness Score	Score for Plan A	Score for Plan B	Score for Plan C
1. Benefit-cost ratio	40	35	25	30
2. Persons relocated	20	10	20	5
3. Transit load factor	20	10	15	3
4. Core accessibility	10	3	5	10
5. Low-income transit availability	10	2	10	8
Total effectiveness score	100	60	75	56

Plan B was selected as being the most responsive to the goal statements that the transportation plan was designed to achieve.

5.6   PREPARATION OF REPORTS, PLANS, AND SPECIFICATIONS

After the preferred design has been selected, it must be communicated to those who must approve it, support it, and translate it into reality. This communication may take the form of an engineering report or a set of plans and specifications. Engineering reports are usually directed to a client or to a supervisor (e.g., if the engineer is employed by a large corporation). Plans and specifications are the engineer's means of describing to a manufacturing division or to a contractor sufficient detail about a design so that it can be produced or constructed. This important phase of the design process is treated more fully in Chapter 6.

5.7   IMPLEMENTATION OF THE DESIGN

It could be argued that once the plans, specifications, and engineering reports have been completed, the design process is finished. Actually, however, the final phase of the design process is implementation, the process of producing or constructing a physical device, product, or system. Engineers must plan and oversee the production of the devices or products and supervise the construction of the engineered projects. Different engineers may, of course, be involved in this final phase. This is the culmination of the design process; to the design engineer, it is the most satisfying phase of all.

Patenting

It is not uncommon for the work of an engineer to be of such value that it should be protected from exploitation by others. This may be accomplished by patenting.

A patent for an invention grants a property right by the government to the inventor or his or her heirs. It excludes others from making, using, or selling the invention. In the United States, patents are administered by the Patent and Trademark Office, a division of the U.S. Department of Commerce.

The patent law classifies subject matter that can be patented as "any new or useful process, machine, manufacture, or composition of matter, or any new and useful improvements thereof" (*10*). This means that patents can be obtained for practically everything that is made by humans as well as the process for making them.

In order for an invention to be patentable it must be new as defined in the patent law. The law states that an invention cannot be patented if:

1. *The invention was known or used by others in this country, or patented or described in a printed publication of this or a foreign country, before the invention thereof by the applicant for patent, or*
2. *The invention was patented or described in a printed publication in this or a foreign country or in public use or on sale in this country*

more than one year prior to the application for patent in the United States. (10)

To apply for a patent, the inventor must submit an application which includes:

1. A *specification*, a clear, concise, and exact description of the invention presented in such manner as to distinguish it from other older inventions.
2. An *oath* or *declaration* made by the inventor asserting the belief that he or she is the original and first inventor of the subject matter of the application.
3. A *filing fee.* Reference 10 gives a schedule of fees, beginning with a basic fee of $630.
4. A *drawing* prepared to Patent Office specifications whenever the nature of the case requires such to understand the invention.

The Scientific and Technical Information Center of the Patent and Trademark Office in Arlington, Virginia has a Search Room where the public may search and examine U.S. patents granted since 1836. There, patents are arranged in over 400 classes and 120,000 subclasses. By searching these classified patents, it is possible to determine, before actually filing an application, whether an invention has been anticipated by a U.S. patent.

Since a patent is not always granted when an application is filed, many inventors attempt to make their own search before applying for a patent. This may be done in the Search Room of the Patent and Trademark Office or at libraries located throughout the United States which have been designated as Patent Depository Libraries.

The preparation and processing of an application for patent is an undertaking requiring the knowledge of patent law as well as knowledge of the scientific or technical matters involved in the particular invention. Most inventors, therefore, employ the services of registered patent attorneys or patent agents. The Patent and Trademark Office maintains a register of attorneys and agents qualified to help inventors with the patenting process (*10*).

Computer-Aided Design

Although digitial computers first appeared in the 1940s, most of the growth in computer technology has occurred within the past two decades. In this relatively brief span of time, the use of computer-based tools for engineering problem solving has become commonplace. These tools are variously referred to as computer-aided engineering (CAE), computer-aided design (CAD), or computer-aided design and manufacturing (CAD/CAM). These systems make the engineering problem solving process much more efficient and free engineers from monotonous and unimaginative tasks, allowing them more time for technical ingenuity. Here we will focus primarily on CAD systems, which are becoming increasingly powerful and pervasive design tools.

With CAD systems, interactive graphics allow the user to communicate easily with the computer in display-screen pictures. With the speed of modern computers, this communication is carried out in real time; that is, the computer's response is practically instantaneous. Furthermore, little knowledge of computers is required to operate these user-friendly systems.

Earlier CAD systems were used primarily to perform automated drafting or to facilitate the solution of simple two-dimensional problems. Interactive graphic systems now allow the user to develop three-dimensional models and to perform a wide range of geometric manipulations and sophisticated analyses.

Assisting the designer in constructing a model are thousands of software aids that automate many of the tedious tasks consuming so much time in traditional manual methods. With the stroke of the pen or the push of a button, the user can move, magnify, rotate, flip, copy, or otherwise manipulate the entire design or any part of it. . . .

In working with a complex model, the user can temporarily "erase" portions of it from the screen to see the area under construction more clearly. Then the deleted area is recalled later to complete the model. Likewise, portions of the model may be enlarged to view and add minute details accurately. And the model may be moved and rotated on the screen for the user to view it at any angle. Furthermore, mechanisms such as linkages and gears in the assembly may be animated on the screen to ensure proper operation and check for interferences. When the design is complete, the system may automatically add dimensions and labels. And automated drafting features may be used to produce detailed engineering drawings. (11)

Learning from Failures

Despite the best efforts of engineering designers, their designs occasionally fail. Bridges collapse, roofs of buildings cave in, and earthen dams fail, threatening human lives and causing millions of dollars of damage to property.

Engineering failures may be attributed to a wide variety of causes, including:

1. Mistakes made by inept or careless designers.
2. Imperfections in building or manufacturing materials and uncertainties as to their variability.
3. Careless workmanship by technicians or craftsmen who implement the design.
4. Poor communications between the managers, engineers, technicians, and craftsmen who produce or construct the engineered design.

Although the object of engineering design is to preclude failure, truly fail-proof design cannot be achieved. An engineering structure or machine can fail in many ways, the results ranging from blemishes to catastrophes. It is a curious fact that we often learn more from our failures than from our successes.

One of the ironies of engineering history is that success ultimately leads to failure. With each engineering success, questions arise from taxpayers, from boards of directors, and from engineers themselves as to how much larger, or how much lighter, or how much more economical the next structure of machine can be made. Thus, in the interests of aesthetics or economy, there is a tendency to be more daring in design and to take greater risks in workmanship and style.

On the other hand, after a failure, there is usually pressure to increase factors of safety, revise building codes, and to generally engage in a more conservative engineering practice (*12*).

When an engineering failure occurs, it is usually important that an investigation be conducted to determine the cause of the failure and to identify remedial actions that can be taken to prevent or lessen the likelihood of a reoccurrence. Such investigations may be carried out by:

1. Government agencies or boards.
2. Private or professional associations.
3. Ad hoc committees or commissions.

For example, the National Transportation Safety Board (NTSB) has a staff of about 300 specialists who investigate hundreds of civil aviation and surface transportation accidents each year. The Board does not have regulatory powers, but it recommends changes for improved safety that other agencies of government may implement.

The National Fire Protection Association (NFPA), a private (but government-assisted) organization, empanels teams of experts to study and report on the causes of major fires. Great benefits have accrued to building owners and to the public from recommendations of the NFPA to improve the nation's fire codes.

The Architectural and Engineering Performance Information Center (AEPIC) was organized at the University of Maryland in 1982 (*13*). AEPIC serves as a focus for activities to collect and disseminate knowledge and experience gained from structural failures. By establishing patterns of structural failures, AEPIC seeks to help engineers and architects to prevent similar future failures and avoid litigation (*13*).

When an especially dramatic or costly engineering failure occurs, a special committee or commission may be empaneled to study the circumstances of the failure and to make appropriate recommendations. Such groups may be convened under the auspices of one or more professional organizations or may be named by a governor or the president of the United States. A notable example of the work of such a commission is given in the *Report of the Presidential Commission on the Space Shuttle* Challenger *Accident* (*14*). The Space Shuttle *Challenger* accident is described as a case study in Chapter 9 of this book.

THE HYATT REGENCY HOTEL WALKWAYS COLLAPSE (15, 16)

On July 17, 1981, during a weekly tea dance, two suspended walkways in the atrium area of the Hyatt Regency Hotel in Kansas City, Missouri collapsed, killing 114 people and injuring 185. The collapse was one of the most serious structural failures in the history of the United States.

The hotel included a 40-story guest room tower, a four-story wing containing restaurants and meeting rooms, and a large, open atrium. The atrium contained three suspended walkways at the second-, third-, and fourth-floor levels which connected the tower section with the restaurants and meeting rooms. Each walkway was 120 feet long and approximately 8 1/2 feet wide.

The second- and fourth-floor walkways were constructed one above another along the west wall of the atrium. The third-floor level walkway was independently suspended from the atrium roof trusses and was built about 13 feet toward the center of the room. The third-floor walkway was not involved in the collapse. The second-floor walkway was suspended from the fourth-floor walkway, which in turn was suspended from the roof framing.

In the aftermath of the tragedy, the mayor of Kansas City requested that the National Bureau of Standards (NBS) conduct an independent investigation to determine the cause of the collapse (16). There were, of course, other investigations and hearings as well as at least 150 lawsuits seeking total damages of $1.5 billion.

Each of the walkways consisted of four spans of about 30 feet. Intermediate supports consisted of three pairs of 1 1/4-inch diameter steel hanger rods. Each walkway was supported from underneath longitudinally by 16-inch deep wide flange steel beams and laterally by 8-inch deep steel box beams. The box beams were made of pairs of 8-inch steel channels that were welded together at their open ends. The walkway deck consisted of a formed steel deck overlain by a 3 1/4-inch lightweight concrete slab which acted compositely with the 16-inch deep stringers. Figure 5.8 shows a cross-section of the walkways as well as the hanger rod connection.

The National Bureau of Standards discovered that a significant design change had been made after the completion of the original design drawings in the way in which the walkways were connected to the hanger rods. The original drawings called for both the fourth- and second-floor walkways to be hung from the same continuous steel rods. As originally conceived, pairs of single rods about 45 feet long would have been passed through the box beams at the fourth-floor walkway and continued down to pass through the box beams at the second-floor level. The walkways were to have been supported by a nut-and-washer connection under the box beams at each level.

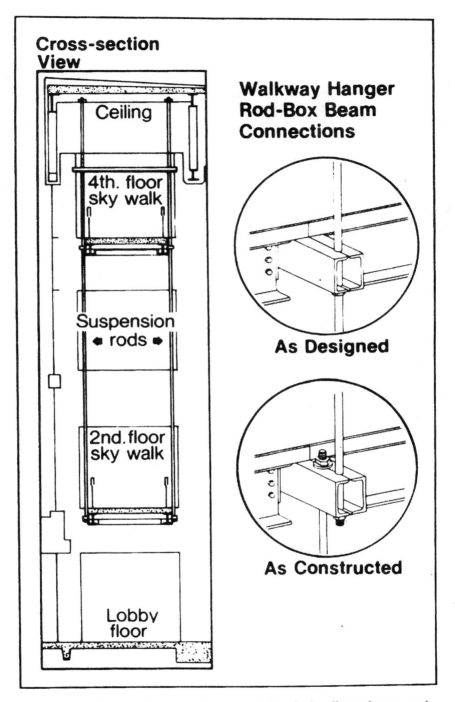

Figure 5.8 *Cross section of walkways and detail of walkway hanger rod-box beam connections. (Source: Neil Schlager, ed.,* When Technology Fails, Gale Research, Inc., *Detroit, 1994.)* (Reprinted by permission of AP/Wide World Photos.)

Instead of using continuous rods, however, the contractor hung the walkways from two separate sets of rods. Each fourth-floor box beam had two holes at each end, one 2 inches from the end and the other 6 inches from the end. The upper hanger rod passed through the outer hole, while the lower hanger rod, onto which hung the second-floor walkway, passed through the inner hole. A nut-and-washer connection was used on the ends of the rods.

The effect of this change was to essentially double the load on the box-beam hanger connection at the fourth floor walkway. In fact, it was concluded that the collapse was initiated when the welding of one of the fourth-floor beams split, and the nut-and-washer connection supporting that part of the walkway slipped through the hole. The load of both walkways was then transferred to the remainder of the fourth floor connections, which also failed. The fourth-floor walkway then collapsed onto the one below it, and both walkways crashed onto the lobby floor.

It was reported that the failed connection was designed by the project's steel erector and fabricator, a common practice in the construction industry. It was noted, however, that the shop drawings submitted by the fabricator had been signed by the chief structural engineer and the project engineer. Missouri law states that: "Any registered engineer who affixes his signature and personal seal to any such plans . . . shall be personally and professionally responsible therefore." The Board of Architects, Professional Engineers, and Land Surveyors voted unanimously to revoke the licenses of these two engineers permanently (*17*) and to revoke the certificate of authority of their firm. The firms' assets were sold to another civil and structural engineering firm.

An expert witness appearing before the Missouri Administrative Hearing Commission stated that the engineer of record usually has to delegate his duties because there is too much work. "But he cannot delegate his responsibility. . . . There has to be a point where the buck stops." (*18*)

REFERENCES

1. CLELAND, DAVID I., AND HAROLD KERZNER, *Engineering Team Management,* Van Nostrand Reinhold Company, New York, 1986.

2. PEARSON, DONALD S., *Creativeness for Engineers*, 3rd Edition, Pennsylvania State University, University Park, PA, 1960.

3. WHITING, CHARLES S., *Creative Thinking*, Rheinhold Publishing Corporation, New York, 1958.

4. DUDERSTADT, JAMES J., GLENN F. KNOLL, AND GEORGE F. SPRINGER, *Principles of Engineering*, John Wiley & Sons, Inc., New York, 1982.

5. WRIGHT, PAUL H., AND J. N. THOMASSON, JR., "Simulation of Traffic at a Two-Way Stop Intersection," *Traffic Engineering*, Vol. 37, No. 11, August 1967.

6. ROLAND, ALEX, *Model Research, The National Advisory Committee for Aeronautics 1915–1958*, Vol. 2, National Aeronautics and Space Administration, Washington, DC, 1985.

7. GRANT, EUGENE L., W. GRANT IRESON, AND RICHARD S. LEAVENWORTH, *Principles of Engineering Economy*, 8th Edition, John Wiley & Sons, Inc., New York, 1990.

8. WRIGHT, PAUL, H. *Highway Engineering*, 6th Edition, John Wiley & Sons, Inc., New York, 1996.

9. WRIGHT, PAUL H., NORMAN J. ASHFORD, AND ROBERT STAMMER, JR., *Transportation Engineering: Planning and Design*, 4th Edition, John Wiley & Sons, Inc., New York, 1998.

10. *General Information About Patents*, U.S. Department of Commerce, Patent and Trademark Office, Washington, DC, Revised December, 1990.

11. KRAUSE, JOHN K., *Computer-Aided Design and Computer-Aided Manufacturing*, Marcel Dekker, Inc., New York, 1982, p. 12. Reprinted by courtesy of Marcel Dekker, Inc.

12. PETROSKI, HENRY, *To Engineer Is Human*, St. Martin's Press, New York, 1985.

13. FITZSIMONS, NEAL, AND DONALD VANNOY, "Establishing Patterns of Building Failures," *Civil Engineering*, Vol. 54, No. 1, American Society of Civil Engineers, January 1984.

14. *Report of the Presidential Commission on the Space Shuttle* Challenger *Accident.* Report to the President, Government Printing Office, 1986.

15. SCHLAGER, NEIL, ed., *When Technology Fails,* Gale Research, Inc., Detroit, 1994.

16. PFRANG, EDWARD O., AND RICHARD MARSHALL, "Collapse of the Kansas City Hyatt Regency Walkways," *Civil Engineering*, July, 1982, pp. 65–68.

17. ALM, RICK, "Hyatt Engineers Lose Licenses in Missouri," *Engineering News Record,* January 30, 1986, p. 11.

18. "Hyatt Hearing Traces Design Chain," *Engineering News Record*, July 26, 1984, pp. 12–13.

EXERCISES

5.1 Write a report comparing the scientific method and the engineering method of problem solving.

5.2 List three ideas for overcoming the problems of drivers locking their keys in their automobiles.

5.3 Describe three ways for reducing or eliminating flying insects from a patio area.

5.4 Give an example of a technological development that was delayed because technologists failed to properly identify the problem.

5.5 Prepare a report describing the Delphi technique for developing ideas for solving problems. Describe the background of the development of this technique. How does it differ from brainstorming? Indicate how it can be used to facilitate the solution of engineering problems.

5.6 Prepare a scheme for developing:
   a.   A system for measuring or monitoring heat loss from a residential house.

    b.   A device to measure the distance a jogger runs.

    c.   A device mounted on the instrument panel of a car to indicate the distance from the edge of a curb.

5.7   List two types of problems that could suitably be modeled by:

    a.   Mathematical models.

    b.   Simulation models.

    c.   Physical models.

5.8   Suppose that you wished to improve the design of bathroom scales. Prepare an attribute list showing how each of the attributes might be improved.

5.9   Using the forced relationship technique, develop a list of ideas for designing a better mousetrap. For the random element, use a mail box.

5.10   Using morphological analysis, prepare a list of possible attributes of a device to remove dust from a warehouse floor.

5.11   Write a report on a significant and well-publicized engineering failure. Discuss any lessons that were learned, and describe any changes in engineering codes and design procedures that resulted from that failure. For ideas, consult Reference 15.

An Exemplary Engineering Achievement

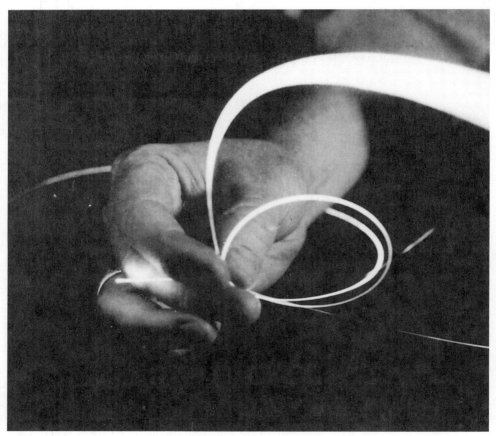

Loops of a hair-thin glass fiber, illuminated by laser light, represent the transmission medium for lightwave systems. Typically, 12 fibers are embedded between two strips of plastic in a flat ribbon, and as many as 12 ribbons are stacked in a cable that can carry more than 40,000 voice channels. (Courtesy of American Council of Engineering Companies.)

CHAPTER SIX

ENGINEERING COMMUNICATIONS

6.1 INTRODUCTION

It is difficult to overstate the importance of effective communications to the success of engineering. No matter how creative and elegant a design may be, it is of no value until it can be communicated to those who must accept it, pay for it, support it, and translate it into physical reality. Successful engineers must be able to communicate effectively with their supervisors, peers, and with the general public. Often, these individuals are not in close proximity, so effective communication via technology and traditional sources is essential. In this chapter, we describe some of the resources and guidelines for effective engineering communications.

6.2 COMMUNICATIONS AND INFORMATION RESOURCES

With developments in computer technology and the rapid growth of the Internet, information has become ubiquitous in our lives. A wealth of information is available in a variety of formats through a vast number of gateways. The World Wide Web, scholarly journals, textbooks, reference sources, virtual communities, colleagues, and full-text databases are examples of the various sources to which engineers turn for information. With information available in such abundance, the problem for modern engineers is not simply locating information but also learning how to filter, evaluate, process, and use it. From the undergraduate student completing a semester project to the professional working on a design problem, engineers are called upon to perform research, use that research to solve problems, and communicate their solutions to others.

How Engineers Find Information
and the Information-Seeking Process

Technology has driven dramatic changes in the information-seeking behaviors and practices of engineers. While still making use of traditional resources such as colleagues, handbooks, print indexes, and technical publications, engineers have integrated new World Wide Web–driven resources into their information-seeking processes. A researcher can just as easily connect to the Web as open a reference book or walk to the nearest library. As a result, engineers physically visit libraries less frequently. As scholarly research gravitates toward online sources, customized Web portals, and desktop access, engineers become more dependent on remote computer access but are, at the same time, more overwhelmed by information noise. The result is twofold. Engineers need training to develop their research and communications skills while at the same time they are performing more and more of their research and communications remotely via the computer.

The best way to ensure that you are locating and using quality information is to understand the steps it takes to do so. There are five basic steps in the traditional research process:

1. Identify and define the topic, research question, or problem.
2. Select the specific keywords or terms that best describe your topic.
3. Select the appropriate information resource and perform a search.
4. Evaluate the search results and identify the specific books, articles, technical papers, chapters, pages, and so on that will give you the most relevant information.
5. Locate the materials and synthesize the information to solve a problem.

Although the Internet has had a profound impact on the process of locating materials, the initial four steps remain essential with any type of search. Locating information resources can be as quick as clicking a hyperlink. Prior to the Internet, engineers would have to either communicate with someone directly (either visit with a colleague in person or over the telephone), consult their own personal library, or visit a research library to locate appropriate materials. Regardless of whether an engineer uses traditional research resources or turns to the Internet, the ability to comprehend the problem at hand, choose the appropriate resource, and perform an effective search remain key skills.

Turning Information into Knowledge:
Evaluating and Processing Information

The Internet, however, is no panacea for the information needs of engineers. If anything, it has made it more difficult to select the appropriate resources and evaluate search results to identify quality information. Quantity and ubiquitous access have not led to information quality, and professors and employers are beginning to take note. Employers are focusing on the need for the integration of "soft skills" such as writing, oral communication, teamwork, and life-long learning into the engineer's skill set. A key part of effective communication and lifelong learning is information literacy and being able to effectively and efficiently locate, process, and evaluate information to aid in research, problem solving, and learning.

The World Wide Web is fraught with opportunity and risk for engineers searching for information. Before the rise of the Web and online full-text documents, it was easier for professors, students, employers, and employees to ascertain the quality of the information they found. Books and journal articles in corporate and university libraries are reviewed by other scholars and carefully screened. On the Web, quality peer-reviewed content coexists with unreliable and unverified content, biased information, and advertising in a primordial soup of information. Anyone can publish on the Internet, and at times it seems that everyone has. Add to that the fact that most libraries have made at least some of the materials they collect available on the Web and it can be difficult to discern quality information from misinformation.

Kari Boyd McBride and Ruth Dickstein (*1*) point to the potential of the Web as an information resource when they write

> Some critics of the World Wide Web question its usefulness as a scholarly resource, especially for undergraduates, who may rely exclusively on it for their research. But the Web will continue to affect learning while serving as a valuable research tool that students enjoy using.

David Rothenberg (*2*) provides a more cynical view of the Web as a scholarly resource when he writes

> Search engines, with their half-baked algorithms, are closer to slot machines than to library catalogues. You throw your query to the wind, and who knows what will come back to you? Perhaps one in a thousand sites might actually help you. But it's easy to be sidetracked or frustrated as you try to go through those Web pages one by one."

He goes on to write

> The placelessness of the Web leads to an ethereal randomness of thought. Gone are the pathways of logic and passion, the sense of the progress of argument. Chance holds sway, and it more often misses than hits. Judgment must be taught, as well as the methods of exploration.

There are strong arguments on both sides. The reality is that the World Wide Web is a valuable research tool for engineers. The potential for exchanging, locating, and publishing engineering information on the Web is vast. However, its current organization, content, and search mechanisms warrant caution. Let us look at an example.

Lawrence Weschler's book *Mr. Wilson's Cabinet of Wonder* (*3*) discusses the evolution of museums in the Western world. The book outlines their origins 300 or so years ago as personal collections developed in rich people's homes. These personal collections were the precursors of the modern museum. One modern example of these thematic personal museums that Weschler discusses is the Museum of Jurassic Technology in Los Angeles. The museum highlights and exhibits unusual discoveries and technologies that stretch the imagination but are also meticulously researched and documented.

Each discovery or oddity is presented with the same type of scholarly documentation, firsthand testimony, and scientific evidence. The similarities between the exhibits, the quality of the research and writing, and the manner in which each discovery is presented convinces the viewer that they must be real. The catch is that some of the discoveries and technologies are planted hoaxes, while others are absolutely true. The viewer cannot tell the real from the imagined because all of them are presented in the same manner with the same look and same detailed research to support the claims. The Museum of Jurassic Technology is an excellent analogy for the Web. Everything on the Web looks very similar at first glance. Items may even be presented in a scholarly looking manner, but it is difficult to be sure because the Web lacks peer review, quality control, and any discernable authority. It takes a careful and discerning mind to find quality information on the Web.

Once the need to carefully evaluate and filter Internet resources is understood, techniques for doing so must be learned. One common method for evaluating information resources is CARDS. CARDS is an acronym for credibility, accuracy, relevancy, date, and source.

Credibility: Who is the source of the information? Is this a well-respected site for credible information? Is the author a professor, graduate researcher, or respected professional? Can you even find out who the author is and a list of their credentials? Any source worth trusting will list the name, contact information, affiliation, and title of the author.

Accuracy: Can you compare the information found on this site to other sources? Are there any obvious errors or statements that seem exaggerated or out of place? Can you verify any of the information the site provides?

Relevancy: Is the site relevant to your research project or problem? Does the site have a clearly defined scope and purpose? Who is the intended audience?

Date: Is the site up-to-date? Do the pages on the site have a lot of dead links? Is there a date on the page that tells you when it was last updated?

Source: Does the page cite other print or electronic resources? Does the page have a bibliography?

No one system will work for every situation, but engineers must ask themselves if a Web page is up-to-date, reliable, credible, and accurate before using any of its information. The CARDS method provides some simple steps engineers can use in evaluating information resources until they gain experience and their information literacy skills become more developed. One basic rule is to not use Web sites simply because they are more convenient. A Web site, like other resources, must add some value and provide quality information.

Where to Locate Information and Good Starting Points

From electronic full-text databases to traditional print reference sources to discussions with colleagues, engineers use a range of information sources to solve problems. With all of the options available, engineers need to have a selection of peer-reviewed sources that they can rely on and trust. An overview of the different types of information resources along with specific examples is outlined here.

1. ***Databases.***   One of the more overwhelming tasks facing an engineer performing research is choosing the appropriate database. With all of the database options made available through libraries and the Internet, electronic research can be quite confusing. Databases come in a variety of formats. Some databases offer selected full-text documents while others index and abstract articles from journals and other sources. Not only are there many different types of databases, but they are presented in an array of distinct interfaces. One database may use AND to combine terms, while another uses the + symbol. Search options, results displays, and record selection can all vary. There are two keys in managing electronic databases. The first is choosing the proper database. If you do not know the right one to use, ask a librarian or a colleague for suggestions. Second, remember that although databases have different interfaces, they generally share some fundamental searching concepts. Tools and techniques that elicit quality results in one system will typically work with other databases. The key point is that a few simple search techniques allow researchers to harness the power of electronic databases. By providing full access to a range of scholarly materials with a few searches, databases save engineers time while helping to ensure that research is accurate and comprehensive. See Table 6.1 for a sampling of different database types with specific examples.

2. ***Print Reference Sources.***   Even with the rise of the Web, print reference materials remain a good source of technical data and research information. These authoritative sources are peer reviewed and have been carefully edited. Engineers should apply the same criteria to print resources that they do to Web sites. However, keep in mind that print resources are generally more authoritative and controlled because the costs of publishing and distributing the books prohibits the randomness of the Web. While the difference in quality between print and online resources is diminishing, it is worth noting. It is a tribute to the growing utility and importance of the Web that a number of these sources are now available in print and through Web gateways. Examples of print information resources include encyclopedias, handbooks, dictionaries, and textbooks. See Table 6.2 for examples.

3. ***Web Resources.***   The unreliability of Web resources and the importance of evaluating and filtering Web pages using such techniques as CARDS has been covered in previous sections. However, there is another technique for performing research on the Web that has not been discussed. Many times

TABLE 6.1   *Examples of Different Database Types*

Type of Database	Examples	Description
Index and abstract	INSPEC	Covers electrical engineering, computer science, and physics. Provides abstracts and indexes for millions of journal articles and conference papers.
	Compendex/ Engineering Index	Provides the broadest range of coverage for engineering. Includes citations and abstracts for millions of articles and papers.
Full-text collection	IEEEXplore	A full-text database of all IEEE publications.
	ScienceDirect	An example of an individual publisher providing access to its publications through a full-text searchable database.
Citation database	Science Citation Index	Allows researchers to search for citations and abstracts as well as track journal citation patterns for specific articles and authors.

TABLE 6.2   *Examples of Print Information Resources*

Type of Print Resource	Example
Technical encyclopedias	*McGraw-Hill Encyclopedia of Science and Technology*
Handbooks	*Perry's Chemical Engineers' Handbook,* 7th Edition, New York, McGraw-Hill, 1997.
	Electronics Engineers' Handbook, 4th Edition, New York, McGraw-Hill, 1997.
Indexes	*Applied Science and Technology Index,* New York, H.W. Wilson Company, 1958–present.
Abstracts	*Chemical Abstracts,* Columbus, OH, American Chemical Society, 1907–present.
Dictionaries	*The IEEE Standard Dictionary of Electrical and Electronics Terms,* 6th Edition, New York, Institute of Electrical and Electronics Engineers, 1997.
Textbooks	Richard C. Dorf and James A. Svoboda, *Introduction to Electric Circuits,* 5th Edition, New York, John Wiley and Sons, Inc., 2001.

the best way to locate quality information on the Web is to start with reliable pages. Web sites from professional engineering organizations, colleges, and universities, and pages maintained and recommended by other engineering professionals are all examples of reliable starting points. Table 6.3 includes a sampling of the different types of pages along with specific examples of quality sites.

TABLE 6.3   *Examples of Quality Web Sites*

Type of Web Site	Examples	Description
Professional organization	www.ieee.org	The IEEE site contains information on the society, their publications, professional involvement, student resources, and electrical engineering news.
	www.asme.org	As is common with other professional Web sites, the American Society of Mechanical Engineers' site contains a wealth of information about mechanical engineering as well as links to other related pages.
Information gateway	www.eevl.ac.uk	The Edinburgh Engineering Virtual Library is a gateway of quality engineering resources selected by subject specialists in each field of engineering.
Academic site	www.avel.edu.au	The Australasian Virtual Engineering Library is a search engine and gateway largely promoted and maintained by universities.
Engineering-specific search engine	www.edie.net/power search/index.cfm	Edie Powersearch is a subject-specific search engine focusing on environmental engineering.
Search engine	www.google.com	Google is an example of the improving power and accuracy of search engines. However, it is important to remember that general search engines like Google do not discriminate in the pages they index.

THE ENGINEER AS A WRITER

During the course of their career, engineers will likely be called upon to write memoranda and letters and prepare technical reports, journal articles, and specifications. Before considering these types of writing in detail, we shall discuss some general guidelines for effective writing.

6.3 GUIDELINES FOR EFFECTIVE WRITING

In this section, we list several suggestions for becoming a more effective writer. Although this list was compiled with the engineering student in mind, these guidelines are applicable for writing of various kinds.

1. **Plan and organize your thoughts before writing.**   In the words of Strunk and White (4), "Planning must be a deliberate prelude to writing. The first principle of composition, therefore, is to foresee or determine the shape of what is to come, and pursue that shape."

2. **Prepare an outline.**   Many writers, especially those that are inexperienced, find it highly desirable to prepare an outline of the proposed work. Such an exercise helps the writer to think through the composition and improve its logic and internal order. It also provides an orderly framework and basis for increased writing productivity and efficiency.

3. **Avoid a boring structure.**   Make the paragraph the unit of composition. It should have a main theme and be introduced by a topic sentence. In technical and other types of writing, it is often desirable to divide a composition into chapters, sections, and subsections with appropriate headings or titles. To improve clarity and provide variety of style, present complex data or information as lists or tables rather than in narrative form.

4. **Strive for brevity and clarity.**   "The secret of good writing," Zinsser (5) states, "is to strip every sentence to its cleanest components." Short sentences generally are preferred over long sentences. Short words usually are better than long words (6). For example,

    near is preferred to *in close proximity to*

    scarce is preferred to *in short supply*

    now is preferred to *at this point in time*

5. **Adapt your writing style to the intended audience.**   Writers must consider the educational background, socioeconomic level, age, and interests of the readers, and choose a writing style that is appropriate to the intended audience. For example, papers for technical journals may contain chemical formulas, theoretical calculations, detailed descriptions of research methodology, and carefully drawn inferences and conclusions. Articles or reports intended for a general audience require a much different style—one that uses plain language and simple illustrations, and that stresses practical, personal implications and applications of the information being transmitted.

6. **Avoid the use of slang and fad words.**   Words such as "O.K.," "terrific," and "tremendous" are not suitable for technical writing, which calls for a formal style. Fad words or expressions such as "prioritize," "finalize," and "the bottom line" should also be avoided.

7. **Avoid redundancies.**   For example,

Avoid	Use instead
component parts	components *or* parts
consensus of opinion	consensus
most unique	unique
surrounded on all sides	surrounded

8. **Avoid euphemisms.**   Pompous and wordy euphemisms tend to clutter good writing and should not be used. Consider these examples:

previously owned vehicle	used car
communications resource center	library
sanitation engineer	garbage collector

9. **Avoid spelling errors and poor grammar.**   If you have a weakness in spelling or grammar, seek to correct it by taking remedial courses. In the meantime, ask a friend to check your writing to spot and correct spelling and grammatical errors that would mar your work.

6.4   TYPES OF ENGINEERING WRITING

Richard M. Davis (*7*) conducted a survey of successful engineers and reported in 1977 that the respondents spent an average of 24 percent of their time writing. Engineers perform a wide variety of writing, including entries in research notebooks and logs, office memoranda, business letters, technical reports and papers, and design specifications.

Logs and Notebooks   Many engineers maintain an informal record of their work by routinely making entries in a diary, log, or notebook. Such writing usually consists of a day-to-day record of the engineer's work, including results of laboratory experiments, notes of meetings, records of conversations with colleagues, and other pertinent matters. Records of this type, carefully made and maintained in a permanent form, provide a ready source of information for memoranda, letters, and technical reports.

Memoranda and Business Letters   In most large companies and organizations, internal correspondence is accomplished by memoranda. Memoranda usually are short and deal with a single subject. Although the format may vary among organizations, this form of communication typically includes the date, the addressee (TO), the writer (FROM), the topic (SUBJECT), and the message. An example of a memorandum is shown in Figure 6.1.

November 5, 2001

MEMORANDUM

TO: Division Engineers

FROM: Jane Gorman, Director of Engineering

SUBJ: Establishment of a Computer Security Committee

A meeting has been scheduled for 11:00 A.M., November 15, 2001, in Conference Room A to discuss the establishment of a Computer Security Committee. The purpose of the committee would be to safeguard and protect departmental data, solutions, and correspondence.

Please attend this meeting or send a representative.

Figure 6.1   *Example of a memorandum.*

External correspondence, that is, with persons not in the writer's organization, is usually accomplished by business letters. Engineers use a standard format for business letters, as exemplified by Figure 6.2. The style and tone of business letters should be clear, concise, complete, and courteous (*8*).

E-mail   Most engineers now routinely communicate by means of e-mail. This means of communication is typically succinct. In general, it is advisable to attempt to keep the e-mail to one screen length. The e-mail should show an appropriate subject line, and lengthy subject matter should be attached to the e-mail rather than embedded in the document.

Technical Reports   Of all of the forms of written communication employed by engineers, technical reports are the most commonly associated with engineering work. Such reports provide the engineer with a vehicle for communicating the results of his or her work to colleagues, clients, supervisors and other management personnel, and the general public.

The format of technical reports may vary depending on the type of report. Progress reports, proposals, and empirical research reports have organizational similarities, but each type of technical writing has a distinguishing format. For a given class of report, the format is fairly standard. Table 6.4 lists some of the components of technical reports. Typically, these parts are not written in the order listed.

The *title page* gives the title of the report, identifies its writer or writers, their company or organization, and the publication date. It may contain additional information such as report number, name and address of sponsoring organization, a distribution list, and restrictions on the report's reproduction and use.

The *abstract* is a concise summary of the content and purpose of the main report. Its purpose is to provide enough information to allow the reader to decide whether or not to obtain and read the complete report. A *descriptive abstract* describes what the full report contains but does not give the findings of the report. An *informative abstract* briefly describes study methodology and states major conclusions and recommendations. Many clients, including many

---

BROWNLOW AND ASSOCIATES
Engineers and Planners
1000 Memorial Building
Columbus, Ohio 43232

June 30, 2001

Mr. Jerome Salter, P. E.
Planning Engineer
Ohio Department of Transportation
Columbus, Ohio 43215

Dear Mr. Salter:

I submit the accompanying report titled "Noise Impacts of the Cross-County Freeway" as the final report for Contract E20-400.

The report discusses the levels of noise likely to be experienced in one-half-mile borders along each side of the 15-mile Cross-County Freeway and evaluates the expected impacts of noise on residential, commercial, and industrial land uses within the study areas.

Thank you for the opportunity to perform this work. Please do not hesitate to contact me if there are questions or if I can be of further service.

Very truly yours,

Jorge Perez, P.E.

Project Engineer

Figure 6.2   *Example of a business letter.*

TABLE 6.4   *Components of a Technical Report*

Title Page

Abstract or Executive Summary

Introduction

Methodology or Procedure

Results

Conclusions

Recommendations

Acknowledgments

Bibliography or List of References

Appendixes

---

federal agencies, require an *executive summary,* which briefly summarizes the results and recommendations of the report.

The *introduction* sets forth the subject, purpose, and scope of the report and its plan of development. It may also contain theoretical or historical background material based on a search of the technical literature.

The *methodology* or *procedure* section gives a detailed account of the steps taken to accomplish the work described in the study or investigation. In reports of experimental investigations, the equipment that was used is normally described in this section.

The *results* section describes the outcome of the project or investigation. This section of the report normally contains figures and tables, as well as a description and interpretation of the results or findings.

The *conclusions* "are the inferences drawn from the factual evidence of the report" (8). In technical reports dealing with complex or controversial matters, many writers precede their conclusions with a summary of the facts and title that section of the report *summary and conclusions.*

The *recommendations* section states a recommended course of action based upon the conclusions. The recommendations are stated simply, often in the form of a list, and need not contain supporting argument.

The *acknowledgments* section recognizes those people and organizations who have made significant contributions to the project.

The *bibliography* lists the books, journal articles, and other references used in the preparation of the report. In technical reports, a list of cited works is usually headed *References.* Many different bibliographic formats are used in technical reports. Figure 6.3 illustrates two such formats. In the body of the report, reference sources may be cited parenthetically by name or number or by superscript, for example:

Research performed at the University of Texas (Carter, 2001).

Research performed at the University of Texas (*1*).

Research performed at the University of Texas ([1]).

Some organizations prefer to list the bibliographic sources as footnotes rather than in a separate list at the end of the main body of the report.

Detailed technical material such as computer programs, tables of data, and the like are usually placed in one or more *appendixes* at the end of the report.

The writer of a technical report usually employs four modes of discourse (8):

1. **Narration,** in which a series of events are related in an ordered and usually chronological sequence.

2. **Description,** a verbal representation of something usually expressed in terms such as size, shape, color, texture, and position.

3. **Exposition,** which sets forth the writer's meaning or intent for the purpose of clarifying or explaining some matter.

4. **Argumentation,** which is for the purpose of convincing the reader of the probability that some proposition is correct.

Alphabetical Arrangement:

BIBLIOGRAPHY

Abel, J. P., and Alex Jones. *An Introduction to Civil Engineering*, John Wiley & Sons, Inc., New York, 1999.

Brown, John. "Priorities for Improvement of the Highway Infrastructure," *Transportation Research Record 1730*, Washington, DC, 2000.

Carter, Joyce. *Modern Pavement Design*, McGraw-Hill Book Company, New York, 2001.

Numerical Arrangement in Order of Use:

LIST OF REFERENCES

1.   Carter, Joyce. *Modern Pavement Design*, McGraw-Hill Book Company, New York, 2001.
2.   Brown, John. "Priorities for Improvement of the Highway Infrastructure," *Transportation Research Board 1730*, Washington, DC, 2000.
3.   Abel, J. P., and Alex Jones. *An Introduction to Civil Engineering*, John Wiley & Sons, Inc., New York, 1999.

Figure 6.3   *Example of bibliographies and reference lists.*

In order to inform or instruct the reader, the writer of a technical report may use examples, definitions, classifications, comparisons, and discussions of cause and effect (*8*).

Journal Papers   Engineers often publish the results of their work in technical journals. Journal papers are usually briefer than technical reports but are similar in organization and content. Journals provide a means for widespread dissemination of technical information.

Specifications   Technical specifications are used by the engineer to communicate to builders, fabricators, and manufacturers detailed information prescribing materials, dimensions, and workmanship for something that is to be built, installed, or manufactured. Specifications must be written with extreme care to ensure completeness and accuracy. Such documents are sometimes made a part of engineering contracts, and they may be used to document the details of a design (*9*). The language for such documents is therefore precise, and the writing style tends to be legalistic. An example of some technical specifications is shown in Figure 6.4.

GRAPHICAL COMMUNICATIONS

Most engineers communicate with each other, and with other specialists, in a universal language of engineering graphical representations. These representations take many forms, from hand sketches to highly sophisticated computer-generated renderings and simulations. The sketches and computer-generated

SECTION 862
WOOD POSTS AND BRACING

862.01   WOOD FENCE POSTS AND BRACING: Wood Posts and Bracing shall be Southern Pine with dimensions as specified on the Plans. Posts and Bracing shall be either round or sawed but all Posts on a single project shall be the same. The Posts and Bracing shall be cut from sound and solid trees and shall contain no unsound knots. Sound knots will be permitted if the diameter of the knot does not exceed one-third of the diameter of the piece at the point where it occurs. The Posts and Bracing shall be free from decayed wood, rot, and red heart, and a ring shake and season checks which penetrate at any point more than one-fourth the diameter of the piece, or are greater than 5 mm wide. The Posts and Bracing shall show not less than four annual rings per 25 mm, and not less than one-third summerwood unless southern pine veneer cores are used.

All Posts and Bracing shall be peeled for their full length and all bark and inner skin removed. Knots shall be trimmed close to the body of the Post before treatment. A line drawn from the center of the top to the center of the butt shall not fall outside the body of the Post, nor at any point be more than 50 mm from the geometric center of the Post. The maximum allowable change in diameter shall not exceed 38 mm in 3 m. Posts and Bracing shall be free from short or reverse bends. All butts and tips shall be sawed square except that for Posts to be driven the butt end may be pointed before treatment.

A.   SEASONING AND PRESERVATIVE TREATMENT: All Posts shall be preservative treated in accordance with the requirements of Section 863.

B.   ACCESSORIES: Metal caps for covering tops of the Posts shall be a minimum of 0.20 mm thickness. The material shall be aluminum, or galvanized steel with 380 g/m^2 coating in accordance with ASTM A 525M. Caps shall be used only when required by the Plans.

862.02   WOOD SIGN POSTS: Unless otherwise specified. Wood Sign Posts shall be surfaced on all four sides to the dimensions specified. All Posts shall be double end trimmed.

A.   QUALITY: Wood Sign Posts shall meet the same quality requirements as Wood Guard Rail Posts as specified in Sub-Section 859.04.

B.   TOLERANCES: The Posts shall not vary from the specified length by more than ±25 mm.

C.   SEASONING AND PRESERVATIVE TREATMENT: The Posts shall be preservative treated in accordance with the requirements of Section 863. Posts shall be bored and framed before preservative treatment.

D.   ACCESSORIES: Metal caps for covering tops of the Posts shall be a minimum of 0.38 mm thickness. The material shall be aluminum, or galvanized steel with 380 g/m^2 coating in accordance with ASTM A 525M. Caps shall be used only when required by the Plans.

Figure 6.4 *Example of engineering specifications. (Source:* Standard Specifications, 1995 Metric Edition, *Georgia Department of Transportation, 1995.)*

representations transcend culture and language. The are specifically created to clearly describe construction and manufacturing details and to avoid ambiguity. Each of these representations are created using industry-adopted conventions and notations that become standards for communication used in hand-created communications as well as digital computer representations. Organizations such as ANSI and ASME write specifications for many of the representations. As an engineer, you must be able not only to create such representations to describe your work, but also to read and interpret graphical representations produced by others. Often, you may be including a part manufactured by someone else into your design, you may be describing a construction operation to a field superintendent who will create the artifact described in a drawing, or you may be asked to prepare a cost estimate for constructing or manufacturing the entities represented in the graphical depictions.

The level of detail in these representations often varies for the intended audience. Sometimes the intent is to show the general design to a client, so details may be left out of the representation so as to focus on the global project issues. Other times, the graphical representation may be used for a machinist or construction worker who needs exact dimensions and tolerances in addition to production/construction information for producing the part or artifact.

6.5   ANSI LINE CONVENTIONS AND LETTERING

The ANSI has published standard line and lettering practices for use in the preparation of engineering drawings (*10*). The standard describes the size, construction, and appropriate use of various types of lines for engineering drawings. Figure 6.5 shows the various types of lines and how they are drawn and used.

Visible lines are solid thick lines that are used for representing visible edges or contours of objects. *Hidden lines* are short, evenly spaced thin dashes that depict the hidden features of an object. *Section lines* are solid thin lines that indicate the cut surfaces of an object in a section view. Special lining symbols are sometimes used to indicate the type of material depicted.

Center lines consist of alternating long and short thin dashes, as Figure 6.5 illustrates. Center lines represent axes of symmetrical parts and features, bolt circles, and paths of motion.

Solid thin lines used for dimensioning include: (1) *dimension lines*, which indicate the extent and direction of dimensions; (2) *extension lines*, which indicate the point or line on the drawing to which the dimension applies; and (3) *leaders*, which direct notes, dimensions, symbols, item numbers, or part numbers to features on the drawing.

Cutting-plane and *viewing-plane lines* indicate the location of cutting planes for sectional views and the viewing position for removed partial views. Typical construction and the use of these lines are shown in Figure 6.5.

Break lines indicate that only a portion of an object is drawn. Such lines are commonly depicted as shown in Figure 6.5. Alternately, long ruled thin dashes joined by zigzags may be used for break lines.

Phantom lines are used to indicate alternate positions of moving parts, adjacent positions of related parts, and repeated detail. Phantom lines are shown as long thin dashes separated by pairs of short thin dashes.

AMERICAN NATIONAL STANDARDS INSTITUTE
LINE CONVENTIONS AND LETTERING   ANSI Y14.2M-1979

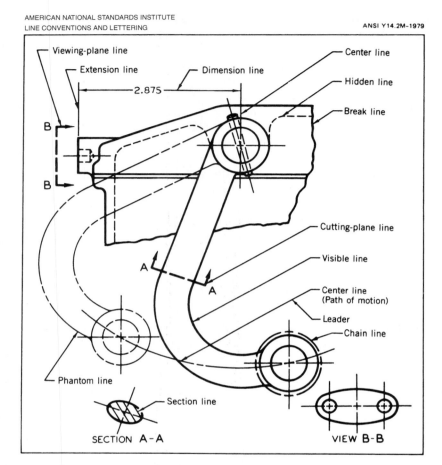

Figure 6.5   *ANSI standard line practice. (Reprinted from ASME Y14.2M-1979 by permission of the American Society of Mechnical Engineers. All rights reserved.)*

The ANSI recommends the use of single-stroke gothic lettering for engineering drawings. The lettering may be either inclined or vertical, as Figure 6.6 illustrates. Uppercase letters are specified for all lettering on drawings unless lowercase letters are required to conform with other established standards or nomenclature. Recommended minimum letter heights for various size drawings are given in the ANSI standard (*10*).

(a)

(b)

Figure 6.6 *ANSI standard lettering practice.* (a) *Inclined letters.* (b) *Vertical letters.* *(Reprinted from ASME Y14.2M-1979 by permissions of the American Society of Mechanical Engineers. All rights reserved.)*

6.6 TYPES OF GRAPHICAL COMMUNICATIONS

A variety of graphical communication types are defined to allow engineering professionals to communicate with each other and with the lay public. These types have associated scales, a defined measurement technique that allows a graphic image to represent either something smaller or larger than the actual drawing, much like a road map has a scale as described in its legend. Often, these representations show construction and manufacturing assembly techniques in addition to geometry and dimensions. The techniques include information about welding, casting, machining, and permissible tolerances. Other times, the drawings may be depictions or schematics of construction and assembly processes, such as consumer instructions for assembly of a plastic model or a piece of premanufactured furniture. Last, the engineer may be representing information in the form of line, bar, or pie graphs. For example, this information could include construction schedules, budgets, and facility capacity.

The engineer may utilize two-dimensional or three-dimensional representations of objects. The choice of which representation to use most often depends on the intended viewer of the information. For communicating with non-engineering professionals, common three-dimensional drawings, called pictorials, such as perspectives and isometric representations are performed. These drawings offer a representation that is more like what one would see with their own eyes but can be deceptive in terms of accurate dimensions. These drawings contain little information about construction or manufacturing techniques. Engineering professionals often create a three-dimensional solid model with two-dimensional views showing orthographic projections, section views, and auxiliary views, provided to describe true unit dimensions, tolerances, and materials. Engineers also use simulations and virtual reality representations to depict, simulate, and interact with objects prior to their manufacture or construction, thus avoiding costly mistakes in fabrication. Each of these representations is described briefly below.

6.7 SKETCHING

Sketching is the art of communicating graphical ideas without using traditional mechanical tools. Sketching is generally thought of as a hasty or undetailed drawing; however, it is a skill used in the preliminary presentation of ideas. Figure 6.7 presents a sketch illustrating a structural detail of a cored pilaster block. Sketches like these should be clear, concise, and to some extent precise.

The ability to make sketches is related to visualization. Visualization is the thinking process that allows the designer to form a mental picture of the device being considered. Sketching ideas rapidly stimulates the design process. Recording ideas in a graphic form makes it possible to evaluate and refine the design.

Many times, engineers will want to produce a sketch of a part, assembly, or process to communicate important information. Sometimes these sketches are computer drawn, but many times sketches are hand drawn. These are quickly

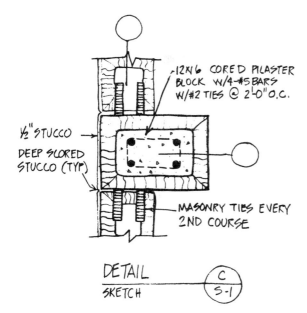

12X6 CORED PILASTER
BLOCK W/4-#5 BARS
W/#2 TIES @ 2'-0" O.C.

½" STUCCO

DEEP SCORED
STUCCO (TYP)

MASONRY TIES EVERY
2ND COURSE

DETAIL
SKETCH
C
S-1

Figure 6.7 *A sketch illustrating a structural detail of a cored pilaster block. (Courtesy of Dr. W. Rodriguez-Ramos.)*

created, but follow standards and conventions for the exchange of information. The use of the standards when drawing the sketch differentiate an engineering sketch from an artistic sketch. The engineering sketch maintains proportionality of dimensions and follows the conventions described above for pictorial representations or orthographic representations. These are useful for quickly exchanging design ideas among colleagues or for describing construction or manufacturing procedures in the field.

6.8   PICTORIAL REPRESENTATIONS

Three-dimensional representations of objects can be drawn using several techniques. Perspective representations provide for a directional reduction in size with apparent distance from the viewer's eye. The illusion of distance is provided by drawing lines that are parallel on the object as lines that converge to a vanishing point. One-point perspectives typically have the depth dimension "vanish," or drawn smaller, as objects are farther from the viewer. Two-point and three-point perspective techniques provide the same illusion of distance from the viewer's eye, but use additional vanishing points along additional directions. Perspective representations can be the most realistic to the human eye of all the pictorial representations and therefore can be useful for describing information to nonengineers. Figure 6.8 shows an object using one-point perspective, while Figure 6.9 shows the same object from a two-point perspective.

Another kind of pictorial representation is called an isometric. These pictorials are similar to two point perspective representations in that the viewer is

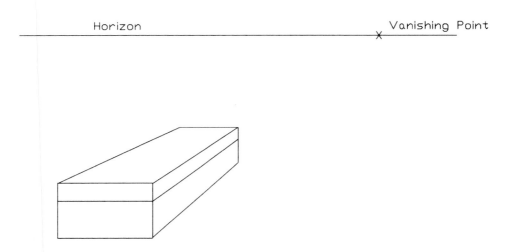

Figure 6.8   *An object drawn using a one-point perspective representation.*

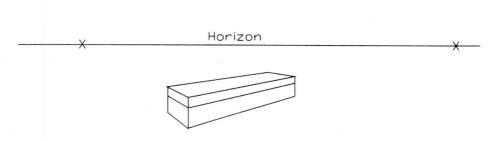

Figure 6.9   *An object drawn using two-point perspective representation.*

usually looking at a corner of an object, but with the isometric, the parallel lines on the object remain parallel to each other in the drawing, rather than converge to a vanishing point. Typically, these sides are drawn at about 30° from the horizontal.

6.9   ORTHOGRAPHIC REPRESENTATIONS

The traditional representation for engineering artifacts has been the orthographic representation. This technique involves looking at an object from three perpendicular directions and drawing the view from each of those perspectives. Figure 6.10 depicts a "glass" viewing box around an object in part (a) of the figure. The three standard views that are typically drawn include the front view, the top view, and a side view. In order to translate these three views of the same object onto a two-dimensional piece of paper, the sides are "unfolded" as shown in part (b) of the figure. Each of the views are now positioned as shown in part (c) of Figure 6.10. This method for representing objects provides for line lengths that are not skewed or dimensionally altered due to the view, as is the situation in perspective representations. In this manner, ambiguity of the object is minimized.

In some disciplines, the different views have other names. For example, the top view is often called a plan view and the front and side views are sometimes called elevations. Figure 6.11 shows an engineering drawing for a railroad crossing gate and its placement along a two-lane road. The top portion of the figure shows two elevations, a front and side view. The lower portion of the figure shows the placement of the crossing gate with respect to the train track and a two-lane road in a plan view.

6.10   SECTION VIEWS

There are times when the three typical views of an orthographic representation for an object does not show sufficient detail to explain (construct or manufacture) the part. In these situations, sections or viewing planes that are located interior to the part are provided. We call the resulting view from the plane a section. There are several types of sections, but most typically a full section, such as that shown in Figure 6.12, is used. Here the interior of the part is more clearly shown by providing a viewing plane in the middle of the part and then drawing a section. The section is differentiated from other views by showing the crosshatching symbols (many diagonal lines) through the material where the viewing plane was placed (see part (c) of Figure 6.12).

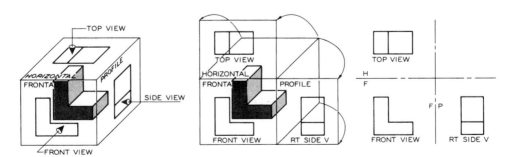

A. The three principal projection planes of orthographic projection can be thought of as planes of a glass box.

B. The views of an object are projected onto the projection planes that are opened into the plane of the drawing surface.

C. The outlines of the planes are omitted. The fold lines are drawn and labeled.

Figure 6.10   *The principal projection planes of orthographic projection. (Source: James H. Earle, Engineering Design Graphics, 5th Edition, Addison-Wesley Publishing Co., Boston, MA, copyright © 1987. Reprinted with permission of Pearson Education, Inc., Upper Saddle River, NJ.)*

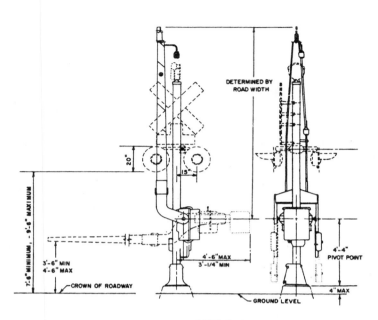

GATE ELEVATIONS

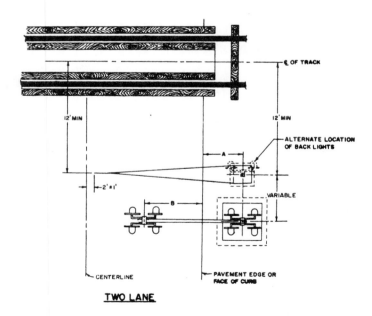

TWO LANE

Figure 6.11   *An example of an engineering drawing.*

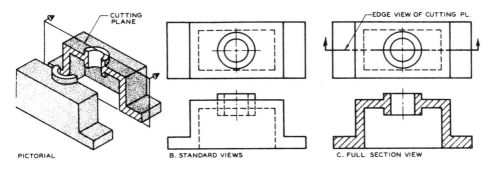

Figure 6.12   *A comparison of a regular orthographic view with a full-section view of the same object. (Source: James H. Earle,* Engineering Design Graphics, *5th Edition, Addison-Wesley Publishing Co., Boston MA, copyright © 1987. Reprinted with permission of Pearson Education, Inc.,Upper Saddle River, NJ.)*

6.11   AUXILIARY VIEWS

When an object has inclined faces, or parts that are not parallel to the viewing planes, the lengths of lines can be distorted from their true dimensions. Engineering drawings are produced so that lines and faces of objects in some view are truly represented. In the situation of inclined faces, auxiliary views are created. These views are obtained by looking from a direction that is normal to the inclined face. Figure 6.13 shows a wedge, or doorstop. The sloped face of this part is not represented in its true dimensions in any of the three standard views in the orthographic representation. Thus, to show the true face, an auxiliary view is drawn. Note that in the auxiliary view, only the inclined face is correctly shown; the flat top of the block is now distorted in the auxiliary view. Engineers must be able to accurately determine views that have distortion so that the correct parts, dimensions, and materials are used during building.

To learn more about engineering graphical communications, please refer to texts such as *Engineering Design Graphics* by James H. Earle (*11*).

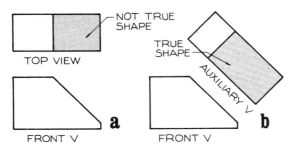

Figure 6.13   *An illustration of an auxiliary view. (Source: James H. Earle,* Engineering Design Graphics, *5th Edition, Addison-Wesley Publishing Co., Boston, MA, copyright © 1987. Reprinted with permission of Pearson Education, Inc.,Upper Saddle River, NJ.)*

6.12   COMPUTER TOOLS FOR CREATING REPRESENTATIONS

The use of computer tools to produce engineering graphic representations is commonplace in engineering practice. Many engineering software tools exist to provide both two-dimensional and three-dimensional models of engineering data. Many engineering organizations have standard part files that they reuse or modify when creating new designs.

Computer-based software provides several advantages over hand-drawn graphical representations. First, the information is easily updated and modified. The information can be quickly exchanged with others who need this information via electronic communications, such as e-mail. Second, many computer-based software tools used today represent the engineering products in databases so that all phases of the engineering design, manufacture, and support cycle can reference the information. This not only allows engineers designing the part to share the data, but engineers and maintenance workers can access details of the part for service requests, marketing departments can obtain information and pictures of the part for sales applications, and inventory systems can be used to reference parts and subparts needed for stocking. Computer-based systems also provide ties to design and analysis software packages so that engineers can study the part for material strength, fatigue, and other properties.

Software tools also support a variety of exchange standards, allowing the software tool to share information about the part, its design, and manufacturing information with other software programs. Specifications and standards such as Initial Graphics Exchange Specification (IGES), created in the early 1980s, Standard for the Exchange of Product (STEP) model data, which is the International Organization for Standardization (ISO) standard 10303, and Product Data Exchange using STEP (PDES) are all efforts to share information between software packages. Many international standards have been created as a result of the specification and standards work for the exchange of design, manufacture/construction, use, maintenance, and disposal information related to the activities of an engineering part's life cycle. Most of these standards are organized by and interfaced with the ISO, via the National Institute of Standards and Technology in the United States.

The software tools for creating graphical and solid model representations for engineering parts can be classified as either explicit representations, or constraint or parametric representations. The explicit representations were the first generation of software tools. They require the user to explicitly define every point in the part's geometry and the edges of the part between these points. Each point is a separate entity in the software database. The constraint or parametric representations are newer systems, allowing the user to specify a variety of points and edges relative to others already defined. In this fashion, the database can keep track of edges that are to remain parallel or perpendicular to other edges, dimensions that are relatively based upon other dimensions, so that as the model is modified these parameters remain constant. Models created in this fashion allow the user to be more expressive in modeling the engineering parameters and the models are more quickly updated than the explicit representations can be.

6.13   SIMULATION AND VIRTUAL REALITY

With most of the software packages, the user can specify a variety of output options. These options range from creating traditional orthographic projections to very complex renderings incorporating light and material models so that the part takes on photo-realistic effects of shadows and sheen. With these kinds of output, engineers can provide not only very realistic images of the final product for presentation to clients, but also can look for engineering interference, manufacturability, or constructability of the part prior to expending large sums of money making the part. These models, when used in virtual reality environments, enable engineers and end users of the products being designed to interact and simulate the usage of the design prior to its manufacture. These models and computing environments allow the engineer and the client to experience the built artifact before it is ever assembled, facilitating quick user input to the design decisions and potentially saving large sums of money.

THE ENGINEER AS A SPEAKER

From time to time, engineers are required to speak to groups of colleagues, make presentations to clients, chair professional meetings, and deliver technical papers at professional conferences. The successful engineer understands the need to develop skills in public speaking and takes advantage of opportunities to refine and advance those skills.

6.14   GUIDELINES FOR EFFECTIVE SPEAKING

Here we list some general guidelines that should help the reader to become a more effective public speaker. These guidelines, which were adapted from a publication of Toastmasters International, are applicable to public presentations of various kinds.

1. **Be prepared.**   By advance preparation, a speaker can speak with confidence, concentrating on what is to be said rather than on self.

2. **Speak clearly and distinctly.**   A speaker cannot hope to communicate successfully if he or she mumbles or uses slovenly language.

3. **Look your hearers in the eye.**   Good eye contact helps to increase the hearers' interest and their participation in the presentation. Experienced speakers learn to analyze their audience and its reactions and make appropriate adjustments based on audience analysis.

4. **Speak sincerely, without hesitation, and with reasonable deliberation.**
   A speaker can maintain or increase audience interest by varying the speech rate, pitch, and volume.

5. **Remember that your audience can think. Don't do all of the thinking for them.**

6. **Use the deeper tones of your voice.**

7. **In preparing a speech, write much.**   Memorize little except stories and quotations.

8. **Never be afraid of your audience or your own opinion.**

9. **Do not try to cover too much ground.**   Be aware of constraints on time, and adjust the length of the presentation accordingly.

6.15   USE OF VISUAL AIDS

Visual aids, properly conceived and employed, can be the key to effective oral communications. They can be especially useful to engineers in explaining complex subjects and summarizing the results of large projects.

The speaker must be willing to put forth the effort to prepare good visual aids and thoughtfully plan for their use. Visual aids should be considered as an integral part of the oral presentation rather than something that is "tacked on" to fill the available time. The use of visuals must therefore be carefully planned, always keeping in mind the overall objectives of the presentation.

A wide variety of visual equipment is available: 35-mm photographic projectors, "overhead projectors" for 8-inch × 10-inch transparencies, 16-mm movie projectors, and so on. However, it is advisable to use visual materials that can be projected with commonly used projection equipment. At engineering meetings, 35-mm slides, and to a lessor extent, 8-inch × 10-inch transparencies, tend to be most widely used.

There are a few simple rules that can be employed that will help a speaker use visuals effectively (*12*).

1. **Show no more on a slide than can be assimilated in about 30 seconds.** Distill from the engineering report or paper the fundamental findings and conclusions, and illustrate them with slides that are crisp, clear, and to the point. Generally speaking, a slide illustrating a table should contain no more than about 15 words.

2. **Photographs that are cluttered or lacking in contrast should not be used.** Take advantage of close-up photography to concentrate the audience's attention on major points of interest. Slides illustrating bar charts or graphs should likewise be simple, showing no more than one or two curves or bars.

3. **Letters and numbers should be large enough that members of the audience seated farthest from the screen can read them.** As a general rule, the height of letters and figures should be at least 2 percent of the longer dimension of the original copy. For example, when preparing a slide from an 8-inch × 12-inch original copy, the minimum letter size should be about 0.25 inch or larger.

4. **It is normally advisable to prepare separate copy for slides.**   It is difficult to make good slides from drawings or tables that are intended for publication in a journal or report.

5. **Check out the visual equipment before the presentation.**   Even if the equipment is provided by someone else, be sure it is in working order. Burned-out projector lamps, equipment that will not focus, and inconvenient electrical outlets can be a source of frustration to both the speaker and the audience and can detract immensely from an oral presentation.

6. **When 35-mm slides are used, be sure slides are arranged in proper order and right side up.**   Slides that are out of order or upside down show that the speaker is unprepared, and interrupting a speech to correct such problems is certain to detract from the presentation and reflect badly on the speaker.

7. **Keep the visual aids simple. For example:**
   - Round off numbers.
   - Substitute symbols for words, such as $ for dollars, % for percent.
   - Do not use footnotes or show sources.
   - Avoid underlines, grids, or other lines that detract.
   - Use color with purpose, not as a decoration.

Use of Computer Technology in Oral Presentations

Engineers often use computer technology to prepare and deliver oral presentations. With presentation software, it is possible not only to create computer-generated slides but also to choose a background and graphics that are appropriate to the message. Software such as PowerPoint allows the speaker to use transitions to move from one slide to the next. Slides can be revealed with a variety of effects such as dissolving from one slide to another, fading out or in, or using "flying text" from any direction. Such effects can enhance the visual impacts of a presentation. The use of computer technology, however, will not guarantee the success of a presentation. All viewers will notice if the presentation has only visual impact and no content. It is important, therefore, that the primary focus be on the topic of the presentation rather than the technology.

6.16   TECHNICAL PRESENTATIONS AT PROFESSIONAL MEETINGS

Engineers commonly share the results of their work by making technical presentations at professional meetings. Professional meetings are usually organized in "sessions" that last approximately three hours and allow for the presentation of four to six technical papers. A moderator presides over each session, introducing the speakers, enforcing time limits, and directing periods of questions and answers. Typically, a technical presentation lasts approximately 20 minutes, and 5 to 10 minutes are reserved for questions and answers.

Papers delivered to technical groups are normally written and published in the conference proceedings. Technical reports that contain complex information or a great deal of statistical material may be read to the assembly. It is generally preferable, however, to summarize the content of the paper and present it in an extemporaneous speech form.

A technical presentation should be well organized, normally following the same format as that of a technical report or paper but in summary form. The presentation usually contains an introduction, the methodology, the results, and the conclusions.

The purpose of the introduction is to create a friendly atmosphere; interest the audience in the topic; and announce the subject matter, purpose, scope, and organizational framework of the presentation (8).

The main body of the presentation consists of a description of the steps that were taken to accomplish the work being reported on and the results or outcome of the project. Because a listener's attention span is limited, experts in public speaking recommend that speeches be planned around intelligent and interesting repetition (8). For a presentation 20 to 30 minutes in length, it is advisable to cover no more than two or three main points. These points should be reinforced with appropriate examples, illustrations, and analogies and may be illustrated with suitable visual aids.

The conclusion of the presentation normally consists of a brief summary of the key points and a list of recommendations, including suggestions for further work.

6.17   THE ENGINEER AS A PRESIDING OFFICER

As leaders in their profession and in their community, engineers may be called upon to serve as the presiding officer for a professional or civic group. They should be prepared to chair on-the-job committees, conduct public hearings, moderate the affairs of professional groups, and serve as the leader of civic associations.

The degree of formality in the conduct of public forums is established by precedence and general consent of the group. Some groups prefer to conduct their affairs informally; others prefer highly formal and structured meetings, insisting that all group decisions be arrived at according to strict rules of parliamentary procedure. In either event, the presiding officer for such groups needs to have a working knowledge of accepted practices in the conduct of organizational business.

The basic principles of parliamentary procedure were clearly defined and practiced as early as the fifth century B.C. in Athens (13). Similarly, the Romans and other civilizations relied on rules of procedure in the conduct of their affairs. These groups were presided over by a chairman, followed a prescribed agenda, provided an opportunity for all those who wished to speak, passed motions, and voted on propositions before them.

Parliamentary procedure evolved over several centuries in England, and many of those rules were used in Colonial America. In modern times, the most popular guide to parliamentary procedure has been *Robert's Rules of Order*, published first by an Army engineer named Henry M. Robert in 1876.

One of the fundamental principles of parliamentary procedure is majority rule. "The voice of the majority decides" is the way that Thomas Jefferson stated it (*13*). The principal reason for using parliamentary procedures is to determine the opinion of the majority fairly, efficiently, and in an orderly manner.

A second fundamental principle of parliamentary procedure is that the apparent minority has a right to be heard—to oppose the position of the majority and to try to persuade others to agree with its point of view.

Other fundamental principles are

- To facilitate action rather than obstruct it.
- To enable the group to express its will.
- To maintain order.

The rules of parliamentary procedure tell how, when, and why to use motions. A motion is an expression used to present ideas to a group for consideration. A motion usually begins with the words: "I move that . . .".

It is not necessary that the chairperson memorize all of the motions that could be used and the rules for their use. He or she needs to know only the rules for those motions that are normally used. Other procedures can be formulated by the assembly by majority vote at the time the need arises.

There are three types of motion: (1) main motions, (2) ordinary or privileged motions, and (3) special motions. Main motions introduce business before the group for its consideration. Main motions are debatable, amendable, and decided by majority vote. Main motions have the lowest rank of all.

Ordinary or privileged motions are those of such urgency or importance that they cannot wait. Examples of ordinary motions, in order of precedence are

1. To adjourn.
2. To recess.
3. To close debate.
4. To limit debate.
5. To postpone.
6. To refer to a committee.
7. To amend.

Special motions include the following:

- Point of order.
- To appeal.
- To withdraw.
- To suspend the rules.
- To reconsider.
- To rescind.

TABLE 6.5   *Summary Chart of Motions*

Motion			Debatable	Amendable	Vote
Ordinary motions[a] (in order of rank)	1.	To adjourn	No	No	Majority
	2.	To recess	No	Yes[b]	Majority
	3.	To close debate	No	No	two-thirds
	4.	To limit (extend the limits of) debate	No	Yes[b]	two-thirds
	5.	To postpone	Yes	Yes	Majority
	6.	To refer	Yes	Yes	Majority
	7.	To amend	Yes	Yes	Majority
Main motion[a] (lowest rank)			Yes	Yes	Majority
Special motions (no rank among themselves	A.	Point of order	No	No	None
	B.	To appeal[a]	Yes	No	Majority
	C.	To withdraw	No	No	Majority
	D.	To suspend the rules	No	No	two-thirds
	E.	To reconsider[a]	No	No	Majority
	F.	To rescind[a]	Yes	Yes	Majority

[a] When ordinary motions are made with no main motion on the floor, they are treated like other main motions. They are debatable, amendable, and their consideration may be referred, postponed, etc. This applies also to the motions to appeal, to reconsider, and to rescind within the limitations stipulated in Chapter 5 of Reference 13.

[b] May be amended regarding time limitations only.

Source: Ray E. Keesey, *Modern Parliamentary Procedure,* Houghton Mifflin Co., Boston, 1974.

Special motions have no rank among themselves.

Table 6.5 summarizes various types of motions and recommended rules for their use. Additional information on parliamentary procedure is given in Reference 13.

REFERENCES

1. McBride, Kari Boyd, and Ruth Dickstein, "The Web Demands Critical Reading by Students," *The Chronicle of Higher Education,* 44, March 20, 1998.

2. Rothenberg, David, "How the Web Destroys Student Research Papers," *The Education Digest,* 63, February, 1998.

3. Weschler, Lawrence, *Mr. Wilson's Cabinet of Wonder,* Pantheon Books, New York, 1995.

4. Strunk, Jr., William, and E. B. White, *The Elements of Style,* 4th Edition, Allyn and Bacon, Needham Heights, MA, 2000.

5. ZINSSER, WILLIAM, *On Writing Well,* 2nd Edition, Harper & Row, New York, 1980.

6. KILPATRICK, JAMES J., *The Writer's Art,* Andrews, McMeel, and Parker, Inc., New York, 1984.

7. DAVIS, RICHARD M., "Technical Writing in Industry and Government," *Journal of Technical Writing and Communications 7,* No. 3, 1977.

8. HOUP, KENNETH W., AND THOMAS E. PEARSALL, *Reporting Technical Information,* 5th Edition, Macmillan Publishing Company, 1984.

9. DUDERSTADT, JAMES J., GLENN F. KNOLL, AND GEORGE S. SPRINGER, *Principles of Engineering,* John Wiley & Sons, Inc., New York, 1982.

10. The American National Standards Institute, *Line Conventions and Lettering,* ANSI Y14.2M, The American Society of Mechanical Engineers, New York, 1979.

11. EARLE, JAMES H., *Engineering Design Graphics,* 9th Edition, Addison-Wesley Publishing Company, Reading, MA, 1999.

12. *Information for Authors,* Transportation Research Board, Washington, DC, 1984.

13. KEESEY, RAY E., *Modern Parliamentary Procedure,* Houghton Mifflin Company, Boston, 1974.

ADDITIONAL REFERENCES NOT CITED

EARLE, JAMES H., *Graphics for Engineers,* 5th Edition, Prentice-Hall, Inc., Englewood Cliffs, NJ, 2000.

National Institute of Standards and Technology, www.nist.gov/.

Product Data Exchange Using STEP, pdesinc.aticorp.org/.

Standard for the Exchange of Product Model Data, ISO 10303, www.nist.gov/sc4, www.stepdocs.htm.

EXERCISES

6.1 Using technical references such as those listed in Table 6.2, prepare a bibliography for a technical paper on one of the following topics:
   a. Design of off-shore drilling platforms.
   b. Design of off-shore terminals for oil tankers.
   c. Recent advances in solar energy.
   d. Maintenance and rehabilation of highway bridge decks.
   e. Advances in computer-aided design/computer-aided manufacturing.
   f. Use of geotextiles in highway pavements.
   g. Reinforced earth construction.
   h. Engineering ethics.
   i. Applications of lasers in research and manufacturing.
   j. The role of robotics in manufacturing productivity.
   k. Artificial intelligence.
   l. Advances in automotive safety.
   m. Recent developments in microprocessors.

6.2 Prepare a 1000-word written report on one of the subjects listed in Exercise 6.1.

6.3 Make a 10-minute oral presentation to your class on one of the topics listed in Exercise 6.1.

6.4   Prepare a plan for visual aids that could be used for the oral presentation required by Exercise 6.3. Describe in detail what each slide, photograph, table, or graph should show.

6.5   Write a memorandum for one of the following situations.

    a.   You are the chief engineer for a consulting engineering firm. You wish to communicate to your department heads a new policy requiring the keeping of travel records of the use of the firm's vehicles.

    b.   As municipal engineer for a city, you need to spell out the policy of the department with respect to weather-related absences from work.

    c.   As director of engineering research for an aerospace corporation, you wish to convene a meeting of key research engineers to plan the preparation of a research proposal for the U.S. Department of Defense.

6.6   With the aid of engineering indexes in the library, identify at least three articles in engineering magazines about engineering salaries. Prepare a brief written report on the subject of "Recent Changes in Engineering Salaries."

6.7   Read an article from a technical journal in your chosen engineering branch. Prepare a descriptive abstract and an informative abstract of the article.

6.8   Prepare an outline of a technical report. Compare the format of the report with that described in Table 6.4.

An Exemplary Engineering Achievement

Penetrating the mysteries of deep space, beyond the range of optical instruments, the 1000-foot-diameter Aericibo Dish, built into a mountain valley in Puerto Rico, detects energy emissions in the radio spectrum. The antenna platform, supported by $3\frac{1}{2}$-inch steel cables and weighing 600 tons, hangs 500 feet above the dish and is held to less than 1-inch sway. (Courtesy of the American Council of Engineering Companies).

CHAPTER SEVEN

ENGINEERING CALCULATIONS

Of all the tools available to the engineer for the solution of engineering problems, none is more valuable than mathematics. Mathematical skills are the very foundation of most engineering work. Successful engineers must develop and maintain their competence in mathematics and learn to apply their mathematical skills with confidence and effectiveness.

In this chapter, we describe certain recommended procedures for the proper handling of engineering data and give accepted standards for the presentation of engineering calculations. We examine the various branches of mathematics, especially those most commonly used by engineers, and discuss the application of common mathematical procedures to the solution of engineering problems.

7.1 THE PRESENTATION OF ENGINEERING CALCULATIONS

Engineering calculations may be complex, often involving many steps and mathematical procedures leading to a final solution. By their nature, engineering calculations provide many opportunities for mistakes, and they must be carefully checked for correctness. In grading homework and examinations, engineering professors often check to see if a student has followed the recommended procedure for the solution of a problem and give partial credit for incorrect solutions provided proper methods have been used. A practicing engineer may lay aside work for a time or give it to another engineer to check or complete. For these reasons, it is vitally important that engineering work be carefully and clearly documented so that it may be checked and validated. It is therefore understandable that in solving engineering problems, a great deal of

importance is attached to neatness and clarity of presentation, a logical documentation of the problem solution, and to the overall appearance of the finished
calculations. Some professors have a very definite format that they ask students
to use when working homework. Similarly, engineering agencies and consulting firms may require their employees to follow a standard format when performing engineering calculations. Although there is no universally accepted
format, it is of utmost importance that engineering work be neatly and clearly
recorded.

| ESM 2201 | 10/23/01 | 6 | Tiernan, Kathleen | 1 / 4 |

Problem No. 6-1

Given: Structure loaded as shown.

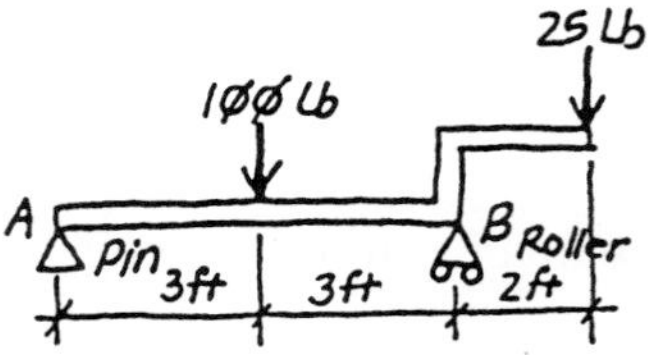

Find: Reaction forces at A and B

Solution: Free body diagram

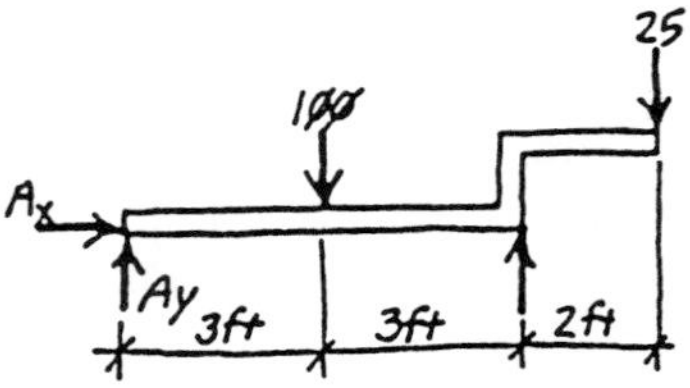

for equilibrium,

$\Sigma F_x = 0$

$\Sigma F_y = 0$

$\Sigma M_A = 0$

$\xrightarrow{+} \quad \Sigma F_x = 0 = A_x$

$+\uparrow \quad \Sigma F_y = 0 = A_y + B_y - 25 - 100$

$\overset{+}{\curvearrowright} \quad \Sigma M_A = 0 = -100(3) + B_y(6) - 25(8)$

$A_x = \underline{\underline{0}}$

$B_y = \frac{1}{6}(300 + 200) = \underline{\underline{83.3 \ LB}}$

$A_y = 100 + 25 - B_y = \underline{\underline{41.7 \ LB}}$

Figure 7.1   *An example of a calculation sheet.*

Figure 7.1 shows an example of a calculation sheet for recording and presenting engineering work. Notice that the work is presented in an orderly manner, beginning with a list of what information is given or known, then setting out what is to be found or required, and followed by a clearly understandable documentation of the steps used in arriving at the solution. A sketch or free body diagram illustrates the significant elements of the problem.

Calculation sheets are usually numbered consecutively, and the total number of sheets in the set is indicated on each page. The name of the person who performed the work and the date it was done are prominently shown. Answers are double underlined or otherwise clearly identified.

7.2   NUMBER SYSTEMS

Intrinsically, engineering involves the analysis, evaluation, and expression of quantities of materials and forces of nature. It requires common symbols for counting objects and a numbering by which the magnitudes of length, mass, time, and other physical properties can be expressed.

Most engineering work employs arabic numerals and is based on the decimal numeration system. With this system, any number, regardless of size, can be expressed with 10 basic numbers or digits. The decimal system represents numbers in groups of 10. Ten is the scale or base of the decimal system.

The value of each digit in the decimal system depends on the symbol and its position in the numeral. Thus the numeral 321 stands for 3 hundreds, 2 tens, plus one. The numeral 123 contains the same digits but represents a different number because the digits are in different positions.

In the decimal system, the position value can also be expressed by powers of 10, the exponent indicating the number of times the number 10 (the base) is to be multiplied by itself:

Place Name	Exponent	Meaning
Ones	0	$10^0 = 1$
Tens	1	$10^1 = 10$
Hundreds	2	$10^2 = 100$
Thousands	3	$10^3 = 1000$, and so forth

There are, of course, other numeration systems that can be used to solve engineering problems, for example, the binary system that forms the basis for the operation of electronic computers. The binary system is based on only two digits, 0 and 1. In computers, this corresponds to the positions of electronic switches: on or off.

The binary system groups numbers by powers of 2. The position of the digit determines the value in terms of powers of two. The value of the rightmost digit is 2^0 or 1; the value of the digit to its immediate left is 2^1; the value of the next digit to the left is 2^2; and on on. Binary numbers can be converted to decimal numbers by summing the place values of the digits in terms of decimal numbers. The meanings of several binary numbers and equivalent decimal numbers are shown in Table 7.1.

7.3   DIMENSIONS

To solve engineering problems, it is necessary that engineers describe or characterize the material world in terms of *dimensions.* We commonly think of dimensions in terms of spatial extent or size, that is, length, width, and height. But many other dimensions are used to describe the physical properties of the objects and materials of engineering. There are *fundamental dimensions* such as length, time, and mass, and combinations of such dimensions called *derived dimensions.* For example, velocity, the ratio of length and time, is a derived dimension. Other examples of fundamental and derived dimensions are shown in Table 7.2.

Some quantities used in engineering calculations have no dimensions. Examples of dimensionless quantities are ratios of quantities having the same dimension, such as π, the ratio of the circumference of a circle to its diameter.

TABLE 7.1   *Examples of Binary Numbers and Equivalent Decimal Numbers*

Binary Number	Meaning	Equivalent Decimal Number
1	$1 \times 2^0 =$	1
10	$(1 \times 2^1) + (0 \times 2^0) =$	2
11	$(1 \times 2^1) + (1 \times 2^0) =$	3
100	$(1 \times 2^2) + (0 \times 2^1) + (0 \times 2^0) =$	4
101	$(1 \times 2^2) + (0 \times 2^1) + (1 \times 2^0) =$	5
110	$(1 \times 2^2) + (1 \times 2^1) + (0 \times 2^0) =$	6

TABLE 7.2   *Examples of Fundamental and Derived Dimensions*

Fundamental Dimensions	Derived Dimensions
Length, L	Area, L^2
Time, T	Volume, L^3
Mass, M	Velocity, L/T
Electric current, I	Acceleration, L/T^2
Temperature	Mass density, M/L^3
Amount of substance, (mole)	Force, ML/T^2
Luminance intensity	Energy, ML^2/T^2

7.4   UNITS

The word *unit* is defined as a precisely stated quantity in terms of which other quantities of the same kind can be stated. For each dimension, there is a need for one or more reference amounts in order to describe quantitatively the physical properties of some object or material. For example, the dimension of length has been measured in units of miles, metres, feet, the distance from a person's nose to fingertip, and many others. We measure time in units of seconds, minutes, hours, months, and so on.

Since we deal with a large number of dimensions, a *system* of units is needed for reliable and reproducible measurements and for good communication. Technological developments in transportation and communications and increasing international trade have emphasized the need for a common language of measurement, a system capable of measuring any physical quantity with units that are clearly and precisely defined and that possess a logical relationship between units to facilitate calculations. The Système Internationale d'Unitès (SI) is widely recognized as such a system. Graham[1] has described the history of the development of the SI system and its essential features in an article published by the American Society for Testing and Materials. The article is reprinted in the following pages with permission of the author and ASTM.

There are many systems of measurement in use throughout the world, but primarily two that have been in use for years—the English system and the metric system. These systems suffer from many variations and problems.

The English system, which is common in the United States, has grown piece by piece over at least 3000 years, with little relationship between units. The element of precision has been provided by the National Bureau of Standards in the United States and the National Physical Laboratory in England since the beginning of the twentieth century, and individual units are adequate to any measuring task. As a system it is poor, and the many differences in its detail between English-speaking countries presents a problem.

The old metric system (speaking of today's common European system) also has problems. In contrast with the English system, which grew in a haphazard fashion, it was commissioned by the French government nearly 200 years ago and was designed to be an integrated, universal measurement system. The United States and the British Commonwealth nations refused to join in its use but Germany, France, Italy, and others proceeded to develop their industries and industrial standards around it. Many variations in the system have developed, however, because no controls were set up to unify use, and the common metric system is as awkward and varied as the English system.

In the late nineteenth century these variations of units of measure, particularly the minor differences that had grown up between countries using the metric system, were an obstacle to the rapidly increasing sophistication of science and industry.

---

[1] J. D. Graham, "The International System of Units (SI)," *Metrification—Managing the Industrial Transition,* ASTM STP 574, American Society for Testing and Materials, 1975, pp. 42–56.

In 1875 five years of international discussion on measurement culminated in the signing by 17 countries (including the United States) of the Metre Convention. An international organization was established to provide a sound basis of precise uniform world measurement units. This organization consisted of an international working committee to provide the technical base (CIPM), an international bureau for laboratory work (BIPM), and the treaty body, the General Conference on Weights and Measures (CGPM), scheduled to meet in Paris every six years. The initials are those of the French names for these societies, and are universally used to designate them.

This organization has developed a basis for the standardization of the world's measurement units by issuing in 1960 the International System of Units, abbreviated SI (from its French name) in all languages. This is a complete, coherent system, is the basis of all official measurement in the world, and is the system that the United States is now beginning to adopt. It is a major obligation of all the world's technical people to understand it, respect it, and use it properly.

The International System of Units

This is a complete system of measurement units including names and symbols for base units from which derived units may be formed so that any physical quantity may be expressed. It includes a system of prefixes by which the base and derived units may be made any convenient size from very small to very large. Finally, the precise basis for its units, and the symbols for expressing them, have received worldwide agreement. It is officially recognized by all industrial nations, is referenced by SAE, ASTM, ASME, and many other societies, is required by ISO in all documents, and is the official basis of our U.S. units (the inch and pound are defined in terms of the metre and kilogram).

Fortunately, there is much about this system that is old and familiar. There is also much that is new.

Base Units   There are seven base units of SI. These units and the quantities for which they are used are listed in Table 7.3.

TABLE 7.3   *Seven Base Units of SI*

Quantity	Unit	Symbol
Length	metre	m
Mass	kilogram	kg
Time	second	s
Electric current	ampere	A
Thermodynamic temperature	kelvin	K
Amount of substance	mole	mol
Luminous intensity	candela	cd

All of these are defined in terms of readily reproducible natural phenomena except for the kilogram. This is based on a prototype kept at the International Bureau of Weights and Measures, copies of which are in use all over the world.

Supplementary Units Two more essential units are included in the system, but agreement could not be reached whether these were base or derived. Accordingly, they were designated as supplementary (see Table 7.4).

Derived Units The nine preceding units may be combined mathematically (by multiplication or division) to provide new units as required, for measurement of any physical quantity. Fifteen of these have been given special names and symbols, and the rest are created at will to suit the need.

Those derived units with special names, including their formulas for definition, are listed in Table 7.5.

All other necessary derived units are produced by multiplying or dividing the base and derived units according to the definition of the quantity to be

TABLE 7.4 *Supplementary Units*

Quantity	Unit	Symbol
Plane angle	radian	rad
Solid angle	steradian	sr

TABLE 7.5 *Derived Units*

Quantity	Unit	Symbol	Formula
Frequency	hertz	Hz	s^{-1}
Force	newton	N	$kg \cdot m/s^2$
Pressure, stress	pascal	Pa	N/m^2
Energy, work	joule	J	$N \cdot m$
Power	watt	W	J/s
Quantity of electricity	coulomb	C	$A \cdot s$
Electric potential	volt	V	W/A
Capacitance	farad	F	C/V
Electric resistance	ohm	Ω	V/A
Conductance	siemens	S	A/V
Magnetic flux	weber	Wb	$V \cdot s$
Magnetic flux density	tesla	T	Wb/m^2
Inductance	henry	H	Wb/A
Luminous flux	lumen	lm	$cd \cdot sr$
Illuminance	lux	lx	lm/m^2

measured. A few are shown here as examples, but of course no list could be complete (see Table 7.6).

Multiplying Prefixes Any of these units are then made larger or smaller if desired by the addition of one of a list of prefixes provided for this purpose (see Table 7.7).

This is the new system. Much is common with the old metric system, but SI differs sharply from customary European metric use. Most of these differences are related to "coherence."

TABLE 7.6 *Other Derived Units*

Quantity	Unit	Symbol and Formula
Area	square metre	m^2
Volume	cubic metre	m^3
Velocity	metre per second	m/s
Acceleration	metre per second squared	m/s^2
Density	kilogram per cubic metre	kg/m^3
Specific volume	cubic metre per kilogram	m^3/kg
Entropy	joule per kelvin	J/K
Radiant intensity	watt per steradian	W/sr
Bending moment, torque	newton-metre	$N \cdot m$
Heat capacity	joule per kilogram-kelvin	$J/kg \cdot K$

TABLE 7.7 *SI Prefixes*

Multiplication Factor	Prefix	Symbol
10^{12}	tera	T
10^9	giga	G
10^6	mega	M
10^3	kilo	k
10^2	hecto	h
10^1	deka	da
10^{-1}	deci	d
10^{-2}	centi	c
10^{-3}	milli	m
10^{-6}	micro	μ
10^{-9}	nano	n
10^{-12}	pico	p
10^{-15}	femto	f
10^{-18}	atto	a

Coherence In SI every derived unit is the result of the equation expressing some physical law. The unit of area is the square of the unit of length, or square metre, because the area of a rectangle is the product of the length of its two sides. Similarly, the unit of velocity is metre per second, since velocity is defined as distance traveled divided by time. When all derived and fundamental units are related in this way, a system is called "coherent," and each of its units is a coherent unit. The factor relating all units to each other is always *one.* The coherence of SI is one of its most important characteristics: *A force of one newton operating through a length of one metre produces energy of one joule. If this energy is produced in one second, the power is one watt.*

Two other major characteristics of SI are directly related to coherence, but merit separate discussion.

An Absolute System The relationship between force and mass is tangled in a complicated history of differing customs. In a *gravitational system* the units of mechanics are all derived from the three fundamentals, length, force, and time, and the unit of mass is a derived unit. In an *absolute system*, on the other hand, the units of mechanics are derived from the three fundamentals, length, mass, and time, and the unit of force is a derived unit. In either of these two systems, the units of mass and force are always related by Newton's law $F = ma$, and in a coherent system these cannot be the same unit. Properly, the units in the world's measurement systems should be as shown in Table 7.8.

Unfortunately, common use all over the world has ignored the existence of these two kinds of systems and has casually used the same units for force and mass. We speak of stress in pounds, pressure in pounds per square inch, mass in pounds, density in pounds per cubic inch, using the pound for both force and mass. The European treats the kilogram in the same fashion.

SI is an absolute system, and must be used as such. A most difficult problem in transition to SI will be to learn to use different units for force and mass.

Mass—unit, the kilogram

Force—unit, the newton

An absolute system has several advantages, the greatest being simplicity of calculations. A force of a newton accelerates a mass of one kilogram one metre per second squared. In contrast, a force of one kilogram accelerates the same mass 9.80665 metres per second squared.

TABLE 7.8 *World's Measurement Systems*

	English System	**Metric System**
Gravitational system		
mass	slug (lbf·s²/ft)	hyl (kgf·s²/m)
force	pound-force	kilogram-force
Absolute system		
mass	pound	kilogram
force	poundal (lb·ft/s²)	newton (kg·m/s²)

Complicating this change is the fact that the term *weight* has traditionally been badly misused. Its formal definition has always been that of a force—loosely the force of gravity acting on a mass—and the unit of weight has been the force of standard gravity on a unit of mass. Early in the development of measurement systems, the word was incorrectly used to mean mass; thus we have a Bureau of Weights and Measures, and we use "weights" on a scale to measure mass. As a result the term has been widely used to mean either a force or a mass.

The future of the term is somewhat uncertain. By far the most common use has been for mass, and strong pressure exists to redefine the term to this meaning. The urgent need, however, is to separate force and mass and use the proper SI units for each, as just shown. The ASTM *Metric Practice Guide* (ASTM E 380-74) states, "In commercial and everyday use on the other hand, the term weight nearly always means mass. Thus when one speaks of a person's weight, the quantity referred to is mass. Because of this dual use, the term weight should be avoided except under circumstances in which its meaning is completely clear."

Uniqueness   SI is a *unique* system in which there is only one unit for each kind of physical quantity, regardless of whether it is mechanical, electrical, or thermal. Power in engines or air conditioners is measured in watts. Of course, this rule does not prevent the use of either a special name or the derived name for a unit—pressure may be expressed either in pascals or in newtons per square metre.

Vector Influence   Some units, such as torque, involve vector quantities, but in common with other systems of measurement units, the symbols and names do not indicate this fact. As a result, an apparent anomaly exists in the use of newton-metre for torque or bending moment, and the use of joule for work ($1 \text{ J} = 1 \text{ N·m}$). These are entirely different units, since the unit of work results from unit force moving through unit distance, while the unit of bending moment involves a force applied normal to a lever of unit length. This would be readily seen if vectors were incorporated in the unit symbols. For this reason it is important not to express moments in joules.

Units Used with SI

As stated earlier, SI units can be used to measure any physical quantity, and the use of other units with them must be carefully and sensibly limited. If this principle is not respected, the new system will soon be as uncontrolled and incoherent as the older ones.

A very limited list of non-SI units has been accepted for use with SI for varying reasons.

> *Time*—Since we live our lives by the sun, it has been widely agreed that the hour and the calendar units will continue to be used with SI, particularly in such quantities as vehicle velocity.

Angle—Due to the much simpler use in geometry, the plane angle unit degree has been accepted for use along with SI unit, radian. The units minute and second, however, are unnecessary, and subdivisions of degree should be produced by decimalizing.

Temperature—Wide acceptance is established of the degree Celsius (formerly called centigrade) in addition to the kelvin, particularly in everyday use. Temperature intervals are identical in the two scales. The kelvin will, of course, be used in thermodynamics.

Volume—The litre has been recognized as a special name for the cubic decimetre, and will be commonly used as a unit of liquid volume. It is strongly recommended that it be used only for this purpose, and that prefixes be avoided. (The millilitre is exactly a cubic centimetre, and the latter, being part of SI, should be used for small volumes.)

Thus the list of non-SI units to be used with the system is shown in Table 7.9. Use of any other units with SI should be carefully avoided unless real need exists for special use, in order that the coherence and simplicity of the system may be preserved. It is particularly important that use of non-SI units such as bar, tonne, and hectare, which have been common in Europe, should be avoided, since proper SI units are available and suitable for use.

For a number of reasons, the United States has been slow in changing to the SI unit system. To a great extent, engineering work in the United States continues to be based on the English gravitational system of units. In that system, force is measured in pounds force (lbf), and mass is measured in lbf sec²/ft.

In solving engineering problems, it is important that the units and dimensions be properly handled. Units used in mathematical equations must be considered carefully and thoughtfully in light of the units desired in the answer. There is a technique for checking the dimensional validity of a mathematical procedure. It involves treating the dimensions or units as if they were numbers and multiplying, dividing, and raising them to powers just as one would do with numbers. This is best explained by an example.

TABLE 7.9   *List of Non-SI Units*

Quantity	Unit	Symbol	Meaning
Time	hour	h	3.6 ks
	minute	min	60 s
	day	d	calendar
	week	...	calendar
	year	...	calendar
Angle	degree	°	$(\pi/180)$ rad
Volume	litre	l	1 dm³
Temperature	degree Celsius	°C	$t_{°C} = t_K - 273.15$

Example 7.1

A petroleum pipeline has a flow rate or throughput of 110,000 barrels per day. Given the following conversion factors, convert the flow rate to units of cubic feet per second.

$$1 \text{ barrel} = 42.0 \text{ gallons}$$
$$1 \text{ ft}^3 = 7.48 \text{ gallons}$$

Solution

$$\text{number of s / day} = 24\frac{\text{h}}{\text{day}} \times 60\frac{\text{min}}{\text{hr}} \times 60\frac{\text{s}}{\text{min}}$$

$$= 86,400\frac{\text{h} \times \text{min} \times \text{s}}{\text{day} \times \text{h} \times \text{min}}$$

This is the same as

$$\text{number of s / day} = 86,400\frac{\text{h} \times \text{min} \times \text{s}}{\text{h} \times \text{min} \times \text{day}}$$

Since the ratios h/h and min/min are 1, it is appropriate to write

$$\text{number of s / day} = 86,400\frac{\text{s}}{\text{day}}$$

The flow rate in cubic feet per second can now be determined as follows:

$$Q \text{ (ft}^3 \text{ / s)} = \frac{110,000\dfrac{\text{bbls}}{\text{day}} \times 42.0\dfrac{\text{gal}}{\text{bbl}}}{86,400\dfrac{\text{s}}{\text{day}} \times 7.48\dfrac{\text{gal}}{\text{ft}^3}}$$

Ignoring the units, the answer is 7.15.

Now consider the matter of units separately.

$$\frac{\text{ft}^3}{\text{s}} = \frac{\dfrac{\text{bbls}}{\text{day}} \times \dfrac{\text{gal}}{\text{bbl}}}{\dfrac{\text{s}}{\text{day}} \times \dfrac{\text{gal}}{\text{ft}^3}}?$$

This can be written as

$$\frac{\text{ft}^3}{\text{s}} = \frac{\dfrac{\text{bbl}}{\text{bbl}} \times \dfrac{\text{gal}}{\text{day}}}{\dfrac{\text{s}}{\text{day}} \times \dfrac{\text{gal}}{\text{ft}^3}} = \frac{\dfrac{\text{gal}}{\text{day}}}{\dfrac{\text{s} \times \text{gal}}{\text{day} \times \text{ft}^3}}$$

$$= \frac{(\text{day} \times \text{ft}^3) \times \dfrac{\text{gal}}{\text{day}}}{\text{s} \times \text{gal}} = \frac{\text{ft}^3 \times \text{gal}}{\text{s} \times \text{gal}} = \frac{\text{ft}^3}{\text{s}}$$

Thus, the answer is 7.15 ft³/s.

This example illustrates the method of unit balancing. By this means, we have multiplied and divided the units as if they were numbers; combining and simplifying the products and quotients to reveal the answer is in the desired units, ft³/s. Dimensional analysis is an extremely useful engineering tool. It serves as a check on the appropriateness of the units that were employed in the calculations. Equally important, it is a check on the validity of the problem-solving methodology and the correctness of the mathematical operations.

7.5   SIGNIFICANT FIGURES

Engineers often work with numbers that contain many digits and must determine how many of them are significant. A significant figure in a number is defined as a figure that may be considered reliable as a result of measurements or calculations. The number of significant figures in a result indicates the number of digits that can be used with confidence. A common mistake is to show too many figures in the answer, which gives the reader the idea that the answer is more accurate than it really is.

For example, suppose that we add the following numbers: 3.51, 2.205, and 0.0142. The sum is 5.7292, but it should be reported to three significant figures as 5.72, or rounded to 5.73. Since one of the numbers used in the sum was accurate only to the nearest hundredth, it would be presumptuous and misleading to report the answer to the thousandth or ten-thousandth place.

In addition and subtraction, the following rule should be observed when determining the number of significant figures: *The answer should show significant digits only as far to the right as is seen in the least precise number in the calculation.* Thus, when subtracting the numbers

$$1725.463$$
$$189.2$$
$$\overline{1536.263}$$

the answer should be recorded as 1536.2 or rounded to 1536.3.

In multiplication and division, the following rule should be used to determine the number of significant figures in the answer: *The product or quotient should contain the number of significant digits that are contained in the number with the fewest significant digits.* For example, the product

$$2.43 \times 17.675 = 42.950\ 25$$

when rounded, should be recorded as 43.0.

If the number 75.22 is divided by 25.1, the quotient should be reported as 3.00, not 2.9968, since the last two digits are unreliable and not significant.

When rounding off numbers, engineers generally observe the following procedure. Look at the number to the right of the number that is to be kept. If the number following the least significant figure is < 5, leave the last figure as it is.

If the number following the least significant figure is > 5, increase the last figure by 1. For example, if the number 5.7242 is to be rounded to three significant digits, it should be recorded as 5.72. If the number 5.7262 is to be rounded to three significant digits, it should be recorded as 5.73.

If the number following the least significant figure is equal to 5, it is not clear whether the number should be rounded up or down. For such instances, many engineers use the following practice: Truncate the number or round it up so that the recorded number is *even*. With this rule, the number 2.525 would be truncated to three significant figures as 2.52; the number 2.535 would be rounded up to 2.54.

7.6 SCIENTIFIC NOTATION

Engineers must frequently perform calculations using extremely large or very small numbers. In such instances, it may become cumbersome to write such numbers in decimal form. For example, consider the following multiplication operation:

$$2\ 340\ 000\ 000 \times 0.000\ 000\ 000\ 041 = 0.096$$

It is more convenient to utilize *scientific notation:*

$$(2.34 \times 10^9) \times (4.1 \times 10^{-11}) = 9.6 \times 10^{-2}$$

Notice that multiplication of numbers with powers of 10 is performed by adding the exponents algebraically. Furthermore, the product is recorded to two significant digits, the fewest significant digits of numbers used in the multiplication.

With scientific notation, the exponents of 10 are used to indicate the decimal place. Thus,

$100 = 1 \times 10^2$	$0.01 = 1 \times 10^{-2}$
$1\ 000 = 1 \times 10^3$	$0.001 = 1 \times 10^{-3}$
$10\ 000 = 1 \times 10^4$	$0.0001 = 1 \times 10^{-4}$ and so forth.

BRANCHES OF MATHEMATICS

The field of mathematics can be divided into pure mathematics and applied mathematics. Pure mathematics is concerned with the study of abstract mathematical properties and systems with no concern for application. Applied mathematics deals with solutions to problems that have practical applications. Engineers use both pure and applied mathematics in the solution of problems.

There are many branches of mathematics, but all of the branches are sometimes grouped broadly into three areas: algebra, geometry, and analysis. Each area has several subspecialties or branches. The branches of mathematics most commonly used by engineers are briefly discussed in the remaining sections of this chapter.

7.7 ALGEBRA

Algebra is a generalization of arithmetic in which symbols are used to represent unknown numbers or sets of numbers called variables. Relationships among the variables are expressed in the form of open mathematical sentences as equations or inequalities. The variables are usually symbolized by the letters of the alphabet, but Greek letters (Table 7.10) are sometimes used.

Mathematicians, scientists, and engineers employ a type of shorthand in which algebraic operations are also expressed by symbols. In addition to the familiar symbols for addition, subtraction, multiplication, and division, many other symbols are used. Table 7.11 illustrates some of the symbols that are commonly used.

7.8 GEOMETRY

Geometry is concerned with the properties, measurement, and relationships of points, lines, surfaces, and solids. It includes:

- Plane geometry — The study of lines, curves, angles, and polygons in a plane.

- Solid geometry — The study of cones, spheres, cylinders, and polyhedra curves in a three-dimensional space.

- Differential geometry — The application of calculus to geometry to study local properties of curves.

- Descriptive geometry — The mathematical techniques used to describe geometrical relationships of three-dimensional surfaces on a plane surface.

TABLE 7.10 *The Greek Alphabet*

Alpha	A	$\alpha\ \alpha$	Nu	N	ν
Beta	B	β	Xi	Ξ	ξ
Gamma	Γ	γ	Omicron	O	o
Delta	Δ	$\delta\ \partial$	Pi	Π	π
Epsilon	E	$\epsilon\varepsilon$	Rho	P	ρ
Zeta	Z	ζ	Sigma	Σ	$\sigma\ \varsigma$
Eta	H	η	Tau	T	τ
Theta	Θ	$\theta\ \vartheta$	Upsilon	Y	υ
Iota	I	ι	Phi	Φ	$\phi\ \varphi$
Kappa	K	κ	Chi	X	χ
Lambda	Λ	λ	Psi	Ψ	ψ
Mu	M	μ	Omega	Ω	ω

TABLE 7.11   *Commonly Used Mathematical Symbols*

Symbol	Meaning
$\pm$	Plus or minus
$=$	Equals
$\neq$	Is not equal to
$>$	Greater than
$<$	Less than
$\geq$	Greater than or equal to
$\leq$	Less than or equal to
$\mid\;\mid$	Absolute value
∞	Infinity
$n!$	Factorial, $n(n-1)(n-2)\ldots 1$
Σ	Sum of a series of numbers
$\therefore$	Therefore

- Analytical geometry   The application of algebraic methods to geometry by which lines and curves are represented by algebraic equations. (See Section 7.12 for a discussion of applications of analytical geometry.)

7.9   TRIGONOMETRY

Trigonometry is an extension of geometry used for computing the unknown sides and angles of a triangle. Trigonometry applies to triangles in a plane or on a spherical surface.

There are many practical applications in engineering for the trigonometric functions: sine, cosine, tangent, secant, cosecant, and cotangent. These functions are defined as the ratios of the sides of plane right triangles. These functions are shown in Table 7.12.

The fundamental theorems and laws of trigonometry are frequently used by engineers. Three of the most frequently used relationships are the Pythagorean theorem, the Law of Sines, and the Law of Cosines.

The Pythagorean theorem, attributed to the sixth-century Greek philosopher Pythagoras, states that the sum of the squares of the lengths of the sides of a right triangle is equal to the square of the length of the hypotenuse. Referring to the sketch that accompanies Table 7.12, the Pythagorean theorem can be stated:

$$A^2 + B^2 = C^2 \tag{7.1}$$

The Law of Sines states:

$$\frac{\text{sine } \alpha}{A} = \frac{\text{sine } \beta}{B} = \frac{\text{sine } \gamma}{C}$$

$$\tag{7.2}$$

TABLE 7.12 *Trigonometric Functions*

Sine $\alpha = \dfrac{A}{C}$

Cosine $\alpha = \dfrac{B}{C}$

Tangent $\alpha = \dfrac{A}{B}$

Secant $\alpha = \dfrac{1}{\text{cosine } \alpha} = \dfrac{C}{B}$

Cosecant $\alpha = \dfrac{1}{\text{sine } \alpha} = \dfrac{C}{A}$

Cotangent $\alpha = \dfrac{1}{\text{tangent } \alpha} = \dfrac{B}{A}$

Hypotenuse C

A

$90°$

B

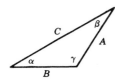

Figure 7.2 *Relationships for the Law of Sines.*

as shown in Figure 7.2. This law is applicable to triangles with $0 < \gamma < 180°$.

The Law of Cosines, which also applies to triangles with $0 < \gamma < 180°$, can be stated as follows:

$$C^2 = A^2 + B^2 - 2AB \cos \gamma \tag{7.3}$$

7.10 CALCULUS

A branch of analysis, calculus deals with rates of changes of functions. There are two principal areas of calculus: differential calculus and integral calculus. Differential calculus provides a way of calculating maxima and minima of functions and instantaneous rates of changes of functions as opposed to an average rate. With integral calculus, we are able to calculate areas and volumes bounded by curves and surfaces with precision, to find lengths of curves, and to determine divergence or convergence of an infinite series of numbers. The following examples illustrate how calculus can be used to solve engineering problems.

Example 7.2

Given: An automobile, traveling at a velocity of 44 ft/s, is accelerated at an average rate of 4 ft/s². The relationship between distance traveled and time is expressed by the equation:

$$S = v_0 t + \tfrac{1}{2} a t^2$$

where S = distance traveled, ft
   v_0 = original velocity, ft/s
   t = time, s
   a = acceleration rate, ft/s²

Find   the instantaneous velocity of the car at time $t = 3$ s.

Solution   Differential calculus allows us to take the derivative with respect to time:

$$\frac{ds}{dt} = v_0 + at = 44 + 4t$$

The derivative, ds/dt, represents the slope of the curve and makes it possible to determine the slope of the curve at any point. See the sketch. In this case, the slope is the instantaneous velocity. Thus, the velocity at $t = 3$ s,

$$\frac{ds}{dt} = 44 + 4(3) = \underline{56 \text{ ft}/\text{s}}   Answer$$

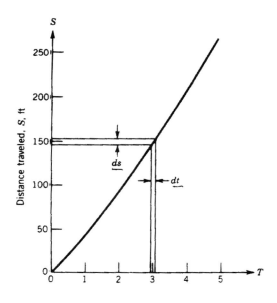

Example 7.3

Given: Water drains from a field at a rate q, which varies with time, t, according to the following equation:

$$q = 3.78t^{-0.37}$$

where q = rate of flow of water, thousands of cubic feet per minute
   t = time, minutes

The relationship is shown by the accompanying graph.

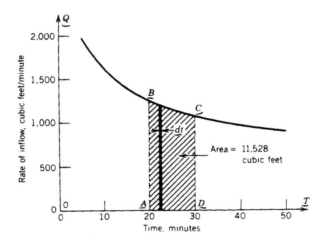

Find   by integral calculus, the total amount of water draining from the field between the time t_1 = 20 min and t_2 = 30 min.

Solution   In this example, the total amount of water draining from the field is represented by the area under the curve, *ABCD*. The area under the curve can be divided into strips by a system of equidistant lines parallel to *OQ*, qdt. It is equal to the sum of all such strips between t_1 and t_2 and can be calculated by integration.

$$\int_{20}^{30} qdt = \int_{20}^{30} (3.78t^{-0.37})\,dt = \frac{3a78}{0.63}\left[t^{0.63}\right]_{20}^{30}$$

$$= 6[(30)^{0.63} - (20)^{0.63}] = \underline{\underline{11.528 \text{ thousand ft}^3}}   \textit{Answer}$$

7.11 ENGINEERING STATISTICS

The science of statistics involves the collection, organization, and interpretation of numerical data. Engineers use statistics for many purposes, including:

1. To understand, control, and account for errors in measurement.
2. To facilitate the collection of adequate and reliable data for the planning of engineering projects.
3. To better understand and account for uncertainties in the demands placed on engineering structures and products.
4. To control the quality of workmanship and materials in manufacturing and construction.

The data that engineers collect may be raw or unorganized; however, when dealing with a large set of raw data, it is helpful to group the data into various classes. The data could be grouped into class intervals to form a *frequency distribution*, which shows the number of observations that occur within a given interval. In fact, it may be possible to classify the data in this way with a tally sheet as they are collected (see Table 7.13).

Engineers often display the frequency or relative frequency of observations graphically in the form of a *histogram* (see Figure 7.3). A smooth curve drawn through the midpoints of the frequency bars of a histogram approximates the *probability distribution* of the variable. The histogram represents the frequency of observations of a sample of data. The probability distribution represents the relative frequencies with which all possible values of the variable occur.

Probability distributions may be *continuous* or *discrete.* In continuous distributions, the variable may take all values in an interval and may be represented by a smooth curve. The distribution shown in Figure 7.3 is a continuous distribution. In discrete distributions, the variable takes on nonnegative inte-

TABLE 7.13 *Example of a Tally Sheet*

Vehicle Speeds	Counts
27–30	
31–34	||||
35–38	||||
39–42	|||| ||||
43–46	|||| |||| ||||
47–50	|||| |||| |||| |
51–54	|||| |||| |||
55–58	|||| ||||
59–62	|||| ||||
63–66	||
67–70	||||
71–74	

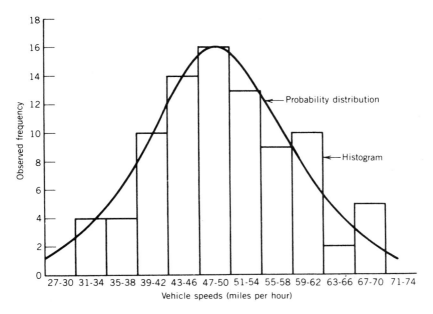

Figure 7.3   *Hypothetical example of a histogram and a continuous probability distribution.*

gers: 0, 1, 2, 3, and so on. Figure 7.4 is a hypothetical example of a discrete distribution. It shows the number of trucks arriving at a loading dock at a manufacturing plant during a specified interval of time.

It is sometimes convenient to describe a set of data by one or two numbers that characterize the entire set. Commonly, two types of measures are used: *measures of central tendency* and *measures of dispersion.*

Measures of central tendency are used to characterize the center or average of the data. Three common parameters of central tendency are the *arithmetic mean,* the *mode,* and the *median.* The arithmetic mean of a sample of n measures is defined as the sum of the measures divided by n. The mode of the sample is the most commonly occurring number. The median is the halfway point in the data when the values have been arranged in order of size.

Consider the following hypothetical set of data: 1, 1, 2, 2, 3, 3, 5, 5, 5, 6, 11. The sum of the 11 numbers is 44, and the arithmetic mean is 4. The mode is 5, and the median is 3.

There are a number of measures or parameters that are used to describe the dispersion or scatter of the data. One such measure is the *range,* the difference between the highest and lowest readings. The range of the data just listed is 10.

Another way of characterizing dispersion is to state various estimates of *percentiles.* For example, one might state the difference between the 95th and the 5th percentiles, $P_{95} - P_{05}$. A percentile is a value contained in a set of data that is not exceeded by a specified percentage of all the values in the set.

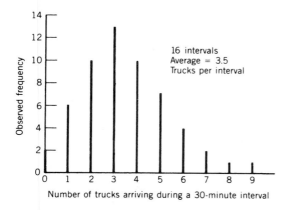

Figure 7.4 *Hypothetical example of a discrete probability distribution.*

Percentiles may be obtained graphically or in the following way. To determine P_{95}, arrange the values in order of size and count off 95 percent of them. The value appearing nearest that point is the 95th percentile.

Another, and probably the most common, measure of dispersion is the *standard deviation*. The standard deviation, s, of a sample of n observations, x_1, x_2, x_3, ..., x_n, is defined as follows:

$$s = \sqrt{\frac{\sum\limits_{j=1}^{n} x_i - \bar{x}^2}{n-1}}$$

(7.4)

where $\bar{x}$ is the arithmetic mean.

It is suggested that the reader verify that the standard deviation of the hypothetical data set given above is equal to 2.9.

Yet another commonly used measure of dispersion is the *variance*, s^2, the square of the standard deviation.

The Normal Distribution

Many probability distributions have been developed to describe empirical engineering data. The description of all or even the most commonly used distributions is beyond the scope of this book. We limit our description here to the *normal probability distribution*. This theoretical curve has widespread use in many forms of engineering research and practice.

The normal distribution for a random variable, x, is defined by the following equation:

$$f(x) = \frac{1}{\sigma\sqrt{2\pi}} e^{-(x-\mu)^2/2\sigma^2}$$

(7.5)

where σ = the standard deviation
μ = the mean
e = the Napierian logarithmic base

Notice that Greek letters are used here for the mean and standard deviation to distinguish these values from sample parameters.

The normal distribution is bell-shaped and symmetrical about the mean. The points of inflection of the curve occur at ± 1 standard deviation from the mean, as Figure 7.5 illustrates. In other words, the curve is concave downward within 1 standard deviation from the mean and concave upward at points farther than 1 standard deviation from the mean.

The total area under the normal curve is equal to 1. If the mean and variance of a normally distributed random variable are known or can be assumed, integration can be used to calculate probabilities such as

$$P(a < x < b) = \int_a^b \frac{1}{\sqrt{2\pi}} e^{-(x-\mu)^2/2\sigma^2}\, dx$$

This, however, is not an elementary function, and its integral is not easily determined. Nor would it be easily tabulated. For this reason, the equation for the normal curve is usually expressed in a standard form with the mean = 0 and the variance = 1. The standardized curve is shown in Figure 7.6 in terms of the variable $z = (x - \mu)/\sigma$. The standardized equation becomes

$$f(z) = \frac{1}{\sqrt{2\pi}} e^{-z^2/2}$$

(7.6)

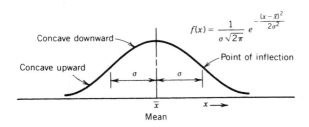

Figure 7.5 *The normal probability distribution.*

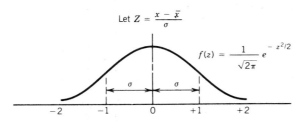

Figure 7.6 *The standardized normal probability distribution.*

This transformation permits the use of one table for all normal distributions. An abbreviated version of the table is shown as Table 7.14.

It will be noted from the normal distribution table that approximately 68 percent of the area under the curve lies within the range $z = -1$ and $z = +1$ or within ± 1 standard deviation from the mean. This is illustrated by Figure 7.6. In other words, about 68 percent of a set of normally distributed data points lie within ± 1 standard deviations from the mean. Similarly, 95.4 percent of such data lie within 2σ from the mean; 99.7 percent of the data lie within 3σ from the mean.

TABLE 7.14   Areas Under the Normal Curve from $-\infty$ to Z

Z	=	0.0000	0.5000	1.0000	1.5000	2.0000	2.5000	3.0000	3.5000
Area	=	0.5000	0.6915	0.8413	0.9332	0.9772	0.9938	0.9987	0.9998

Example 7.4

An engineer supervising the construction of an earth embankment determines that the mean of the dry density of the soil is 120 lb/ft³ and the standard deviation is 10 lb/ft³. Assuming that the densities are normally distributed, what is the probability that a random measurement will be less than 100 lb/ft³?

Solution

$$Z = \frac{100 - 120}{10} = -2.0$$

From Table 7.14,

$$P(Z \leqslant +2.0) = 0.9772 = P(Z \geqslant -2.0)$$
$$P(Z < -2.0) = 1.0 - P(Z \geqslant -2.0)$$
$$= 1.0 - 0.9772 = \underline{0.0228} \; Answer$$

Suppose earlier laboratory tests of the soil used in the earth embankment indicated that a density of less than 100 lb/ft³ would be highly undesirable and likely to cause subsidence of the structure. The results shown in this example indicate that even though the *mean* densities are 120 lb/ft³, there is still a small likelihood (probability = 0.0228) that unacceptably low densities (<100 lb/ft³) would result. In this case, the engineer would probably attempt to improve the field construction procedures in order to achieve higher and less variable densities, decreasing the likelihood of failure.

7.12   GRAPHICAL ANALYSIS

Often it is possible to gain a better understanding of the relationship between two variables by plotting the data on a graph. Conventionally, engineers designate the variable plotted on the abscissa or horizontal scale as x; the variable plotted on the ordinate or vertical scale is designated as y. On such a graph, data can be arranged in an infinite variety of patterns. However, most of the relationships with which engineers must deal fall into one of four types:

1.   Straight lines.
2.   Parabolic curves.
3.   Hyperbolic curves.
4.   Exponential curves.

Figure 7.7 illustrates the simplest type of relationship, a straight line. The equation of a straight line is expressed as

$$y = mx + b \qquad (7.7)$$

where m = the slope of the line
b = the zero intercept or the value of y at $x = 0$

Parabolic curves may be concaved upward, as in Figure 7.8a, or downward, as in Figure 7.9a. A parabola such as these, which passes through the origin of the graph, may be expressed mathematically as

$$y = ax^m, \, m > 0 \qquad (7.8)$$

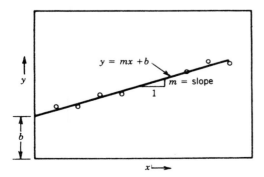

Figure 7.7   *A straight-line relationship.*

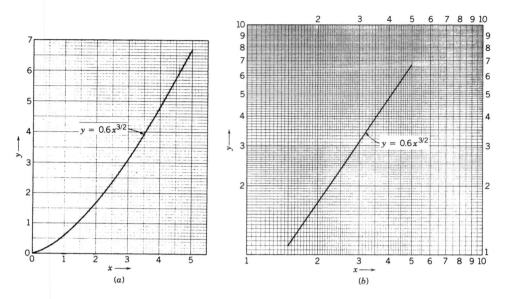

Figure 7.8   *A parabolic curve plotted (a) on rectangular coordinate graph paper and (b) on logarithmic graph paper.*

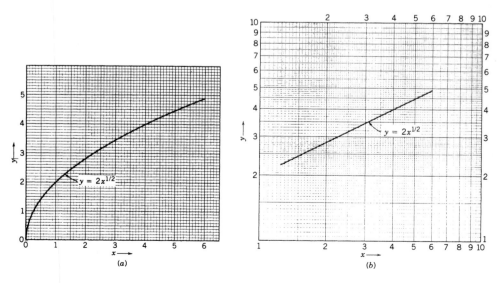

Figure 7.9   *A parabolic curve plotted on (a) rectangular coordinate graph paper and (b) on logarithmic graph paper.*

If we take the logarithms of Equation (7.8), the relationship takes on the form of a straight line.

$$\ln y = m \ln x + \ln a$$

Thus, when a parabola is plotted on logarithmic graph paper with logarithmic scales for both the ordinate and abscissa, the relationship appears as a straight line with a slope $= m$ and an intercept on the y-axis $= \ln a$. See Figures 7.8b and 7.9b.

Notice from the figures that when $m > 1$, the parabola is concaved upward on rectangular coordinate graph paper. When $m < 1$, the curve is concaved downward.

Parabolic curves may not intersect the ordinate at zero but at some value c. In that case, the equation for the relationship takes the form

$$y = ax^m + c \tag{7.9}$$

Hyperbolic curves are expressed by the equation:

$$y = ax^m, \, m < 0 \tag{7.10}$$

Figures 7.10a and 7.10b illustrate a hyperbolic relationship on rectangular coordinate graph and logarithmic paper, respectively. This type of equation may also include a constant c, which would shift the ordinates by a value of c.

Exponential curves may be described by an equation of the form:

$$y = ae^{mx} \tag{7.11}$$

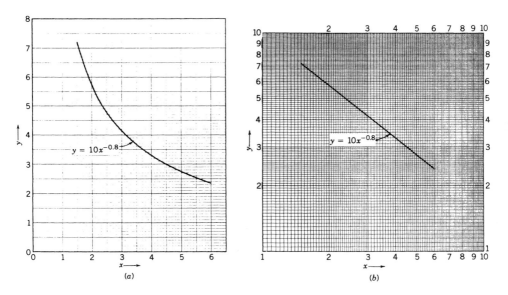

Figure 7.10 *A hyperbolic curve plotted (a) on rectangular coordinate graph paper and (b) on logarithmic graph paper.*

A typical exponential relationship is shown as Figure 7.11a. If we take logarithms of both sides of the equation, the relationship becomes:

$$\ln y = mx + \ln a$$

The equation shows that in this type of relationship, logarithms of the y-values are related linearly to the x-values. Therefore, exponential relationships plotted on semilog graph paper, with the ordinates plotted on a logarithmic scale, are seen as straight lines (see Figure 7.11b).

An exponential relationship with positive values of m is an increasing relationship appearing as a "growth" curve (Figure 7.11a). With negative values of m, the y-values decrease with increases in x, and the graph is known as a "decay" curve (see Figures 7.12a and 7.12b).

Developing an Equation for a Straight-line Relationship

Several methods can be used to develop an equation for a straight-line relationship, including: (1) the graphical method, (2) the method of selected points, (3) the method of averages, and (4) the method of least squares.

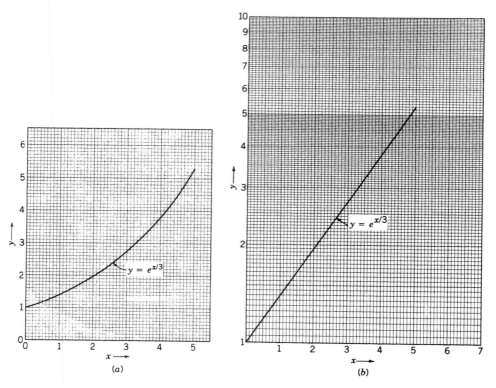

Figure 7.11   *An exponential curve plotted (a) on rectangular coordinate graph paper and (b) on semilogarithmic graph paper.*

Graphical Method   With the graphical method, the slope, m, and the y-intercept of the line are simply determined directly from the figure. The method involves two steps:

Step 1   For the value of the intercept:

      a.   Read the y-value corresponding to $x = 0$ for straight lines and exponential curves.

      b.   Read the y-value corresponding to $x = 1$ for parabolic and hyperbolic curves that are plotted on log paper.

Step 2   For the slope, select two widely separated points and calculate the ratio of the difference in the ordinates and the difference in the abscissa values:

$$m = \frac{\Delta Y}{\Delta X}$$

Method of Selected Points   The following procedure is used for the method of selected points. Select two widely separated points. Substitute the coordinates

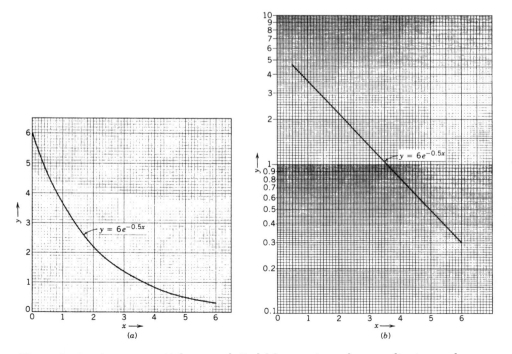

Figure 7.12   *An exponential curve plotted (a) on rectangular coordinate graph paper and (b) on semilogarithmic graph paper.*

of these points in the equation of the line. This will produce two equations that can be solved simultaneously for the intercept, b, and the slope, m.

Example 7.5

Suppose a study revealed that a student's grade on an examination is a function of the number of hours studied. Empirical data are listed in Table 7.15 and shown graphically as Figure 7.13.

Develop a straight-line equation using the method of selected points.

Solution   Using judgment, a "best fit" line was drawn on the figure. Two widely separated points from the "best fit" line were chosen:

$$(x_1 = 1.5, y_1 = 69) \text{ and } (x_2 = 4.5, y_2 = 97)$$

The equation for a straight line is $y = mx + b$. Substituting the above values in this equation,

$$
\begin{aligned}
69 &= m(1.5) + b \\
97 &= m(4.5) + b \\
\hline
28 &= m(3.0) \\
m &= 9.33 \\
b &= 69 - 9.33(1.5) = 55.
\end{aligned}
$$

The equation is

$$\underline{\underline{y = 9.33x + 55}} \quad Answer$$

Method of Averages   This method assumes that the sum of the residuals for the various points is zero. The residual is the vertical distance from the plotted point to the selected curve.

$$\Sigma[Y - (mX + b)] = 0$$

$$\Sigma[Y - mX - b] = 0$$

$$\Sigma Y - m\Sigma X - nb = 0 \qquad (7.12)$$

TABLE 7.15   *Example of Empirical Data*

x, Number of Hours Studied	y, Grade on Examination
0	50
1	70
2	86
3	85
4	90
5	98

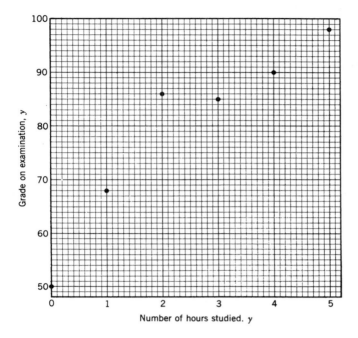

Figure 7.13   *A plot of the hypothetical relationship given in Example 7.5.*

The procedure is to divide the experimental data into two equal groups of adjacent observations. Then determine ΣX, ΣY, and n. Substitute these values in Equation (7.12). Solve the resulting equations simultaneously for the slope, m, and the intercept, b.

Example 7.6

Develop a straight-line equation for the data given above using the method of averages.

Solution

Group I Data		Group II Data	
X	Y	X	Y
0	50	1	70
2	86	3	85
4	90	5	98
$\Sigma x = 6$	$\Sigma y = 226$	$\Sigma x = 9$	$\Sigma y = 253$

Equation $\Sigma y - m\Sigma x - nb = 0$

$$226 - m(6) - 3b = 0$$
$$253 - m(9) - 3b = 0$$
$$\overline{}$$
$$3m = 27 \qquad m = 9.0$$

$$b = \frac{226 - (9)6}{3} = 57.3$$

$$\underline{y = 9.0x + 57.3} \quad Answer$$

Method of Least Squares   The "best fit" curve according to the principle of least squares is that curve for which the sum of squares of the residuals is a minimum. That is,

Σe^2 = a minimum, where e is the difference between the computed and observed Ys.

It can be shown that for the sum of squares of the residuals to be a minimum, the following equations must be true:

$$\Sigma(XY) - m\Sigma X^2 - b\Sigma X = 0 \tag{7.13}$$

$$\Sigma Y - m\Sigma X - nb = 0 \tag{7.14}$$

By calculating the sums of the Xs, Ys, the products (XY)s, and the X^2s, we obtain two equations with two unknowns, m and b. These equations can be solved simultaneously for m and b to yield an equation of the form:

$$Y = mX + b$$

Example 7.7

Develop a straight-line equation for the data given above using the method of least squares.

Solution

x No. of Hours Studied	y Grade on Exam	xy	x²
0	50	0	0
1	70	70	1
2	86	172	4
3	85	255	9
4	90	360	16
5	98	490	25

$\Sigma x = 15$ $\Sigma y = 479$ $\Sigma(xy) = 1347$ $\Sigma x^2 = 55$

(1) $\Sigma y - m\Sigma x - nb = 0$
(2) $\Sigma(xy) - m\Sigma x^2 - b\Sigma x = 0$
(1) $479 - m(15) - 6b = 0$
(2) $1347 - m(55) - b(15) = 0$

Multiply

(1) $\times \dfrac{15}{6}$ $1198 - m(37.5) - 15b = 0$

(2) $1347 - m(55) - 15b = 0$

$\overline{ - 149 + 17.5m = 0 \quad\quad m = 8.52 }$

(2) $15b = 1347 - (8.52)(55) = 879$

$$b = \frac{879}{15} = 58.6$$

Least Squares Model $y = mx + b$

$\underline{y = 8.52x + 58.6}$ *Answer*

Example 7.8

Suppose that it is desired to fit an equation to the data of the form $Y = ax^m + c$. (It appears to be parabolic.)

Solution   We can choose the value of c from curve, $c = 50$. In this case the function Y for ordinates is $\ln(y - c)$ and the function X for abscissas is $\ln x$.

X	Y	ln x	(y − c)	ln (y − c)
0	50	—	0	—
1	70	0	20	3.00
2	86	0.693	36	3.584
3	85	1.099	35	3.555
4	90	1.386	40	3.689
5	98	1.609	48	3.871

Form of rectified equation: $\ln(y - c) = m \ln x + \ln a$
Solve for m and $\ln a \to a$.
Use the method of selected points.

Select points: $x_1 = 1$ $x_2 = 5$

$(y - c)_1 = 20$ $(y - c)_2 = 48$

$$y = mx + b$$

1. $3.00 = m(0) + \ln a$ $\ln a = 3.00$

2. $3.871 = m(1.609) + \ln a$ $a = 20$

$$m = \frac{3.871 - 3.00}{1.609} = 0.54$$

$$Y = 20X^{0.54} + 50$$

X	Actual Y	Computed Y Values
0	50	50
1	70	70
2	86	79
3	85	86
4	90	92
5	98	98

EXERCISES

7.1   Determine the number of significant figures in each of the following numbers.
  a.   7,123,600
  b.   7.1236
  c.   0.00026
  d. 4.167×10^5
  e.   0.0007
  f. 2.23×10^{-3}

7.2   Determine the number of significant figures in each of the following numbers.
  a.   0.0027
  b.   722.6
  c.   0.0403
  d. 8.91×10^4
  e.   2 000 001
  f.   0.000 000 7

7.3   Round off each of the following answers to the proper number of significant figures.
  a. $6.0 + 1.01 + 0.904 = 7.914$
  b. $42. + 0.52 + 0.229 = 42.749$
  c. $92.01/0.4 = 230.025$
  d. $4.02 \times 21.1 = 84.822$

7.4 Round off each of the following answers to the proper number of significant figures.

   a. 27. + 0.322 = 27.322
   b. 36.7/0.021 = 1 747.619
   c. 6.36 × 21.03 = 133.7508
   d. 7.9 + 4.31 + 6.444 = 18.654

7.5 Express the following numbers in scientific notation.

   a. 0.0007
   b. 27 922.76
   c. 0.063400
   d. 4 billion

7.6 Express the following numbers in scientific notation.

   a. 0.0033
   b. 43 561.7
   c. 0.725 300
   d. 10 trillion

7.7 Shown below are data giving speeds of vehicles traveling along a major highway.

   a. Estimate the standard deviation.
   b. Estimate the probability that a randomly chosen vehicle will exceed the speed limit of 65 miles per hour. Assume the data to be distributed by a normal distribution.

Speed, mph	Speed, mph
65	62
64	67
57	54
50	59
71	61

7.8 Shown below are data giving the length of life of lights in a tunnel.

   a. Estimate the standard deviation.
   b. Estimate the probability that a randomly chosen light will last as long as 7 months after installation. Assume the data to be described by a normal distribution.

Length of Life, months	Length of Life, months
9.0	7.0
8.2	8.3
7.8	8.1
7.5	7.6
9.1	7.4

7.9 Given the data shown below, develop an equation between y (dependent variable) and x (independent variable). Show the results as a plot on rectangular coordinate graph paper.

   a. By the method of selected points. Use values for $x_1 = 1.0$ and $x_5 = 5.0$.
   b. By the method of averages.
   c. By the method of least squares.

x	y
0.5	1.4
1.0	2.0
2.0	2.8
3.0	3.4
4.0	4.0
5.0	4.5

7.10 The following data shows the increase of strength, s, with time, t. Develop an equation between strength (dependent variable) and time (independent variable).
   a. By the method of selected points (first and last points).
   b. By the method of averages.
   c. By the method of least squares.

Time, t, years	Strength, s, psi
0	615
1	650
2	675
3	720
4	765
5	790

An Exemplary Engineering Achievement

The Metro, serving the nation's capitol, extends over 103 mile of track, through the District of Columbia and its Maryland and Virginia suberbs. (Courtesy of the American Council of Engineering Companies.)

CHAPTER EIGHT

A CASE STUDY— ATLANTA'S FREEDOM PARKWAY PROJECT

In earlier times, there was little concern about the harmful social and environmental effects from engineering projects. The works of engineers were welcomed by people and looked upon as a means to economic progress. Complaints about environmental problems were rare and viewed by political leaders and professional engineers as minor impediments to progress.

A dramatic reversal in professional and political attitudes about the social and environmental impact of technology developed in the late 1960s. Political and professional leaders began to realize that technological progress is often accompanied by relocation of families and businesses, disruption of communities, and harmful changes to the natural environment.

Beginning in the 1960s, several federal laws were enacted to insure that engineers give appropriate consideration to social and environmental issues when planning and designing engineering works. By the 1990s, professional engineers had become more sensitive to these issues, and public attitudes and concerns had become an integral ingredient of the engineering design process.

This chapter is intended to demonstrate that engineering is much more than solving mathematical equations and that engineers must be concerned about possible harmful effects of their designs on people and the earth's environment.

8.1 BACKGROUND

By 1960, the Georgia Department of Transportation (GDOT), working in concert with the Atlanta Regional Commission, had completed plans for the construction of segments of two controlled-access highways located just east of Atlanta's central business district. These highways were designed to Interstate highway standards and were intended to ease traffic congestion near the city center. The north-south portion of this development, designated Interstate Route I-485, would generally parallel and relieve the traffic on Interstate Routes I-75/85 which are located near the center of the city. The east-west segment, called the Stone Mountain Tollway, would serve as a major carrier of commuter traffic from the eastern suburbs. A general vicinity map of these projects is shown as Figure 8.1.

These controlled-access projects featured generally straight alignment, relatively level gradients, and wide shoulders and had two lanes in both directions separated by a median. They were designed for speeds up to 70 miles per hour and would have accommodated heavy trucks.

The Department of Transportation began acquiring rights-of-way for these projects in 1961. The highways were to be built through established neighborhoods and were opposed by many of the residents. Opposition, however, was not well organized or extensive, and landowners who were unable to negotiate an acceptable offer for their land were left with little recourse but to seek more compensation for their land in the courts on a case-by-case basis.

8.2   SOCIAL AND ENVIRONMENTAL LEGISLATION

It should be remembered that significant social and environmental legislation did not appear until several years after the planning and design of Route I-485 and the Stone Mountain Tollway had been completed. Landmark federal legislative provisions related to the evaluation of social and environmental impacts of highways were included in the Department of Transportation Act of 1966, the National Environmental Policy Act of 1969, the Clean Air Act of 1963, the Uniform Relocation Assistance and Real Property Acquisitions Policies Act of 1970, and the Federal-Aid Highway Act of 1970.

The most significant legislative provisions relating to evaluation of social and environmental consequences of highways were contained in the Department of Transportation Act of 1966, the National Environmental Policy Act of 1969, the Clean Air Act of 1963 (and subsequent acts dealing with air pollution), the Uniform Relocation Assistance and Real Property Acquisitions Policies Act of 1970, and the Federal-Aid Highway Act of 1970.

The Department of Transportation Act, passed October 16, 1966, declared it to be the national policy that a special effort should be made to preserve the natural beauty of the countryside. Section 4(f) of that act stated that the Secretary of Transportation shall not approve any program or project that requires any land from a public park, recreation area, wildlife and waterfowl refuge, or historic site unless there is no feasible and prudent alternative to the use of such land. It further stated that transportation programs that require land from such areas must include all possible planning to minimize environmental harm.

The National Environmental Policy Act of 1969 declared it to be a national policy that the federal government would use all practicable means and measures "to create and maintain conditions under which man and nature can

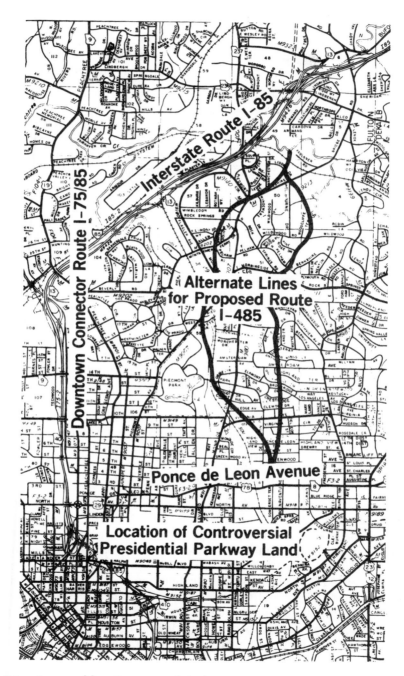

Figure 8.1   *A general location map of study area.*

exist in productive harmony." It established a three-member Council on Environmental Quality in the Executive Office of the President to develop guidelines for agencies affected by the law. Section 102 of the act, quoted in part below, established the requirement for environmental impact statements (EISs).

Sec. 102. The Congress authorizes and directs that, to the fullest extent possible: (1) the policies, regulations, and public laws of the United States shall be interpreted and administered in accordance with the policies set forth in this Act, and (2) all agencies of the Federal Government shall—

(A) utilize a systematic, interdisciplinary approach which will insure the integrated use of the natural and social sciences and the environmental design arts in planning and in decision making which may have an impact on man's environment;

(B) identify and develop methods and procedures, in consultation with the Council on Environmental Quality established by title II of this Act, which will insure that presently unquantified environmental amenities and values may be given appropriate consideration in decision making along with economic and technical considerations;

(C) include in every recommendation or report on proposals for legislation and other major Federal actions significantly affecting the quality of the human environment, a detailed statement by the responsible official on—

(i) the environmental impact of the proposed action,

(ii) any adverse environmental effects which cannot be avoided should the proposal be implemented,

(iii) alternatives to the proposed action,

(iv) the relationship between local short-term uses of man's environment and the maintenance and enhancement of long-term productivity, and

(v) any irreversible and irretrievable commitments of resources which would be involved in the proposed action should it be implemented.

The Clean Air Act of 1963 encouraged increased state and local programs for the control of air pollution. The act also provided for the development of air quality standards. In 1965, Congress passed the Motor Vehicle Control Act, which initiated controls on motor vehicle manufacturers to require the installation of air pollution control devices on all new vehicles. Since that time, there have been additional laws that further involved both state and federal agencies in controlling air pollution.

In 1970, Congress passed the Uniform Relocation Assistance and Real Property Acquisitions Policies Act in an effort to establish uniform treatment of all people affected by public projects financed with federal funds. The act sets forth standard policies and procedures for the determination of just compensation, for negotiation with property owners, for taking possession of property, and, when required, for instituting formal condemnation proceedings.

The Federal-Aid Highway Act of 1970 required the Secretary of Transportation to publish guidelines designed to insure that possible adverse eco-

nomic, social, and environmental effects are properly considered during the
planning and development of federal-aid highway projects.(*1*)

8.3 SIGNIFICANT STATE LEGISLATION

It is important to remember that in the United States, major highways are usually planned and built under a cooperative cost-sharing arrangement between
the federal government and the state in which the highway is located. Like
other agencies of government, the state highway agency (in this example, the
Georgia Department of Transportation) must operate under the provisions
of state laws. For example, in the state of Georgia, its laws contain specific
instructions for purchasing land for highways and disposing of land no longer
needed for a transportation purpose. This provision of the state law was to
become a major impediment to solving the controversy of the parkway project.

Because of its importance, those sections of Georgia state law that are relevant to this case are quoted below:

Section 32-3-1 (a), (b)
Any property may be acquired in fee simple or in any lesser interest,
including scenic easements, airspace, and rights of access, by a state
agency or a county or municipality through gift, devise, exchange, purchase, prescription, dedication, eminent domain, or any other manner
provided by law for present or future public road or other transportation
purposes.

Public road purposes shall include rights of way; detours; bridges;
bridge approaches; ferries; ferry landings; overpasses; underpasses;
viaducts; tunnels; fringe parking facilities; borrow pits; offices; shops;
depots; storage yards; buildings and other necessary physical facilities of
all types; roadside parks and recreational areas; the growth of trees and
shrubbery along rights of way; scenic easements; construction for
drainage, maintenance, safety, or esthetic purposes; the elimination of
encroachments, private or public crossings, or intersections; the establishment of limited-access public roads; the relocation of utilities; and
any and all other purposes which may be reasonably related to the development, growth, or enhancement of the public roads of Georgia.

32-2-2 (8)
The department shall have the authority to exercise the right and power
of eminent domain and to purchase, exchange, sell, lease, or otherwise
acquire or dispose of any property or any rights or interests therein for
public road and other transportation purposes or for any activities incident thereto, subject to such express limitations as are provided by law;

32-3-3 (a)
The department or any county or municipality is authorized to accept
donations, transfers, or devises of land from private persons, from the

federal government, or from other state agencies, counties, or municipalities, provided that such land is suitable for present or future public road purposes. Any property may be so acquired in fee or any lesser interest, provided that the state agency, county, or municipality thereby obtains an interest sufficient to ensure reasonable protection of the public investment which it may thereafter make in such land. The instrument which conveys such property or interest shall be recorded in the county or counties where such property or interest lies and, in the case of property or interests acquired by the department, shall also be kept in the records of the department.

8.4   THE ABANDONMENT OF INTERSTATE ROUTE I-485

A court decision in 1971 suspended action on the I-485 project pending the completion of an EIS under the provisions of the National Environmental Policy Act of 1969. In the same year, hearings were held on the proposed Stone Mountain Tollway. These hearings indicated that this project also had become controversial.

As a result of questions raised, a commission was appointed by Governor Jimmy Carter to examine the issues and make recommendations to him regarding the Stone Mountain Tollway. The Commission recommended that the Stone Mountain Tollway not be built until the effect of the impending construction of the MARTA[1] East Rail Line could be assessed. The Commission noted that while the decision to build would be irreversible, the decision not to build is reversible, leaving open the option to proceed at a later time. Governor Carter announced acceptance of the Commission's recommendation in December, 1972.

In 1973, the City of Atlanta reversed its position of approval of the I-485 project, and in 1974, the Atlanta Regional Commission deleted I-485 from regional plan alternatives. The decision of the State Transportation Board to withdraw I-485 from the Interstate Highway System was made in November, 1974. The Federal Highway Administration approved the withdrawal in 1975.

> *Until recently, I thought I had made a mistake by not killing the controversial project. Now I am pleased with it. All the Department of Transportation ever wanted was the highest and best use of the property for the community.*
>
> *Mr. Tom Moreland, Former Commissioner,*
> *Georgia Department of Transportation*

---

[1] Metropolitan Atlanta Rapid Transit Authority.

In 1977, the State Transportation Board moved to dispose of all of I-485 properties north of St. Charles Avenue. Efforts to provide the north–south traffic service that I-485 was intended to provide resulted in the modification of planned improvements to a portion of the down-town connector, Interstate Routes I-75/I-85 that run in a north–south direction through the city. Both the State Transportation Board and the Atlanta Regional Commission (ARC), however, recognized the contin-ued need for transportation improvements in the east–west corridor. The ARC sought to address this need by adopting the Decatur Parkway and the Decatur Parkway Connector. In a separate action, the Trans-portation Board reserved the 219 acres of rights-of-way south of St. Charles Avenue and Ponce de Leon Avenue for future transportation purposes.

8.5   LOCAL PLAN DEVELOPMENT

As controversy continued over the use of rights-of-way cleared for I-485 and the Stone Mountain Tollway, ideas for its use were being developed in many quarters of the public and private sector. These proposals, described in the environmental impact statement for the Presidential Parkway (2), are abstracted in the following paragraphs.

In October, 1975, a conceptual plan entitled "The Great Park, A Proposal by The City of Atlanta" was published. This plan was produced through the com-bined efforts of a citizen ad hoc committee, a consultant (Arkhora Associates, Inc.), and the city. The Great Park concept plan called for a mix of parkland and housing uses with improvements to local and regional transportation systems. The transportation aspect of the Great Park plan involved an extension from the existing I-75/I-85 stub on new location southward to DeKalb Avenue. It required additional rights-of-way, cutting across existing residential and indus-trial property; it contained a reversed curvature alignment and an expensive skewed railroad crossing; and it did not address the problem of east–west movement in the Ponce de Leon corridor. The plan made no use of the cleared right-of-way for major transportation solutions, the purpose for which the land had been acquired. Since the Great Park concept did not address the legal and financial requirements of transferring land owned by GDOT for purposes other than transportation, the Department could not support this plan. It was not a viable option. No substantive action was therefore taken on this concept.

In March of 1976, Atlanta Great Park Planning, Inc. (AGPP) was created, rep-resenting neighborhood organizations, the City of Atlanta, the City of Decatur, DeKalb County, and the State of Georgia. Building on the Great Park concept, AGPP prepared a study entitled "Great Park II: Opportunities for Residential, Recreation and Economic Development." This report, published in 1977, acknowledged that "the Great Park could serve not only as a major recreation area for the Atlanta Metro Area, but can also provide a stimulus for industrial and economic development, neighborhood and housing restoration and a gen-eral revitalization of in-town communities." It was concluded, however, that further study was needed.

In 1978, AGPP received a grant from the National Endowment for the Arts to study detailed housing opportunities in the rights-of-way, with matching funds from the City of Atlanta. "The Great Park III—Housing Study" was prepared for AGPP by H. Randal Roark and was published in October, 1979. Although this study focused on housing, it recognized the need to consider other major issues "including a solution for providing adequate east-west through traffic movement, and improvement of local traffic conditions in the adjacent neighborhoods." Therefore, it adopted the transportation, open space, and economic development recommendations from the Great Park concept plan and the Great Park II study as a framework for other major elements of rights-of-way reuse. As previously discussed, no use of existing rights-of-way for transportation improvement was called for, and therefore the same legal restrictions previously cited applied in this case as well.

In August, 1978, the GDOT presented a park and road concept for use of the 219 acres. The plan proposed the use of 80 acres for a four-lane east–west roadway and a four-lane north–south roadway through the existing rights-of-way. The remaining 139 acres would be developed as a park, providing various recreational activities. The City of Atlanta and AGPP both opposed this plan as being excessively oriented toward transportation.

Another plan, "The Land Use Plan for I-485/Stone Mountain Freeway Property," was developed in 1979 by Land Use Consultants, Inc., John C. Portman, Jr., at the request of Governor George Busbee. This plan, presented to the governor in November, 1979, included a transportation element which called for an extension from the I-75/I-85 stub through the rights-of-way property, connecting DeKalb Avenue, which would become the Decatur Parkway, near the Inman Park–Reynoldstown MARTA station. This proposal involved the extensive use of tunneling in order to have the least disruption on the development of the "Great Park," costing an estimated $64 million. It also provided for a Presidential Library located just east of Moreland Avenue. Tunneling made this a very expensive alternative which did not address the transportation need through the Ponce de Leon Corridor.

In 1980, the Georgia General Assembly created the Great Park Authority to examine the Portman plan and other proposals and to "develop a master plan for the most appropriate utilization of the property constituting the Great Park and for the development of the Great Park."

The Authority presented a plan to the 1981 General Assembly similar to the Portman plan entitled "The Great Park Plan, A Master Plan and Development Strategy." This plan, also calling for a park and for housing facilities, included several alternative road alignments. The estimated cost of these alternatives ranged from about $34 million to $57 million, and their impacts included the displacement of 69 to 97 residences and 36 to 78 businesses. The General Assembly took no specific action on the Authority's proposal.

In the decade following the purchase of the rights-of-way for expressway facilities, a wide range of other uses for this land were proposed. Public and private interests, organizations, and individuals expressed ideas and opinions on how this land should be used. Selling the property, developing a large park, redeveloping housing, and a number of combinations of land uses including various transportation facilities were proposed and studied. Each of the reuse concepts met needs recognized by those who proposed them, but no one plan encompassed the wide spectrum of needs that had been identified. Thus, a consensus of support for any given plan could not be reached, and progress toward implementation of any reuse of the vacant land was thwarted.

This large tract of land within the city remained vacant year after year as efforts to resolve the impasse on how the land should be used continued unsuccessfully. It was from this background that the concept of the Presidential Parkway evolved.

> *Engineers need to understand that a highway project is not simply an engineering project. There are important social problems that must be taken into account in a meaningful and responsible way, preferably early in the planning process.*
>
> Mr. Charles M. Richards
> Senior Assistant Attorney General, Georgia

8.6   THE PRESIDENTIAL PARKWAY

When former President Jimmy Carter returned to Georgia in January, 1981, Andrew Young, his friend and former member of his cabinet, had been elected Mayor of Atlanta. Commissioner of Transportation Tom Moreland, who had served as Governor Carter's Commissioner, remained in that position. At that juncture, Mr. Carter was formulating plans to establish a Presidential Library but had not yet developed a plan to finance the library project. The large tract of unused highway land had become an eyesore and a place for crime. Public officials were weary of the controversy and the failed efforts to resolve the impasse as to how the highway land would be used.

The former president was much more actively involved in the selection of a library site and the promotion of the Presidential Parkway than was publicly revealed. The Portman plan, which had been presented to Governor George Busbee in November, 1979, provided for a Presidential Library located just east of Moreland Avenue. When that property was rejected as a library site, Commissioner Moreland invited Mr. and Mrs. Carter to view a location near the center of the cleared rights-of-way. That land, located on Copenhill[2] and possessing an excellent view of Atlanta's skyline, was readily approved as a

---

[2] Copenhill was the place from which Civil War General William Tecumseh Sherman stood and watched Atlanta burn.

library site, and plans for the library moved ahead without delay. Construction of suitable roadway access to the library would begin more than a decade later.

It was from this background that Mayor Andrew Young "confronted the need to develop a balance of uses for this land that together would serve the broadest public interest." Under the Mayor's direction, old and new ideas were blended into a composite plan to return the land to productive use without further delay and to enhance the quality of life in the City of Atlanta and in the State. The plan included the Jimmy Carter Presidential Library and a parkway consisting of a pair of two-lane roadways, one traveling east and one traveling west, that diverge to circumscribe the Presidential Complex.

The proposal offered the state a way to finally use the vacant 219 acres that had been purchased for highway purposes. It would provide the city with a prestigious tourist attraction not far from the central business district. It would provide the former President with a superb site for his library for minimal cost.[3] The Presidential Library complex is shown as Figure 8.2.

One group, however, was adamantly opposed to the proposal: the residents of the affected neighborhoods. Their position remained as it had been from the beginning: "No road." Furthermore, if a roadway had to be built, a four-lane parkway was not, in their view, an acceptable choice.

Solicitation of Support

In early 1982, Mayor Andrew Young organized a multidisciplinary team of professionals to assist him in communicating with and seeking the support of citizens and public officials. The team included an architect, an engineer, a professor of economics and finance, a professor of city planning, and an urban anthropologist. The mayor and individuals of the team conducted more than 70 meetings with citizens groups, individuals, and state and federal agencies. These meetings were held in churches, restaurants, schools, offices, homes, and at other locations in the affected area, with groups ranging in size from two up to 300 people. It was from these meetings that the details of a plan for the Presidential Parkway evolved and was adopted by the City of Atlanta. Engineering plans for the project were then developed by the Georgia Department of Transportation.

Design Features and Location

The proposed parkway was a pair of 24-foot roadways with a median ranging from 8 to 20 feet in width except at the Presidential Library. It extended 2.4 miles from the Downtown Connector stub to Ponce de Leon Avenue just east

---

[3] With the exception of the actual "footprints" for the buildings, the required land was declared a roadside park and made available to the Carter Center at no cost. The Center purchased highway rights-of-way elsewhere and exchanged it with GDOT for the building sites.

Figure 8.2   *The Carter Presidential Library. (Photo courtesy of the Carter Presidential Center.)*

of Lullwater Road (see Figure 8.3). A cross-sectional view of the parkway is shown as Figure 8.4.

The parkway was designed for a speed of 45 miles per hour. The design featured visual barriers to shield adjacent homes from automobiles on the parkway and bridges with bas-relief keystone panels depicting a presidential theme. Ornamental lighting bollards were proposed with low to medium intensity lighting to reduce light spill onto residential areas. About 40 percent of the parkway was to have been depressed. The design of the other areas featured earth berms, walls, or vegetation to lessen visual intrusion (2).

The project design included bicycle paths, jogging trails, and grading and landscaping for rest stops, picnic areas, and play lots.

The project would have used lands from four parks, a historic district included in the National Register of Historic Places, and one district eligible for inclusion in the National Register. The alignment impacted six neighborhoods, located as shown in Figure 8.5: the Old Fourth Ward, Poncey-Highland, Inman Park, Candler Park, Lake Claire, and Druid Hills. The environmental impact statement describes these neighborhoods as follows:

The residents of these neighborhoods are very diverse and represent a broad spectrum of the city's population. Likewise, the socio-economic characteristics of the neighborhoods are greatly varied. For example, the

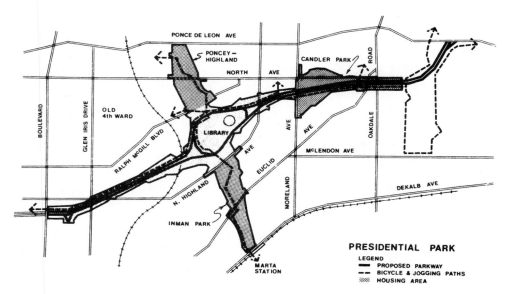

Figure 8.3   *Location map of the Presidental Parkway.*

Old Fourth Ward neighborhood residents, which are predominantly Black and live in an industrial setting, have a comparatively low average income level and have few voluntary community associations representing the neighborhood. Druid Hills residents in their suburban setting, on the other hand, have a rather high average income level and a well-organized community network represented by many voluntary associations. Also, the Druid Hills neighborhood is listed in the National Register of Historic Places.

The remaining neighborhoods found in the study area—Poncey-Highland, Inman Park, Candler Park, and Lake Claire—have a mixture of older residents and newcomers which are mostly younger, professional people who have moved into these neighborhoods over the past decade. Together many younger and older citizens share a sense of community, family, and spirituality. They are well represented in voluntary associations for the neighborhoods. . . .

The total number of households for all six of the above neighborhoods is 9,184; about 50% of the people are renters, with the highest percentage of ownership in Druid Hills. A comparison of the ethnic makeup of the neighborhoods shows that the Old Fourth Ward is 6.8% White and 92.7% Black; Candler Park is 84.4% White and 15.6% Black; Lake Claire is 81.6% White and 18.4% Black; and Druid Hills is 94.3% White, 3.3% Black, and 2.4% Asian. (2)

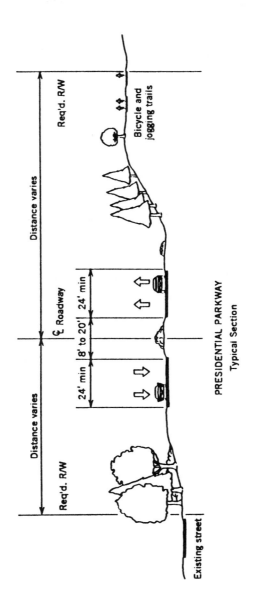

Figure 8.4 *Typical cross-section of the Presidential Parkway. (Courtesy of the Georgia Department of Transportation.)*

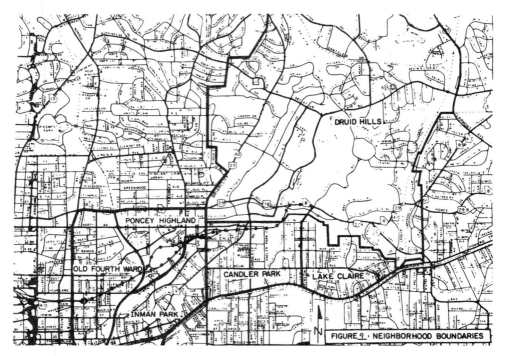

Figure 8.5   *Neighborhoods affected by the Presidential Parkway.*

Social and Environmental Assessment

By April 1983, the draft EIS for the Presidential Parkway had been prepared and approved by the Federal Highway Administration. Nearly 1000 copies of the draft EIS were distributed to individuals who had expressed an interest in the project.

Reference 2 describes the public meetings that were conducted to explain the Presidential Parkway to interested citizens as follows:

> *Between May 31 and June 2, 1983, three public information meetings were conducted in neighborhoods adjacent to the project. The meetings were informal where individuals could review displays, could ask questions, and could speak to a court reporter if they wished to enter their comments into the public record. These comments were made a part of the hearing transcript.*
>
> *Public response was light at the Howard School but several hundred people attended the Little Five Points Community Center meeting and a great many made statements to the court reporter. Because of the great turnout and expected interest in the Candler Park neighborhood two court reporters were available at the third meeting at the Epworth Methodist Church.*

A fourth public meeting was held at the Atlanta Civic Center on the afternoon of the public hearing, June 7, 1983. Again court reporters were available and questions were individually answered. Later that evening the public hearing was conducted which consisted of a formal presentation followed by a public comment session. Five court reporters were available in the lobby and one in the auditorium to receive spoken comments, and written comments were also accepted. GDOT estimated 1500 to 2000 people attended the public hearing, although opponents of the project would estimate 3000 or more. The hearing record and public comment period were held open until July 25, 1983 in response to public request.

Regardless of the estimates of hearing attendees 728 people submitted written comments and some of these comments contained signed petitions with as many as 700+ signatures. Also 742 people spoke to a court reporter at one or more of the public meetings. Although there was a substantial amount of duplication in which individuals spoke more than once at information meetings or the hearing, or both spoke, wrote letters, or signed petitions; the total number of people involved in some manner was in excess of 2000. (2)

Comments on the draft EIS were sought and received from six federal agencies and eight state and local agencies.

Public Opposition to the Presidential Parkway

By the time of the public information meetings in June 1983, public opposition to the parkway was strong and well-organized. CAUTION, Inc.[4], a coalition of neighborhood groups, had been organized in 1982 and empowered to represent the organizations within narrow, well-defined areas in opposition to the parkway. The determination and commitment of the neighborhood residents to fight the project is shown by the fact that CAUTION, Inc. was able to raise more than $800,000 during the course of the controversy.

The emotional intensity of the opposition to the project was unprecedented, at least in the State of Georgia (see Figure 8.6). For approximately two years, opposition was manifest in statements at the public hearings, letters to GDOT, petitions and resolutions, and display advertisements in the Atlanta newspapers.[5] Overall, there were more than 1700 public statements concerning the

---

[4] CAUTION is an acronym which stands for Citizens Against Unnecessary Thoroughfares In Older Neighborhoods.

[5] On February 4, 1985, CAUTION, Inc. placed a full-page advertisement in the Atlanta newspapers entitled "The Carter Library is being built. But why, Mr. President, are you determined to destroy historic neighborhoods in Atlanta with a 'parkway' built on lies and deceit?" The strongly worded message was also critical of Mayor Andrew Young who was accused of betraying his supporters by withdrawing his public opposition to the parkway after he was elected.

Figure 8.6   *Flyer used by CAUTION, Inc. in opposition to the Presidential Parkway.*

project. Not all of the statements were in opposition to the project; however, the predominant tone of the comments was unfavorable to the proposed work.

Administrative Actions

On August 4, 1983, ten days after the expiration of the period for comment on the draft EIS, the GDOT made the decision to proceed with preparation of the final EIS around the build, that is, parkway, option. The GDOT and FHWA also began preparation of a preliminary case report (PCR) pursuant to section 106 of the National Historic Preservation Act of 1966 to evaluate the impact of the project on historic and archeological resources. The PCR was forwarded to the United States Advisory Council on Historic Preservation (ACHP) on November 3, 1983. Copies of the PCR were made available for public comment.

After a review of this preliminary report, the ACHP recommended that the GDOT and FHWA give further consideration to the Moreland Avenue termination alternative in conjunction with other transportation improvements. The

FHWA responded that the Moreland Avenue alternative and others had been adequately considered but were not feasible or prudent. Later, the Council recommended that the parkway not be built but that the Carter Complex should be constructed on the site. The Council's written findings, forwarded to the Secretary of the USDOT on March 13, 1984, were largely critical of the stated need for the project and of the attempt to link the parkway and the Complex. The FHWA responded to the comments on April 17, 1984.

On May 22, 1984, the FHWA approved the final EIS. Copies of the statement were distributed to interested parties and notice of the approval was published in the *Federal Register*. In addition to alternatives raised in the draft EIS, the final EIS discussed MARTA, a light rail proposal, one-way pairings of streets, staggered work hours, and toll charges and provided a more detailed discussion of the Decatur Parkway alternative.

The Department of Interior (DOI), Environmental Protection Agency (EPA), individuals, and organizations submitted comments on the final EIS. The DOI decided that the statement did not adequately respond to the department's comments on the draft EIS and was not responsive to the requirements of section 4(f) (see Section 8.2). Accordingly, the department objected to section 4(f) approval of the project.

On June 25, 1984, the chairman of the ACHP filed a formal notice of referral with the Council on Environmental Quality (CEQ). The CEQ solicited written comments from the public on the national importance of the parkway and held a public meeting on July 17, 1984. On September 20, 1984, the CEQ determined that the proposed parkway was not of national importance and declined to further review the project. The CEQ requested the FHWA to resume its normal decision-making process. On September 21, 1984, the FHWA, acting through William Van Luchene, the designee of the Secretary of USDOT, approved and executed a record of decision. (*3*)

8.7 LITIGATION

Roadway opponents brought suit in the U.S. District Court in Atlanta in September, 1984 challenging the environmental impact statement and seeking an injunction to stop construction of the project. Thus began a series of court actions in opposition of the parkway construction that would last more than seven years and cost hundreds of thousands of dollars. These actions would not stop the roadway, but they would significantly change its length, function, and design features.

The initial trial was held on October 22–25, 1984. District Judge William O'Kelly ruled against the plaintiffs and refused to stop the parkway construction. The matter was appealed to the U.S. Court of Appeals which, in September, 1985, agreed with the overall adequacy of the EIS but sent the order back to the Secretary of Transportation for a clarification of section 4(f) findings regarding three alternative plans. The court stated:

In summary, the case must be remanded to the Secretary for adequate findings of the impact on 4(f) properties caused by the Decatur Parkway and the two Moreland Avenue plans. This review should encompass an accurate assessment of the characteristics of the property that will be affected by the alternative, e.g., if the property is in a historic district, whether it has been previously impacted by commercial development and if so, to what extent. The Secretary's review must also address the quantity of harm that will accrue to the park or historic site and the nature of that harm, e.g., visual impact or physical taking. It will not suffice to simply state that an alternative route would affect 4(f) properties without providing some rational, documented basis for such a conclusion. In short, the same consideration must be given to whether these alternative routes would minimize harm to the section 4(f) properties as was accorded the adopted route. (3)

In response to this ruling, GDOT produced an addendum to the Section 4(f) statement which was published in December 1985 (4).

Ultimately, it was in the political arena that the citizens were successful. The actions in the courts were simply a way of postponing construction until the political battle could be won.

Ms. Gail Waldorff, Member of CAUTION, Inc.
Member of Mediation Panel

Civil Disobedience

There was great concern among the parkway opponents that GDOT would inflict great damage to the parks before the project could be stopped in the courts. There could be a remedy at law but not a remedy in fact. In early 1985, a road protest group known as "Roadbusters" erected a tent city in historic Shady Side Park. Eventually, 50 of the protestors were arrested. Meanwhile, the controversy continued to be argued in the courts.

By the autumn of 1984, it appeared that the Presidential Parkway would finally be built. On October 26, bids were received on the project, and Shepherd Construction Company was announced as the apparent low bidder for the grading and paving work, and Arapaho Construction Co., Inc. was reported to be the low bidder for the construction of the bridges. On November 19, 26 days later, the Atlanta City Council, chaired by Council President Marvin Arrington, approved an ordinance transferring parklands owned by the city to GDOT for the parkway in exchange for state-owned property for the improvement of a golf course. Work started on the parkway project on December 6, 1984.

Several events then transpired which resulted in additional litigation.

December 18, 1984.   WGST radio reported that Arrington Enterprises, with City Council President Marvin Arrington as majority owner, was a Disadvantaged Business Enterprise (DBE) subcontractor on the Presidential Parkway Project.

January 15, 1985. The Attorney General of Georgia released the results of an investigation that had been requested by Transportation Commissioner Tom Moreland. The investigation concluded that Mr. Arrington's participation in the Presidential Parkway project constituted a conflict of interest.

January 25, 1985. Parkway opponents filed two lawsuits in Fulton County Superior Court:

1. One lawsuit asked the court to set aside the contract between GDOT and Shepherd Construction Company because of alleged improprieties in the bidding process. In this case, the trial court judge ruled in favor of the residents, but the ruling was reversed on appeal.

2. The other lawsuit was filed against the City of Atlanta seeking to declare the land transfer for the parkway null and void because of Mr. Arrington's conflict of interest. The ruling in this case was also reversed by the Court of Appeals. The appellate court invalidated the land transfer but left the City Council free to take whatever action it deemed fit to dispose of the parklands.

On May 20, 1985, the Atlanta City Council passed another ordinance which authorized a second transfer of four parks for the parkway. Unlike the first ordinance, however, this one imposed a number of restrictions on the transfer, such as, a 35 mph speed limit on the parkway, a ban on trucks and heavy vehicles, and a ban against widening Ponce de Leon Avenue east of Moreland Avenue. GDOT accepted the deed after objecting to the conditions and its "reverter" clause. The GDOT then filed a petition in DeKalb Superior Court asking it to condemn the reverter and any other interest the city might have retained.

Residents asked for and were granted permission to intervene in the case. On July 1, 1985, the trial judge dismissed GDOT's condemnation petition. On the following day, two of the residents filed suit to void the land transfer from the City of Atlanta and to enjoin any further construction of the parkway. On September 4, trial court Judge Clarence Seeliger issued an order voiding the land transfer and a permanent injunction against further construction on any portion of the parkway.

This order was appealed to the state supreme court, which sided with the roadway opponents and vacated the land transfer. The court said, in effect, that the current state law did not permit the state to condemn municipal property but that the General Assembly could "certainly provide the DOT with the authority and procedures to condemn any municipal property." The court also lifted the trial court's permanent injunction on construction on land not included in the parklands controversy and allowed GDOT to proceed as it desired "at its peril."

In 1986, the Georgia General Assembly created a condemnation commission, giving GDOT the legal mechanism to condemn the parkland. GDOT then filed an action in DeKalb County Superior Court to condemn the city's parkland, whereupon the residents were again allowed to intervene and filed an action to set aside the declaration of taking. Trial Court Judge Clarence Seeliger enjoined GDOT from further construction of the Presidential Parkway until the merits of the case could be determined. GDOT appealed this injunction but lost in the Georgia Supreme Court.

During those proceedings, Judge Seeliger also ordered the parties to mediate the case and fixed a deadline for the parties to furnish the names of those who would represent them in mediation. The Georgia Supreme Court reversed Judge Seeliger's order but stated:

> *We wish to encourage the use of mediation as a means of dispute resolution. At the same time we recognize that parties may not be ordered to settle their disputes. A great service a court may provide for litigants is a referral to mediation. There are times when parties have reached a standstill in settlement negotiations such that for either party to suggest mediation is to perhaps admit a weakness or at least suggest he is willing to yield further. At this point a referral to mediation by the court may secretly be welcomed by both sides. Then too, it may be that the parties are simply unaware of the benefit which may flow from mediation and a referral by a court may serve to introduce them to the process. In any event the court should simply make the referral and leave it to the parties from that point. . . .*
>
> *It is incongruous to say one may order another to mediate a dispute as that violates the first premise of mediation, that it is a voluntary process. However, we hold a trial court has the authority to refer the parties to mediation. (5)*

8.8 MEDIATION

By early 1991, the political climate had changed in Atlanta. The state had new leadership in Governor Zell Miller and Lt. Governor Pierre Howard, and Mayor Maynard Jackson had replaced Andrew Young. At a press conference at the state capitol in February, 1991, 33 elected officials from Atlanta and Fulton and DeKalb Counties went on record in opposition to the Presidential Parkway. By then, the controversy had endured for 30 years, and the parties had been engaged in the courts for seven years.

DeKalb County Superior Court Judge Clarence Seeliger wanted the matter settled and exerted pressure on the litigants to agree to mediation. Commissioner Hal Rives, a civil engineer and career employee of GDOT, was nearing retirement and decided to try to bring the long controversy to a conclusion. Having established their legal right not to be forced to mediate, the GDOT agreed to do so.

Mediation began in March, 1991. The participants included:

Representing the State	Commissioner Hal Rives
	Mr. Charles M. Richards, Attorney
	Mr. George Shingler, Attorney
Representing the City	Mr. Leon Eplan, Commissioner of Planning
	Mr. John Reid, Chief Executive Officer
	Mr. Michael Coleman, Attorney
	Mr. Kendric E. Smith, Attorney
Representing CAUTION, Inc.	Mr. Richard Ossof
	Ms. Gail Waldorff
	Ms. Catherine Bradshaw
	Mr. Robert B. Remar, Attorney
Professional Mediators	Mr. J. Michael Keating, Attorney
	Ms. Edith B. Prim, Attorney

After an initial organizational meeting at a downtown office building, the mediation was carried out in conference rooms located in neutral locations, first, at a motor hotel, and later in a downtown church.

Commissioner Rives brought to the mediation a significant concession by his department. He proposed that the parkway terminate at Moreland Avenue. This would remove the impact of the project on four public parks and the Druid Hills and Candler Park Historic Districts. Nevertheless, subsequent negotiations did not proceed smoothly, and in fact, after several meetings, on July 3, 1991, the proceedings dissolved without an agreement. On the following day, Commissioner Rives was stricken with illness and was unable to return to work until August 19.

One of the important lessons to be learned from this controversy is that you must be persistant but not be afraid to compromise. The parkway not only had to provide access to the Carter Library. It had to fulfill at least a sizeable portion of the transportation need in the corridor. I felt that it should become an asset to the communities involved, and I was willing to give assurance that it would not be extended.

Mr. Hal Rives, Former Commissioner
Georgia Department of Transportation

There remained a strong desire on the part of all of the participants in the mediation to settle the matter. Judge Seeliger had set a trial date for September 3, and neither GDOT nor CAUTION, Inc. wanted the matter settled in the courts. After several meetings between CAUTION, Inc. representatives and public and political leaders, arrangements were made to resume negotiations.

On August 1, 1991, a new Transportation Commissioner, Wayne Shackelford, was named by the Transportation Board. Although he would not take office until November 1, 1991, Mr. Shackelford became actively involved in the mediation process. Thus, when the mediation resumed on Tuesday, August 27, GDOT was represented by both the commissioner and the commissioner-elect.

When the mediators reconvened, Atlanta Planning Commissioner Leon Eplan presented a plan that would form the basis for the resolution of the controversy. During the morning of August 27, however, all the distrust between GDOT and CAUTION, Inc. remained. Commissioner Rives recommended several changes to the city's proposal, and when the meeting adjourned for lunch, an agreement did not appear near.

During the lunch hour and extending into the afternoon, representatives of GDOT and CAUTION, Inc. caucused separately. During this period, Commissioner-Elect Shackelford met with Lt. Governor Howard who pressed GDOT to try harder to reach an agreement.

The mediators reassembled at 4:00 P.M. By 6:30 P.M., they had reached agreement on the essential elements of the parkway plan.

State engineers worked into the night on a preliminary engineering plan that embodied the terms of the agreement. Engineers Walker Scott and Joe Palladi devised a design feature that would be a key to making the parkway more acceptable to the neighborhood representatives. Where originally a grade separation structure had been proposed (and constructed) for the parkway's intersection with Boulevard, the engineers suggested that a hill be built to create a signalized at-grade intersection, creating a more natural transition from the I-75/85 freeway to the parkway environment.

The mediators reconvened the following day at 11:00 A.M. and developed the formal language of the agreement. There was, at this juncture, according to one of the participants, a feeling of euphoria. The governor, the lieutenant governor, the mayor, and other political leaders were summoned for a press conference where the agreement was publicly announced. (There would be additional meetings to work out the details, and the formal agreement would not be signed by Judge Clarence Seeliger until June 25, 1992.)

What I learned from about the process is that mediation can and does work provided every participant is allowed to fully express his or her fears, frustrations and committments. People-friendly cities are going to have to be the focus of all of us who are responsible for infrastructure. We must balance the abilities of roadways to move people and vehicles with what is acceptable and what should be acceptable to a community.

Mr. Wayne Shackelford, Commissioner
Georgia Department of Transportation

8.9   THE FREEDOM PARKWAY

The agreement reached by the mediators was set forth in great detail in a formal 47-page document signed by all of the principals and approved by Judge Seeliger (6). The new parkway would be known as Freedom Parkway.

The settlement provided, in part, for the following: (1) the construction of a meandering parkway with six at-grade intersections, a four-lane termination point at Ponce de Leon Avenue west of Barnett Street, a one-lane directional loop around the Carter Center, and a two-lane termination point at Moreland Avenue; (2) the coordinated and comprehensive disposition of project rights-of-way not utilized for road purposes, including rights-of-way previously acquired for the I-485 and Stone Mountain Tollway projects . . . for parks and housing in a comprehensive manner pursuant to a plan mutually developed by the City, the affected neighborhoods, and DOT; (3) creation of a significant amount of park land, along with linkage of the Martin Luther King, Jr. Historic District and the Carter Center; (4) the mutual agreement to support legislation necessary to effectuate the settlement; and (5) the agreement of DOT to build no further limited-access highways in the project area. (6)

In addition, the settlement provided that, at the time specified, the GDOT would dismiss the condemnation action then pending in the DeKalb County Superior Court.

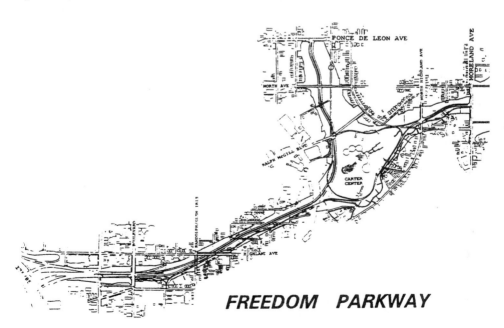

Figure 8.7   *Plan view of the Freedom Parkway. (Courtesy of the Georgia Department of Transportation.)*

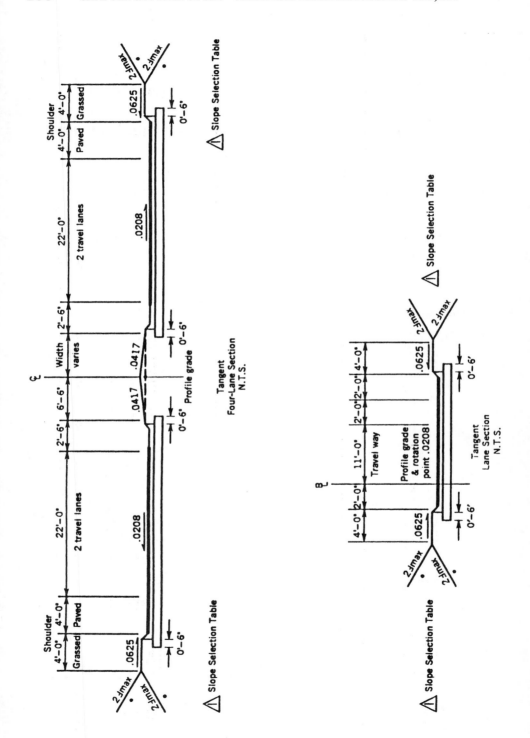

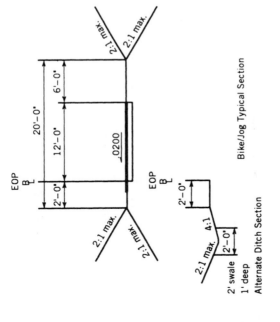

Figure 8.8 *Typical cross-section of Freedom Parkway. (Courtesy of the Georgia Department of Transportation.)*

Design Features of the Freedom Parkway

The Freedom Parkway design incorporated curvilinear alignments with features intended to slow traffic to 35 mph. Trucks with gross weights in excess of 10,000 lb would not be permitted to use the parkway. The design called for travel lanes of 11 feet, a 2-foot curb and gutter on the left side, and a 2-foot paved shoulder bordered by a mountable curb and 2-foot gutter on the right. A grassy shoulder at least 4 feet in width was also to be provided along the outer edges of the traveled way. The design also featured gentle slopes that flow with existing topography and landscaped medians approximately 14 feet in width. The planned amenities for the Presidential Parkway were incorporated into the approved Freedom Parkway plans. These included a bicycle-jogging path, landscaping, playgrounds, and special treatments and facings for bridges, walls, and structures.

A plan view of the Freedom Parkway is shown as Figure 8.7, and a sketch of the cross-section is shown as Figure 8.8.

Congressional Approval

To avoid the need to repeat the environmental assessment mandated by federal laws, the U.S. Congress passed legislation on November 26, 1991 that stated in part:

> *Notwithstanding any other provision of law, the Secretary shall approve the construction of the Department of Transportation project MEACU-9152(2) in Fulton County, Georgia, as described in the legal settlement agreed to for the project by the Georgia Department of Transportation, the city of Atlanta, and CAUTION, Inc. Execution of the settlement agreement by those parties and approval of the settlement agreement by the DeKalb County, Georgia Superior Court shall be deemed to constitute full compliance with all Federal laws applicable to carrying out the project. (2)*

8.10 CONCLUSION

From concept to the approval of a final design, Atlanta's Freedom Parkway project extended over a period of more than 30 years. The protracted controversy over this project involved to varying degrees five mayors, six transportation commissioners, seven governors, and a former president of the United States (see Figure 8.9). It involved all three branches of government: executive, legislative, and judicial; and all three levels of government: federal, state, and local.

The final design of the parkway barely resembles the highway facility that was originally envisioned.

Because of the long and bitter dispute, there remains among the affected residents some distrust of the GDOT. Following the resolution of the controversy, however, feelings of relief and satisfaction were shared by major actors on both sides of the dispute: relief that the controversy had finally been settled and

Year	Major Events Relating to Parkway Controversy
1960	
1961	GDOT begins to purchase land for freeways.
1962	
1963	
1964	
1965	
1966	
1967	
1968	
1969	National Environmental Policy Act becomes law.
1970	
1971	Action suspended on I-485 pending EIS.
1972	Gov. Carter agrees to suspend work on Stone Mtn. Tollway.
1973	City of Atlanta reverses its approval of I-485.
1974	Atlanta Regional Comm. deletes I-485 from regional plan.
1975	FHWA approves withdrawal of I-485 from interstate system.
1976	Great Park Plans published (1975–78).
1977	GDOT agrees to sell some land but retains 219 acres.
1978	GDOT publishes plan for park and roadway.
1979	Portman plan proposed and rejected.
1980	Ga. General Assembly creates Authority to study proposals.
1981	Authority presents plan but Assembly takes no action in proposal.
1982	Presidential Parkway is proposed; CAUTION, Inc. is formed.
1983	Draft EIS published; over 3,000 opponents attend hearing.
1984	Final EIS published and approved by FHWA; litigation begins.
1985	
1986	
1987	
1988	Litigation (1984–1991)
1989	
1990	
1991	Mediation begins in March; agreement reached in October.
1992	Freedom Parkway contract let for bids in July.

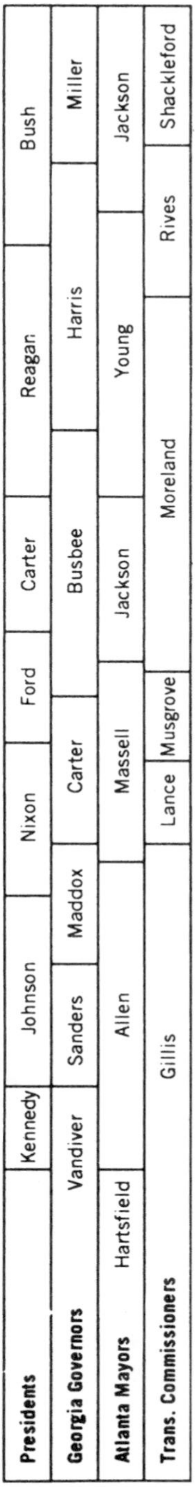

Presidents
Kennedy
Johnson
Nixon
Ford
Carter
Reagan
Bush
Georgia Governors
Vandiver
Sanders
Maddox
Carter
Busbee
Harris
Miller
Atlanta Mayors
Hartsfield
Allen
Massell
Jackson
Young
Jackson
Trans. Commissioners
Gillis
Lance
Musgrove
Moreland
Rives
Shackleford

Figure 8.9 *Time chart of major events relating to Presidential Parkway controversy.*

satisfaction that they had played a part in bringing the matter to a satisfactory conclusion.

The engineer in the public sector may face special perils. In the private sector, it is generally clear who the client is and what his interests and objectives are. Public engineering, however, is to a large degree, a political process. That is as it should be. But though intended to serve the "public good", public engineering is particularly vulnerable to manipulation to serve inherently corrupt ends. It can be painfully difficult for the ambitious junior engineer to keep his integrity intact.

Mr. Richard Ossof, Member of CAUTION, Inc.
Member of Mediation Panel

The essential elements of this case study are by no means unique. Many engineering projects involve complex interactions between engineers, public officials, and citizens. Views of various segments of society vary over time, and those views may or not be reflected in the positions taken by public leaders. One segment of citizens who perceive public and individual benefits from an engineering project may strongly support the project. Another segment may focus on the negative impacts of the project and oppose it with great anger and emotion. The ensuing controversy may stop, delay, or change the engineer's concept of the desired elements of design. In such cases, it is imperative that engineers work closely with elected officials and listen carefully to concerned citizens in seeking a solution that is most suitable for the public as a whole.

REFERENCES

1. WRIGHT, PAUL, H. *Highway Engineering,* 6th Edition, John Wiley & Sons, Inc., New York, 1996.

2. *Final Environment Impact Statement, Presidential Parkway, Atlanta, Georgia, Project M-9152(2),* U.S. Department of Transportation, Federal Highway Administration, and Georgia Department of Transportation, May, 1984.

3. *Druid Hills Civic Association, Inc., et al., Plaintiffs-Appellants, v. The Federal Highway Administration, et al., Defendants-Appelles. 772 Federal Reporter, 2d Series (1985).*

4. *Project M-9152(2), Fulton/DeKalb Counties, Addendum to Section 4(f) Statement,* Federal Highway Administration and Georgia Department of Transportation, December, 1985.

5. *Department of Transportation v. City of Atlanta, et al.,* Case No. 46479, (380 SE2d 265), April Term, 1989.

6. *Settlement Agreement Between Department of Transportation, State of Georgia, Condemnor, and 7.802 Acres of Land; Certain Easement Rights; and the City of Atlanta, Condemnees, and David Vaughn, et al., Intervenors,* Superior Court of DeKalb County, State of Georgia, June 17, 1992.

EXERCISES

8.1 Discuss the following statements:
   a. Engineering is much more than solving mathematical equations.
   b. Engineers are best equipped to design engineering projects. Politicians and the public should not interfere with their work.
   c. Engineering educators are doing a poor job of describing to students a true picture of what engineering is really like. More training is needed in how to communicate with people and to make their concerns and desires an essential part of the engineering design process.
   d. An engineering work may use scarce resources or may do irreparable harm to the environment. An engineer has a responsibility to future generations to protect and preserve the earth.

8.2 Discuss the role of the judiciary in helping to resolve disputes among engineering planners and designers, those who use their works, and those who are negatively impacted by them. Cite an example in your locality where it has become necessary for the courts to resolve such a dispute.

8.3 This case study illustrates the impacts of a *public* facility on neighborhoods and the environment. In what ways might *private corporations* impact their neighbors and the environment? What major federal laws and regulations exist to minimize social and environmental impacts of actions by private corporations?

8.4 How does an engineer weigh the benefits of his or her designs for certain segments of society against the possible negative impacts of those designs to other segments of society and the environment? Give two examples of such tradeoffs.

An Exemplary Engineering Achievement

Space Shuttle Atlantis streaks into the sky on
September 8, 2000. On the 11-day mission to the
International Space Station, the seven-person crew
performed support tasks in orbit, transferred
supplies, and prepared the living quarters for the
newly arrived Zvezda Service Module. (Courtesy
of the National Aeronautics and Space
Administration.)

CHAPTER NINE

A CASE STUDY— THE SPACE SHUTTLE *CHALLENGER* ACCIDENT

Here we examine the circumstances and events leading to the aftermath of one of the most dramatic engineering failures of the twentieth century: the Space Shuttle *Challenger* accident. This material was largely abstracted from the *Report of the Presidential Commission on the Space Shuttle* Challenger *Accident* (1). It also draws from two NASA documents: *NASA, The First 25 Years, 1958–1983* (2), and *The Space Shuttle at Work* (3).

9.1 BACKGROUND

In 1958, a unique federal agency was established: the National Aeronautics and Space Administration (NASA). NASA was charged to "plan, direct, and conduct aeronautical and space activities." NASA was not an entirely new organization. It had as its nucleus the National Advisory Committee for Aeronautics (NACA), an organization that had provided leadership in aeronautical research since 1915.

NASA was created in the wake of the successful orbiting of the Russian space satellite Sputnik on October 4, 1957. It was organized as a civilian agency "devoted to peaceful programs for the benefit of mankind." NASA became a network of research and development centers and facilities across the United States with its headquarters in Washington, DC.

Since 1958, NASA has achieved an extraordinary array of advancements in aeronautics and space flight. The agency's application satellites have enhanced weather forecasting, revolutionized communications, and provided earth resources information for a wide range of interests including land use and water resources management, agriculture, geology, forestry, and mapping and charting. These and other benefits can be traced to NASA's work in the development of launch vehicles to overcome gravitational forces and in space flight.

In 1961, President John F. Kennedy proclaimed a national commitment to land a man on the moon and to return him safely to earth. NASA achieved this goal with three projects: Mercury, Gemini, and Apollo.

Project Mercury's solo flights demonstrated the ability to orbit a manned spacecraft around the earth and showed that humans could function in space and return safely to earth.

Project Gemini showed the capability of conducting space flights up to two weeks in duration. This project also showed that it was possible for a spacecraft to rendezvous with other orbiting vehicles and to precisely and safely enter the atmosphere and land at a preselected point on earth. Gemini involved 10 flights with two-man crews.

Project Apollo achieved the national goal of landing Americans on the moon and returning them safely to earth. In addition, it carried out a program of scientific explorations of the moon and developed man's capability to work in the lunar environment. Apollo employed three-man crews and a three-part spacecraft. In the Apollo project, there were 11 flights, including six landings on the lunar surface.

9.2   THE SPACE SHUTTLE

The space shuttle concept had its genesis in the 1960s, when the Apollo lunar landing spacecraft was in full development but had not yet flown. From the earliest days of the space program, it seemed logical that the goal of frequent, economical access to space might best be served by a reusable launch system.

The first space shuttle design was based on a "fly back" concept in which two stages, each manned, would fly back to a horizontal, airplane-like landing. The first stage was a huge, winged, rocket-powered vehicle that would carry the smaller second stage piggyback; the carrier would provide the thrust for liftoff and flight through the atmosphere, then release its passenger—the orbiting vehicle—and return to earth. The orbiter, containing the crew and payload, would continue into space under its own rocket power, complete its mission, and then fly back to earth.

The "fly back" concept was discarded in 1971 as government and industry studies sought developmental economies in the configuration. A major design change involved the elimination of the orbiter's internal tanks and carrying the propellant in a single, disposable external tank. For the launch system, NASA examined a number of possibilities but chose recoverable solid rocket boosters because of their low development costs.

What emerged from these design decisions was a three-element system composed of the orbiter, an expendable external fuel tank carrying liquid propellants for the orbiter's engines and two recoverable solid rocket boosters (see Figure 9.1). It would cost about half what the two-stage "fly back" design would have cost. To achieve that reduction, NASA had to accept somewhat higher system operating costs and sacrifice full reusability. The compromise

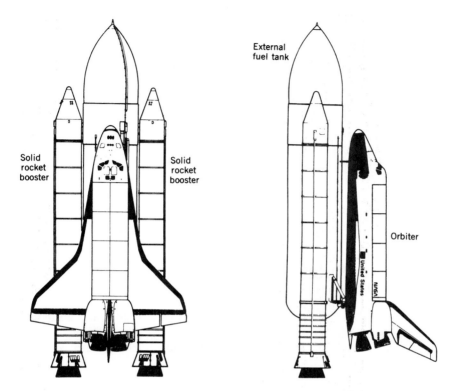

Figure 9.1   *An artist's drawing depicts the space shuttle stacked for launch in view from dorsal side of orbiter (left) and from the left side of stack.* (Source: *Reference 1.*)

design retained recoverability and reuse of two of the three elements and still promised to trim substantially the cost of delivering payloads to orbit.

The final configuration was selected in March 1972.

In an increasingly austere fiscal environment, NASA struggled through the shuttle development years of the 1970s. The planned five-orbiter fleet was reduced to four. Budgetary difficulties were compounded by engineering problems and, inevitably in a major new system whose development pushes the frontiers of technology, there was cost growth. This combination of factors induced schedule slippage. The initial orbital test flights were delayed by more than two years.

The first shuttle test flights were conducted at Dryden Flight Research Facility, California, in 1977. The test craft was the Orbiter *Enterprise*, a full-size vehicle that lacked engines and other systems needed for orbital flight. The purpose of these tests was to check out the aerodynamic and flight control characteristics of the Orbiter in atmospheric flight. Mounted piggyback atop a modified Boeing 747, the *Enterprise* was carried to altitude and released for a gliding approach and landing at the Mojave Desert test center. Five such flights were made.

The *Enterprise* test flights were followed by extensive ground tests of the shuttle systems, including vibration tests of the entire assembly at the Marshall Space Flight Center, Huntsville, Alabama (hereafter called Marshall). Main engine test firings were conducted at the National Space Technology Laboratories at Bay St. Louis, Mississippi, and on the launch pad at the Kennedy Space Center, Merritt Island, Florida (hereafter called Kennedy).

By early 1981, the space shuttle was ready for an orbital flight test program. The program consisted of four flights with more than 1000 tests and data collection procedures.

The orbital test program came to an end in July 1982, with 95 percent of its objectives accomplished. NASA declared the space shuttle "operational" and began the "operational phase" of the space shuttle program.

A total of 21 shuttle missions were launched from late 1982 to January 1986. Thus, including the initial orbital tests, the space shuttle flew 24 successful missions over a 57-month period. *Columbia* made seven trips into space, *Discovery* six, and *Atlantis* two. *Challenger* flew most frequently—nine times prior to its fateful last flight.

In those 24 flights, the shuttle demonstrated its ability to deliver a wide variety of payloads, its ability to serve as an orbital laboratory, its utility as a platform for erection of large structures, and its use for retrieval and repair of orbiting satellites.

9.3   FROM EARTH TO ORBIT

Getting the orbiter into space follows a familiar pattern tested by earlier manned flights and hundreds of unmanned ones: simply dropping off parts of the vehicle, as they run out of fuel, while the rest continues into orbit.

The first to go are the solid rocket boosters (see Figure 9.2). Standing 150 feet from nozzle to nose and 12 feet in diameter, the boosters are attached near their ends to the external tank, slightly taller and twice as fat, which in turn is attached to the Orbiter. A shuttle booster is the largest solid-fuel rocket ever

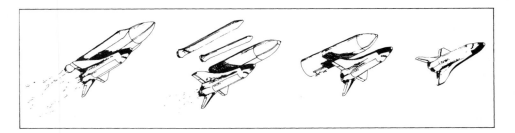

Figure 9.2   *The launching of the space shuttle. (Source: Reference 3.)*

flown, the first built for use on a manned spacecraft, and the first designed for reuse. It is assembled from seamless segments of half-inch steel, lined with heavy insulation, that are filled with propellant at the manufacturing site in Utah and shipped on railway flat cars to Kennedy for assembly—or, for south-north flights, Vandenberg Air Force Base north of Los Angeles.

The propellant looks and feels like the hard rubber of a typewriter eraser. It is a mixture of aluminum powder as fuel, aluminum perchlorate powder as an oxidizer, a dash of iron oxide as a catalyst to speed the burning rate, and a polymer binder that also served as a fuel. It is not sensitive to ignition by static, friction, or impact; and it will not detonate during storage.

For launch, the propellant—1.1 million pounds in each booster—is ignited by a small rocket motor. Flame spreads over the exposed face of the propellant in about 0.15 second, and the motor is up to full operating pressure in less than half a second. As the propellant burns, at a temperature of about 3200°C, huge quantities of hot gases speed through the nozzle, which restricts their flow and increases the pressure, producing thrust as they spew from the exit cone. The two boosters' thrust of 5,200,000 pounds augments the 1,125,000-pound thrust of the Orbiter's three main engines through the first two minutes of ascent.

After burning out, the solid rocket boosters are cut loose from the external tank by electrically fired explosive devices and are moved away by small rocket separation motors, four near the nose of each and four aft, fired by command from the orbiter. The spent boosters coast upward and then fall earthward for almost four minutes, reaching a speed of 2900 mph before being slowed by atmospheric drag. From about 3 miles each is lowered by a succession of parachutes to a splashdown of about 60 mph.

Since the empty rocket enters the water with the nozzle down, air is trapped in the upper end to float it upright until one of two recovery vessels, summoned by a radio beacon and flashing light, attaches lines to tow it back to the launch center. There the booster is taken apart and the rocket segments are shipped to the Utah factory, where they are cleaned out, inspected for cracks, pressure-tested, relined, reloaded, and reshipped to the site. There the booster is refurbished and reassembled to fly again.

The second element of the shuttle that is discarded during ascent to orbit, and the only major part not used again, is the external tank. As tall (153 feet) as a 15-story building and as big (27.5 feet in diameter) as a farm silo, the tank contains the liquid hydrogen and liquid oxygen that fuel the shuttle's three main engines in the stern of the orbiter. The external tank forms the backbone of the entire vehicle during launch.

Made of aluminum alloy up to 2 inches thick, the external tank is actually two propellant tanks connected by a cylindrical collar that houses control equipment. The nose curves to a point tipped by a lightning rod. The forward tank is loaded with 140,000 gallons of liquid oxygen, chilled to minus 147.2°C, weighing 1,330,000 pounds The one forming the aft section, 2½ times larger, contains 380,000 gallons of liquid hydrogen at minus 250°C. This weighs only 223,000 pounds because liquid hydrogen is 16 times lighter.

After the solid rocket boosters separate at 31 miles altitude, the orbiter, with the main engines still firing, carries the external tank to near orbital velocity at about 70 miles above earth. There, eight minutes after takeoff, the now-empty tank separates and falls in a planned trajectory into the Indian Ocean on missions from Kennedy or the South Pacific on flights from Vandenberg Air Force Base in California.

9.4   EVENTS LEADING UP TO THE *CHALLENGER* MISSION

Preparations for the launch of the *Challenger* (known as mission 51-L) were not unusual, although they were complicated by changes in the launch schedule. The sequence of complex, interrelated steps involved in producing the detailed schedule and supporting logistics necessary for a successful mission always requires intense effort and close coordination.

Flight 51-L of the *Challenger* was originally scheduled for July, 1985, but it had to be rescheduled for late January, 1986.

Challenger cargo included two satellites in the cargo bay and equipment in the crew compartment for experiments that would be carried out during the mission. The payloads flown on mission 51-L were

Tracking and Data Relay Satellite-B.

Spartan–Halley Satellite.

Comet Halley Active Monitoring Program.

Fluid Dynamics Experiment.

Phase Partitioning Experiment.

Teacher in Space Project.

Shuttle Student Involvement Program.

Radiation Monitoring Experiment.

On January 27, 1985, one year before launch, NASA announced the names of the astronauts assigned to mission 51-L:

Commander	Francis R. Scobee
Pilot	Michael J. Smith
Mission Specialist One	Ellison S. Onizuka
Mission Specialist Two	Judith A. Resnik
Mission Specialist Three	Ronald E. McNair

Payload specialists are members of a space shuttle crew who are not career astronauts. Two such specialists, Christa McAuliffe and Gregory B. Jarvis, were added to the crew of mission 51-L. McAuliffe was selected as the Teacher in Space and assigned to the 51-L crew in July, 1985. Jarvis, an electrical engineer, was assigned to the 51-L crew in October 1985, as a representative of the Hughes Aircraft Company.

The objectives of mission 51-L were to

1. Place a tracking and data relay satellite in orbit.
2. Deploy and retrieve the Spartan satellite, which would have made observations of Halley's comet.
3. Conduct six experiments.

The crew began training 37 weeks before launch, and the training process was unremarkable. All NASA crew members exceeded the number of training hours required and were certified proficient in all mission tasks. The two payload specialists also fulfilled their training requirements.

The Level I Flight Readiness Review for mission 51-L took place on January 15, 1986. The Flight Readiness Review should address all aspects of flight preparation about which any questions have arisen. In addition, attendees confirm that all equipment and operational plans have been certified by the responsible manager within NASA. Solid rocket booster joints were not discussed during the review on January 15.

9.5   LAUNCH DELAYS

The launch of mission 51-L was postponed three times and scrubbed once from the planned date of January 22, 1986. The first postponement was announced on December 23, 1985. That change established the launch date as January 23, 1986, in order to accommodate the final integrated simulation schedule that resulted from the slip in the launch date of mission 61-C.

On January 22, 1986, the Program Requirements Change Board first slipped the launch from January 23 to January 25. That date subsequently was changed to January 26, 1986, primarily because of Kennedy work requirements produced by the late launch of mission 61-C.

The third postponement of the launch date occurred during an evening management conference on January 25, 1986, to review the weather forecast for the Kennedy area. Because the forecast was for unacceptable weather throughout the launch window on January 26, early countdown activities that had already started were terminated.

The launch attempt of January 27 began the day before as the complex sequence of events leading to liftoff commenced. Fueling of the external tank began at 12:30 A.M., eastern standard time (EST). The crew was awakened at 05:07 A.M., and events proceeded normally with the crew strapped into the shuttle at 07:56 A.M. At 09:10, however, the countdown was halted when the ground crew reported a problem with an exterior hatch handle. By the time the hatch handle problem was solved at 10:30 A.M., winds at the Kennedy runway designated for a return-to-launch-site abort had increased and exceeded the allowable velocity for crosswinds. The launch attempt for January 27 was canceled at 12:35 P.M. (EST); the *Challenger* countdown was rescheduled for January 28.

The weather was forecast to be clear and very cold, with temperatures dropping into the low twenties overnight. The management team directed engineers to assess the possible effects of temperature on the launch. No critical issues were identified to management officials, and while evaluation continued, it was decided to proceed with the countdown and the fueling of the external tank.

Ice had accumulated in the launch pad area during the night and it caused considerable concern for the launch team. In reaction, the ice inspection team was sent to the launch pad at 01:35 A.M., January 28, and returned to the Launch Control Center at 03:00 A.M. After a meeting to consider the team's report, the space shuttle program manager decided to continue the countdown. Another ice inspection was scheduled at launch minus three hours.

Also, during the night, prior to fueling, a problem developed with a fire detector in the ground liquid hydrogen storage tank. Although it was ultimately tracked to a hardware fault and repaired, fueling was delayed by two and one-half hours. By continuing past a planned hold at launch minus three hours, however, the launch delay was reduced to one hour. Crew wake-up was rescheduled for 06:18 A.M., January 28, but by that time the crew was already up.

Because of forecast rain and low ceilings at Casablanca, the alternate abort site, that site was declared a "no-go" at 07:30 A.M. The change had no mission impact, however, because the weather at the primary transatlantic abort landing site at Dakar, Senegal, was acceptable. The abort-once-around site was Edwards Air Force Base, California.

With an extra hour, the crew had more than sufficient time to eat breakfast, get a weather briefing and put on flight gear. At the weather briefing, the temperature and ice on the pad were discussed, but neither then nor in earlier weather discussions was the crew told of any concern about the effects of low temperature on the shuttle system. The seven crew members left the crew quarters and rode the astronaut van to launch pad B, arriving at 08:03. They were in their seats in the *Challenger* at 08:36 A.M.

At 08:44 A.M. the ice team completed its second inspection. After hearing the team's report, the program manager decided to allow additional time for ice to melt on the pad. He also decided to send the ice team to perform one final ice assessment at launch minus 20 minutes. When the count was resumed, launch had been delayed a second hour beyond the original liftoff time of 09:38 A.M. (EST).

At 11:15 the ice inspection was completed, and during the hold at launch minus nine minutes, the mission 51-L crew and all members of the launch team gave their "go" for launch. The final flight of the *Challenger* began at 11:38:00.010 A.M. (EST), January 28, 1986.

From liftoff until the signal from the shuttle was lost, no flight controller observed any indication of a problem. The shuttle's main engines throttled down to limit the maximum dynamic pressure, then throttled up to full thrust as expected. Voice communications with the crew were normal. The crew called to indicate the shuttle had begun its roll to head due east and to establish communication after launch. Fifty-seven seconds later, Mission Control informed the crew that the engines had successfully throttled up and all other systems were satisfactory. The commander's acknowledgment of this call was the last voice communication from the *Challenger*.

There were no alarms sounded in the cockpit. The crew apparently had no indication of a problem before the rapid break-up of the space shuttle system. The first evidence of an accident came from live video coverage. Radar then began to track multiple objects. The flight dynamics officer in Houston confirmed to the flight director that "RSO [range safety officer] reports vehicle exploded," and 30 seconds later he added that the range safety officer had sent the destruct signal to the solid rocket boosters.

During the period of the flight when the solid rocket boosters were thrusting, there are no survivable abort options. There was nothing that either the crew or the ground controllers could have done to avert the catastrophe.

9.6   THE PRESIDENTIAL COMMISSION AND ITS ACTIVITIES

President Ronald Reagan, seeking to ensure a thorough and unbiased investigation of the *Challenger* accident, announced the formation of the Commission on the Space Shuttle *Challenger* Accident on February 3, 1986. (Table 9.1 lists the members of the Commission.) The mandate given by the president, contained in Executive Order 12546, required Commission members to

1.   Review the circumstances surrounding the accident to establish the probable cause or causes of the accident.

2.   Develop recommendations for corrective or other action based upon the Commission's findings and determinations.

Following their swearing in by Chairman Rogers on February 6, Commission members immediately began a series of hearings during which NASA officials outlined agency procedures covering the shuttle program and the status of NASA's investigation of the accident.

Shortly thereafter, on February 10, Dr. Alton G. Keel, Jr., Associate Director of the Office of Management and Budget, was appointed Executive Director. Dr. Keel began gathering a staff of 15 experienced investigators from various government agencies and the military services, and administrative personnel to support Commission activities.

During a closed session on February 10, 1986, the Commission began to learn of the troubled history of the solid rocket motor joint and seals. Moreover, it discovered the first indication that the contractor[1] initially recommended

---

[1] Several contractors were employed in the development and operation of the space shuttle system. In this chapter, the term contractor will designate the developer of the solid rocket motor. The company name is not used.

TABLE 9.1 *Members of the Presidential Commission on the Space Shuttle* Challenger *Accident*

Name	Affiliation/Expertise
William P. Rogers Chairman	Former Secretary of State under President Nixon and Attorney General under President Eisenhower and a practicing attorney in the law firm of Rogers and Wells
Neil A. Armstrong Vice-Chairman	Former astronaut, Chairman of the Board of Computing Technologies for Aviation, Inc.
David C. Acheson	Former Senior Vice-President and General Counsel, Communications Satellite Corporation, a partner in the law firm of Drinker, Biddle & Reath
Dr. Eugene E. Covert	Professor and Head, Department of Aeronautics and Astronautics, Massachusetts Institute of Technology
Dr. Richard P. Feynman	Professor of Theoretical Physics at California Institute of Technology
Robert B. Holz	Former editor-in-chief, *Aviation Week & Space Technology*
Major Gen. Donald J. Kutyna	Director of Space Systems and Command, Control, Communications, U.S. Air Force
Dr. Sally K. Ride	Astronaut, physicist, the first American woman in space
Robert W. Rummel	Former Vice-President of Trans World Airways, President of Robert W. Rummel, Inc.
Joseph F. Sutter	Aeronautical engineer, Executive Vice-President of Boeing Commercial Airplane Company
Dr. Arthur B. C. Walker, Jr.	Professor of Applied Physics, Stanford University
Dr. Albert D. Wheelon	Physicist, Executive Vice-President, Hughes Aircraft Company
Brig. Gen. Charles Yeager USAF (retired)	Former experimental test pilot, the first person to penetrate the sound barrier, and the first to fly at a speed of more than 1600 mph
Dr. Alton G. Keel, Jr. Director	Detailed to the Commission from his executive position of Associate Director for National Security and International Affairs, Office of Management and Budget

against launch on January 27, 1986, the night before the launch of 51-L, because of concerns regarding low temperature effects on the joint and seal. To investigate this disturbing development, additional closed sessions were scheduled for February 13 and 14 at Kennedy. The February 13, 1986, session was an extensive presentation of film, video, and telemetry data relating to the *Challenger* accident. It provided the Commission the first evidence that the solid rocket motor joint and seal may have malfunctioned, initiating the accident.

The session on February 14 included NASA and contractor participants involved in the discussion on January 27, 1986 not to launch 51-L. After testimony was received, an executive session of the Commission was convened. The following statement was subsequently issued by the chairman on February 15, 1986, reflecting the conclusion and view of the Commission:

> *In recent days, the Commission has been investigating all aspects of the decision-making process leading up to the launch of the* Challenger *and has found that the process may have been flawed. The President has been so advised.*
>
> *Dr. William Graham, Acting Administrator of NASA, has been asked not to include on the internal investigating teams at NASA persons involved in that process.*
>
> *The Commission will, of course, continue its investigation and will make a full report to the President within 120 days.*

The role of the Commissioners thus changed from that of overseers to that of active investigators and analysts of data presented by NASA and its contractors.

9.7 THE ACCIDENT

Flight of the space shuttle *Challenger* on mission 51-L began at 11:38 A.M. (EST) on January 28, 1986. It ended 73 seconds later in an explosive burn of hydrogen and oxygen propellants that destroyed the external tank and exposed the orbiter to severe aerodynamic loads that caused complete structural breakup. All seven crew members perished. The two solid rocket boosters flew out of the fireball and were destroyed by the Air Force range safety officer 110 seconds after launch.

The ambient air temperature at launch was 36 degrees Fahrenheit measured at ground level approximately 1000 feet from the 51-L mission launch pad 39B. This temperature was 15 degrees colder than that of any previous launch.

The following description of the flight events is based on visual examination and image enhancement of film from NASA-operated cameras and telemetry data transmitted from the space shuttle to ground stations. The last telemetry data from the *Challenger* was received 73.618 seconds after launch.

At 6.6 seconds before launch, the *Challenger's* liquid-fueled main engines were ignited in sequence and run up to full thrust while the entire shuttle structure was bolted to the launch pad. Thrust of the main engines bends the shuttle assembly forward from the bolts anchoring it to the pad. When the shuttle assembly springs back to the vertical, the solid rocket boosters' restraining bolts are explosively released. During this prerelease "twang" motion, structural loads are stored in the assembled structure. These loads are released during the first few seconds of flight in a structural vibration mode at a frequency of about 3 cycles per second. The maximum structural loads on the aft field joints of the solid rocket boosters occur during the "twang," exceeding even those of the maximum dynamic pressure period experienced later in flight.

Just after liftoff at 0.678 seconds into the flight, photographic data show a strong puff of gray smoke was spurting from the vicinity of the aft field joint on the right solid rocket booster (see Figure 9.3). The two pad 39B cameras that would have recorded the precise location of the puff were inoperative. Computer graphic analysis of film from other cameras indicated the initial smoke came from the 270- to 310-degree sector of the circumference of the aft field joint of the right solid rocket booster. This area of the solid booster faces the external tank. The vaporized material streaming from the joint indicated there was not complete sealing action within the joint.

Figure 9.3   *The space shuttle* Challenger *just prior to launch. The arrow points to puff of smoke coming from the right solid rocket booster.* (Source: Reference 1.)

Eight more distinctive puffs of increasingly blacker smoke were recorded between 0.836 and 2.500 seconds. The smoke appeared to puff upward from the joint. While each smoke puff was being left behind by the upward flight of the shuttle, the next fresh puff could be seen near the level of the joint. The multiple smoke puffs in this sequence occurred at about four times per second, approximating the frequency of the structural load dynamics and resultant joint flexing. Computer graphics applied to NASA photos from a variety of cameras in this sequence again placed the smoke puff's origin in the 270- to 310-degree sector of the original smoke spurt.

As the shuttle increased its upward velocity, it flew past the emerging and expanding smoke puffs. The last smoke was seen above the field joint at 2.733 seconds. At 3.375 seconds the last smoke was visible below the solid rocket boosters and became indiscernible as it mixed with rocket plumes and surrounding atmosphere.

The black color and dense composition of the smoke puffs suggest that the grease, joint insulation, and rubber O-rings in the joint seal were being burned and eroded by the hot propellant gases.

Launch sequence films from previous missions were examined in detail to determine if there were any prior indications of smoke of the color and composition that appeared during the first few seconds of the 51-L mission. None were found. Other vapors in this area were determined to be melting frost from the bottom of the external tank or steam from the rocket exhaust in the pad's sound suppression water trays.

Shuttle main engines were throttled up to 104 percent of their rated thrust level, the *Challenger* executed a programmed roll maneuver, and the engines were throttled back to 94 percent.

At approximately 37 seconds, *Challenger* encountered the first of several high-altitude wind shear conditions, which lasted until about 64 seconds. The wind shear created forces on the vehicle with relatively large fluctuations. These were immediately sensed and countered by the guidance, navigation, and control system. Although flight 51-L loads exceeded prior experience in both yaw and pitch planes at certain instants, the maxima had been encountered on previous flights and were within design limits.

The steering system (thrust vector control) of the solid rocket booster responded to all commands and wind shear effects. The wind shear caused the steering system to be more active than on any previous flight.

At 45 seconds into the flight, three bright flashes appeared downstream of the *Challenger's* right wing. Each flash lasted less than one-thirtieth of a second. Similar flashes have been seen on other flights. Another appearance of a separate bright spot was diagnosed by film analysis to be a reflection of main engine exhaust on the orbital maneuvering system pods located at the upper rear section of the orbiter. The flashes were unrelated to the later appearance of the flame plume from the right solid rocket booster.

Both the shuttle main engines and the solid rockets operated at reduced thrust approaching and passing through the area of maximum dynamic pressure of 720 pounds per square foot. Main engines had been throttled up to 104 percent thrust and the solid rocket boosters were increasing their thrust when the first flickering flame appeared on the right solid rocket booster in the area of the aft field joint. This first very small flame was detected on image enhanced film at 58.788 seconds into the flight. It appeared to originate at about 305 degrees around the booster circumference at or near the aft field joint.

One film frame later from the same camera, the flame was visible without image enhancement. It grew into a continuous, well-defined plume at 59.262 seconds. At about the same time (60 seconds), telemetry showed a pressure differential between the chamber pressures in the right and left boosters. The right booster chamber pressure was lower, confirming the growing leak in the area of the field joint.

As the flame plume increased in size, it was deflected rearward by the aerodynamic slipstream and circumferentially by the protruding structure of the upper ring attaching the booster to the external tank. These deflections directed the flame plume onto the surface of the external tank. This sequence of flame spreading is confirmed by analysis of the recovered wreckage. The growing flame also impinged on the strut attaching the solid rocket booster to the external tank.

At about 62 seconds into the flight, the control system began to react to counter the forces caused by the plume and its effects. The left solid rocket booster thrust vector control moved to counter the yaw caused by reduced thrust from the leaking right solid rocket booster. During the next 9 seconds, space shuttle control systems worked to correct anomalies in pitch and yaw rates.

The first visual indication that swirling flame from the right solid rocket booster breached the external tank was at 64.660 seconds when there was an abrupt change in the shape and color of the plume. This indicated that it was mixing with leaking hydrogen from the external tank. Telemetered changes in the hydrogen tank pressurization confirmed the leak. Within 45 milliseconds of the breach of the external tank, a bright sustained glow developed on the black-tiled underside of the *Challenger* between it and the external tank.

Beginning at about 72 seconds, a series of events occurred extremely rapidly that terminated the flight. Telemetered data indicate a wide variety of flight system actions that support the visual evidence of the photos as the shuttle struggled futilely against the forces that were destroying it.

At about 72.20 seconds the lower strut linking the solid rocket booster and the external tank was severed or pulled away from the weakened hydrogen tank permitting the right solid rocket booster to rotate around the upper attachment strut. This rotation is indicated by divergent yaw and pitch rates between the left and right solid rocket boosters.

At 73.124 seconds, a circumferential white vapor pattern was observed blooming from the side of the external tank bottom dome. This was the beginning of the structural failure of the hydrogen tank that culminated in the entire aft dome dropping away. This released massive amounts of liquid hydrogen from the tank and created a sudden forward thrust of about 2.8 million pounds, pushing the hydrogen tank upward into the intertank structure. At about the same time, the rotating right solid rocket booster impacted the intertank structure and the lower part of the liquid oxygen tank. These structures failed at 73.137 seconds as evidenced by the white vapors appearing in the intertank region.

Within milliseconds there was massive, almost explosive, burning of the hydrogen streaming from the failed tank bottom and the liquid oxygen breach in the area of the intertank.

At this point in its trajectory, while travelling at a Mach number of 1.92 at an altitude of 46,000 feet, the *Challenger* was totally enveloped in the explosive burn. The *Challenger's* reaction control system ruptured and a hypergolic burn of its propellants occurred as it exited the oxygen-hydrogen flames. The reddish brown colors of the hypergolic fuel burn are visible on the edge of the main fireball. The Orbiter, under severe aerodynamic loads, broke into several large sections, which emerged from the fireball. Separate sections that can be identified on film include the main engine/tail section with the engines still burning, one wing of the Orbiter, and the forward fuselage trailing a mass of umbilical lines pulled loose from the payload bay.

Evidence in the recovered wreckage from the mission 51-L hardware supports this final sequence of events.

9.8   THE CAUSE OF THE ACCIDENT

The Commission reviewed in detail all available data, reports, and records; directed and supervised numerous tests, analyses, and experiments by NASA, civilian contractors, and various government agencies; and then developed specific failure scenarios and the range of most probable causative factors. The areas of inquiry included

1.   Launch pad systems.
2.   The external tank.
3.   Space shuttle main engines.
4.   Orbiter subsystems (propulsion and power, avionics, thermal and environmental control, life support, and mechanical and interface systems).
5.   Payload.
6.   Left solid rocket booster.

The Commission found that none of these items of equipment or systems contributed to or caused the *Challenger* accident. In addition, the Commission examined the possibility of sabotage but found no evidence to suggest that sabotage had been committed either at the launch pad or during the other processes prior to or during launch. Thus, as the investigation progressed, elements assessed as being improbable contributors to the accident were eliminated from further consideration. This process of elimination brought focus to the right solid rocket booster, specifically to its motor. (A cutaway view of the Booster is shown as Figure 9.4.) As a result, four areas related to the function of that motor received detailed analysis to determine their part in the accident:

1. Structural load evaluation.
2. Failure of the case wall (the half-inch-thick steel wall of the rocket between the joints).
3. Propellant anomalies.
4. Loss of the pressure seal at the case joint.

Based on a thorough assessment of these possible failure mechanisms, the Commission ruled out the first three as being a contributor or cause of the accident and examined further the possible failure of the pressure seal at the case joint.

Joint Seal Failure   Enhanced photographic and computer-graphic positioning determined that the flame from the right solid rocket booster near the aft field joint emanated at about the 305-degree circumferential position. (Figure 9.5 shows the angular coordinate system used for the boosters/motors.) The smoke at liftoff appeared in the same general location. Thus early in the investigation the right solid rocket booster aft field joint seal became the prime failure sus-

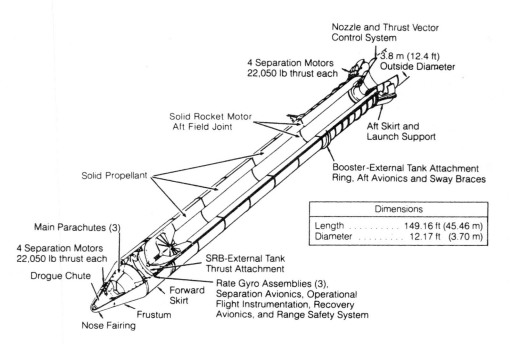

Figure 9.4 *Cutaway view of the solid rocket booster showing the solid rocket motor propellant and aft field joint.* (Source: *Reference 1.*)

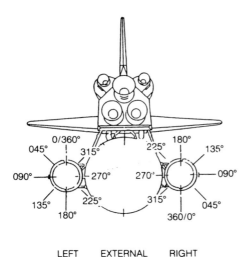

LEFT   EXTERNAL   RIGHT
SRB   TANK   SRB

Figure 9.5   *Angular coordinate system for the Solid Rocket Boosters/Motors. (Source: Reference 1.)*

pect. This supposition was confirmed when the Salvage Team recovered portions of both sides of the aft joint containing large holes extending from 291 degrees to 318 degrees. Several possible causes could have resulted in this failure. These possible causes are treated in the following paragraphs.

During stacking operations at the launch site, four segments are assembled to form the solid rocket motor. The resulting joints are referred to as field joints, located as depicted in Figure 9.4. Joint sealing is provided by two rubber O-rings with diameters of 0.280 inches (+0.005, −0.003), which are installed, as received from the SRB Contractor, during motor assembly. O-ring static compression during and after assembly is dictated by the width of the gap between the tang and the inside leg of the clevis. (The tang is a tongue or projection part of a rocket segment that fits into and is secured by pins to the U-shaped clevis of the adjoining segment. See Figure 9.6.) This gap between the tang and clevis at any location after assembly is influenced by the size and shape (concentricity) of the segments as well as the loads on the segments. Zinc chromate putty is applied to the composition rubber (NBR) insulation face prior to assembly. In the assembled configuration the putty was intended to act as a thermal barrier to prevent direct contact of combustion gas with the O-rings. It was also intended that the O-rings be actuated and sealed by combustion gas pressure displacing the putty in the space between the motor segments (Figure 9.6). The displacement of the putty would act like a piston and compress the air ahead of the primary O-ring, and force it into the gap between the tang and clevis. This process is known as pressure actuation of the O-ring seal. This pressure-actuated sealing is required to occur very early during the solid rocket motor ignition transient, because the gap between the tang and clevis increases as pressure loads are applied to the joint during ignition. Should pressure actuation be delayed to the extent that the gap has opened

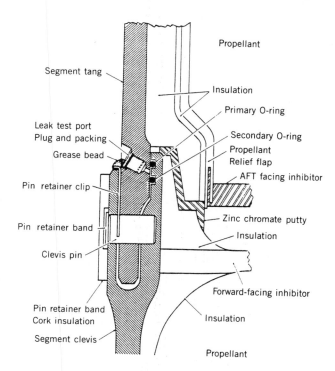

Figure 9.6 *The solid rocket motor cross-section shows the position of tang, clevis, and O-rings. Putty lines the joint on the side toward the propellant.* (Source: Reference 1.)

considerably, the possibility exists that the rocket's combustion gases will blow by the O-ring and damage or destroy the seals. The principal factor influencing the size of the gap opening is motor pressure, but gap opening is also influenced by external loads and other joint dynamics. The investigation showed that the joint-sealing performance is sensitive to the following factors, either independently or in combination:

1. Damage to the joints/seals or generation of contaminants as joints are assembled as influenced by
   a. Manufacturing tolerances.
   b. Out-of-round due to handling.
   c. Effects of reuse.
2. Tang/clevis gap opening due to motor pressure and other loads.
3. Static O-ring compression.
4. Joint temperature as it affects O-ring response under dynamic conditions (resiliency) and hardness.

5. Joint temperature as it relates to forming ice from water intrusion in the joint.
6. Putty performance effects on
    a. O-ring pressure actuation timing.
    b. O-ring erosion.

The sensitivity of the O-ring sealing performance to these factors was investigated in extensive tests and analyses. The sensitivity to each factor was evaluated independently and in appropriate combinations to assess the potential to cause or contribute to the 51-L aft field joint failure. Most of the testing was done on either laboratory or subscale equipment. In many cases, the data from these tests are considered to be directly applicable to the seal performance in full scale. However, in some cases there was considerable uncertainty in extrapolating the data to full-scale seal performance. Detailed descriptions of these tests and analyses are not given here but may be found in Reference 1.

Findings   The Commission's findings about the cause of the *Challenger* accident follow.

1. *A combustion gas leak through the right solid rocket motor aft field joint initiated at or shortly after ignition eventually weakened and/or penetrated the external tank initiating vehicle structural breakup and loss of the space shuttle* Challenger *during STS Mission 51-L.*
2. *The evidence shows that no other STS 51-L shuttle element or the payload contributed to the causes of the right solid rocket motor aft field joint combustion gas leak. Sabotage was not a factor.*
3. *Evidence examined in the review of space shuttle material, manufacturing, assembly, quality control, and processing of nonconformance reports found no flight hardware shipped to the launch site that fell outside the limits of shuttle design specifications.*
4. *Launch site activities, including assembly and preparation, from receipt of the flight hardware to launch were generally in accord with established procedures and were not considered a factor in the accident.*
5. *Launch site records show that the right solid rocket motor segments were assembled using approved procedures. However, significant out-of-round conditions existed between the two segments joined at the right solid rocket motor aft field joint (the joint that failed).*
    a. *While the assembly conditions had the potential of generating debris or damage that could cause O-ring seal failure, these were not considered factors in this accident.*
    b. *The diameters of the two solid rocket motor segments had grown as a result of prior use.*
    c. *The growth resulted in a condition at time of launch wherein the maximum gap between the tang and clevis in the region of the joint's O-rings was not more than 0.008 inches and the average gap would have been 0.004 inches.*
    d. *With a tang-to-clevis gap of 0.004 inches, the O-ring in the joint would be compressed to the extent that it pressed against all three walls of the O-ring retaining channel.*

e.   *The lack of roundness of the segments was such that the smallest tang-to-clevis clearance occurred at the initiation of the assembly operation at positions of 120 degrees and 300 degrees around the circumference of the aft field joint. It is uncertain if this tight condition and the resultant greater compression of the O-rings at these points persisted to the time of launch.*

6.   *The ambient temperature at time of launch was 36 degrees Fahrenheit, or 15 degrees lower than the next coldest previous launch.*

a.   *The temperature at the 300-degree position on the right aft field joint circumference was estimated to be 28 degrees ± 5 degrees Fahrenheit. This was the coldest point on the joint.*

b.   *Temperature on the opposite side of the right solid rocket booster facing the sun was estimated to be about 50 degrees Fahrenheit.*

7.   *Other joints on the left and right solid rocket boosters experienced similar combinations of tang-to-clevis gap clearance and temperature. It is not known whether these joints experienced distress during the flight of 51-L.*

8.   *Experimental evidence indicates that due to several effects associated with the solid rocket booster's ignition and combustion pressures and associated vehicle motions, the gap between the tang and the clevis will open as much as 0.017 and 0.029 inches at the secondary and primary O-rings, respectively.*

a.   *This opening begins upon ignition, reaches its maximum rate of opening at about 200–300 milliseconds, and is essentially complete at 600 milliseconds when the solid rocket booster reaches its operating pressure.*

b.   *The external tank and right solid rocket booster are connected by several struts, including one at 310 degrees near the aft field joint that failed. This strut's effect on the joint dynamics is to enhance the opening of the gap between the tang and clevis by about 10–20 percent in the region of 300–320 degrees.*

9.   *O-ring resiliency is directly related to its temperature.*

a.   *A warm O-ring that has been compressed will return to its original shape much quicker than will a cold O-ring when compression is relieved. Thus a warm O-ring will follow the opening of the tang-to-clevis gap. A cold O-ring may not.*

b.   *A compressed O-ring at 75 degrees Fahrenheit is five times more responsive in returning to its uncompressed shape than a cold O-ring at 30 degrees Fahrenheit.*

c.   *As a result it is probable that the O-rings in the right solid booster aft field joint were not following the opening of the gap between the tang and clevis at time of ignition.*

10. *Experiments indicate that the primary mechanism that actuates O-ring sealing is the application of gas pressure to the upstream (high-pressure) side of the O-ring as it sits in its groove or channel.*

a.   *For this pressure actuation to work most effectively, a space between the O-ring and its upstream channel wall should exist during pressurization.*

b.   *A tang-to-clevis gap of 0.004 inches, as probably existed in the failed joint, would have initially compressed the O-ring to the degree that no clearance existed between the O-ring and its upstream channel wall and the other two surfaces of the channel.*

c.   *At the cold launch temperature experienced, the O-ring would be very slow in returning to its normal rounded shape. It would not follow the opening of the tang-to-clevis gap. It would remain in its compressed position in the*

O-ring channel and not provide a space between itself and the upstream channel wall. Thus it is probable the O-ring would not be pressure actuated to seal the gap in time to preclude joint failure due to blow-by and erosion from hot combustion gases.

11. The sealing characteristics of the solid rocket booster O-rings are enhanced by timely application of motor pressure.

   a. Ideally, motor pressure should be applied to actuate the O-ring and seal the joint prior to significant opening of the tang-to-clevis gap (100 to 200 milliseconds after motor ignition).

   b. Experimental evidence indicates that temperature, humidity, and other variables in the putty compound used to seal the joint can delay pressure application to the joint by 500 milliseconds or more.

   c. This delay in pressure could be a factor in initial joint failure.

12. Of 21 launches with ambient temperatures of 61 degrees Fahrenheit or greater, only four showed signs of O-ring thermal distress, that is, erosion or blow-by and soot. Each of the launches below 61 degrees Fahrenheit resulted in one or more O-rings showing signs of thermal distress.

   a. Of these improper joint-sealing actions, one-half occurred in the aft field joints, 20 percent in the center field joints, and 30 percent in the upper field joints. The division between left and right solid rocket boosters was roughly equal.

   b. Each instance of thermal O-ring distress was accompanied by a leak path in the insulating putty. The leak path connects the rocket's combustion chamber with the O-ring region of the tang and clevis. Joints that actuated without incident may also have had these leak paths.

13. There is a possibility that there was water in the clevis of the STS 51-L joint, since water was found in the STS-9 joints during a destack operation after exposure to less rainfall than STS 51-L. At time of launch, it was cold enough that water present in the joint would freeze. Tests show that ice in the joint can inhibit proper secondary seal performance.

14. A series of puffs of smoke was observed emanating from the 51-L aft field joint area of the right solid rocket booster between 0.678 and 2.500 seconds after ignition of the shuttle solid rocket motors.

   a. The puffs appeared at a frequency of about three puffs per second. This roughly matches the natural structural frequency of the solids at lift-off and is reflected in slight cyclic changes of the tang-to-clevis gap opening.

   b. The puffs were seen to be moving upward along the surface of the booster above the aft field joint.

   c. The smoke was estimated to originate at a circumferential position of between 270 degrees and 315 degrees on the booster aft field joint, emerging from the top of the joint.

15. This smoke from the aft field joint at shuttle liftoff was the first sign of the failure of the solid rocket booster O-ring seals on STS 51-L.

16. The leak was again clearly evident as a flame at approximately 58 seconds into the flight. It is possible that the leak was continuous but unobservable or nonexistent in portions of the intervening period. It is possible in either case that thrust vectoring and normal vehicle response to wind shear as well as planned maneuvers reinitiated or magnified the leakage from a degraded seal in the period preceding the observed flames. The estimated position of the flame, centered at a point 307 degrees around the circumference of the aft

field joint, was confirmed by the recovery of two fragments of the right solid rocket booster.

   a.   *A small leak could have been present that may have grown to breach the joint in flame at a time on the order of 58 to 60 seconds after lift-off.*

   b.   *Alternatively, the O-ring gap could have been resealed by deposition of a fragile buildup of aluminum oxide and other combustion debris. This resealed section of the joint could have been disturbed by thrust vectoring, space shuttle motion, and flight loads induced by changing winds aloft.*

   c.   *The winds aloft caused control actions in the time interval of 32 seconds to 62 seconds into the flight that were typical of the largest values experienced on previous missions.*

Conclusion   The Commission concluded that the cause of the *Challenger* accident was the failure of the pressure seal in the aft field joint of the right solid rocket motor. The failure was due to a faulty design unacceptably sensitive to a number of factors. These factors were the effects of temperature, physical dimensions, the character of materials, the effects of reusability, processing, and the reaction of the joint to dynamic loading.

9.9   THE CONTRIBUTING CAUSE OF THE ACCIDENT

In addition to analyzing all available evidence concerning the material causes of the accident on January 28, the Commission examined the chain of decisions that culminated in approval of the launch. It concluded that the decision-making process was flawed in several ways.

Testimony before the Commission revealed failures in communication that resulted in a decision to launch 51-L based on incomplete and sometimes misleading information, a conflict between engineering data and management judgments, and a NASA management structure that permitted internal flight safety problems to bypass key shuttle managers.

The shuttle flight Readiness Review is a carefully planned, step-by-step activity, establish by NASA program directive SPO-PD 710.5A, designed to certify the readiness of all components of the space shuttle assembly. The process is focused upon the Level I Flight Readiness Review, held approximately two weeks before a launch. The Level I review is a conference chaired by the NASA Associate Administrator for Space Flight and supported by the NASA Chief Engineer, the Program Manager, the center directors, and project managers from Johnson,[2] Marshall, and Kennedy, along with senior contractor representatives.

The formal portion of the process is initiated by directive from the Associate Administrator for Space Flight. The directive outlines the schedule for the Level I Flight Readiness Review and for the steps that precede it. The process begins at Level IV with the contractors formally certifying—in writing—the flight readiness of the elements for which they are responsible. Certification is

---

[2] Lyndon B. Johnson Space Center, Houston, Texas.

made to the appropriate Level III NASA project managers at Johnson and Marshall. Additionally, at Marshall the review is followed by a presentation directly to the Center Director. At Kennedy the Level III review, chaired by the Center Director, verifies readiness of the launch support elements.

The next step in the process is the Certification of Flight Readiness to the Level II Program Manager at Johnson. In this review each space shuttle program element endorses that it has satisfactorily completed the manufacture, assembly, test, and checkout of the pertinent element, including the contractors' certification that design and performance are up to standard. The Flight Readiness Review process culminates in the Level I review (see Figure 9.7).

In the initial notice of the review, the Level I directive establishes a Mission Management Team for the particular mission. The team assumes responsibility for each shuttle's readiness for a period commencing 48 hours before launch and continuing through post-landing crew egress and the safing of the orbiter. On call throughout the entire period, the Mission Management Team supports the Associate Administrator for Space Flight and the program manager.

A structures Mission Management Team meeting, called L-1, is held 24 hours, or one day, prior to each scheduled launch. Its agenda includes closeout of any open work, a closeout of any Flight Readiness Review action items, a discussion of new or continuing anomalies, and an updated briefing on anticipated weather conditions at the launch site and at the abort landing sites in different parts of the world. It is standard practice of Level I and II officials to

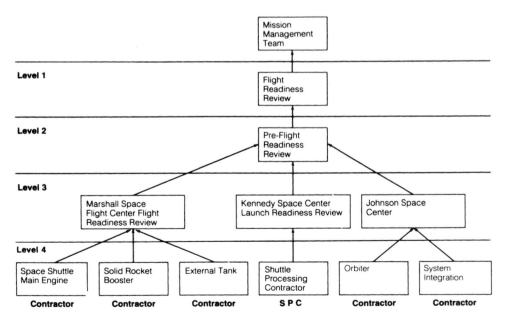

Figure 9.7   *Readiness reviews for both the launch and the flight of a shuttle mission are conducted at ascending levels that begin with contractors. (Source: Reference 1.)*

encourage the reporting of new problems or concerns that might develop in the interval between the Flight Readiness Review and the L-1 meeting, and between the L-1 and launch.

In a procedural sense, the process described was followed in the case of flight 51-L. However, in the launch preparation for 51-L relevant concerns of Level III NASA personnel and element contractors were not, in the following crucial areas, adequately communicated to the NASA Level I and II management responsible for the launch:

> The objections to launch voiced by the SRB Contractor's engineers about the detrimental effect of cold temperatures on the performance of the solid rocket motor joint seal.

> The degree of concern of the contractor and Marshall about the erosion of the joint seals in prior shuttle flights, notably 51-C (January 1985) and 51-B (April 1985).

On January 23, NASA's Associate Administrator for Space Flight[3] issued a directive stating that the Flight Readiness Review had been conducted on the 15th and that 51-L was ready to fly pending closeout of open work, satisfactory countdown, and competition of remaining Flight Readiness Review action items, which were to be closed out during the L-1 meeting. No problems with the solid rocket booster were identified.

Since December 1982, the O-rings had been designated a "Criticality 1" feature of the solid rocket booster design, a term denoting a failure point—without backup—that could cause a loss of life or vehicle if the component failed. In July 1985, after a nozzle joint on STS 51-B showed erosion of a secondary O-ring, indicating that the primary seal failed, a launch constraint was placed on flight 51-F and subsequent launches. These constraints had been imposed and regularly waived by the solid rocket booster project manager at Marshall.

Neither the launch constraint, the reason for it, nor the six consecutive waivers prior to the 51-L were known to appropriate Level I or Level II personnel or the Director, Launch and Landing Operations, at the time of the Flight Readiness Review process for 51-L.

It should be noted that there were other and independent paths of system reporting that were designed to bring forward information about the solid rocket booster joint anomalies. One path was the task force of contractor engineers and Marshall engineers who had been conducting subscale pressure tests during 1985, a source of documented rising concern and frustration on the part of some of the contractor participants and a few of the Marshall participants. But Level II was not in the line of reporting for this activity. Another path was the examination at each Flight Readiness Review of evidence of earlier flight anomalies. For 51-L, the data presented in this latter path, while it reached

---

[3] NASA officials and contractor employees directly involved in decisions leading to the *Challenger* launch are referred to by title rather than by name. Names appear in Reference 1.

Levels I and II, never referred to either test anomalies or flight anomalies with O-rings.

In any event, no mention of the O-ring problems in the solid rocket booster joint appeared in the Certification of Flight Readiness, signed for the contractor on January 9, 1986 by the vice president, Space Booster program.

Similarly, no mention appeared in the certification endorsement, signed on January 15, 1986 by appropriate NASA and contractor officials. No mention appears in several inches of paper comprising the entire chain of readiness reviews for 51-L.

In the 51-L readiness reviews, it appears that neither contractor management nor the Marshall Level III project managers believed that the O-ring blow-by and erosion risk was critical. The testimony and contemporary correspondence show that Level III believed there was ample margin to fly with O-ring erosion, provided that the leak check was performed at 200 pounds per square inch.

Following the January 15 Flight Readiness Review each element of the shuttle was certified as flight-ready.

The L-1 Mission Management Team meeting took place as scheduled at 11:00 A.M. (EST) on January 25. No technical issues appeared at this meeting or in the documentation and all Flight Readiness Review actions were reported closed out.

At approximately 2:30 P.M. (EST), on the afternoon preceding the launch, at the contractor's plant, the manager, SRB Igniter and Final Assembly, convened a meeting with several of the engineers. The participants discussed concerns about the predicted low temperatures at Kennedy.

Later in the afternoon, the manager called the contractor's liaison for the Solid Rocket Booster (SRB) project at Kennedy and expressed concern about the performance of the SRB field joints at low temperatures. The liaison obtained and relayed updated temperature predictions, notified the vice president, Engineering, and contacted the resident for Marshall at Kennedy who arranged for a teleconference between appropriate NASA and contractor representatives.

The first phase of the teleconference began at 5:45 P.M. (EST) and involved NASA's Manager and Deputy Manager of the Shuttle Projects Office at Marshall plus other personnel at Kennedy, Marshall, and at the SRB contractor's plant in Utah. The conferees discussed concerns regarding low temperature effects on the O-rings, and contractor personnel expressed the opinion that the launch should be delayed. A recommendation was made that the program manager at Johnson (Level II) be informed of these concerns. It was decided to arrange a second teleconference at 8:15 P.M. (EST) to transmit data to all of the parties and to have more personnel involved.

At approximately 8:45 P.M. (EST), Phase 2 of the teleconference commenced, the contractor charts and written data having arrived at Kennedy by telefax.

The charts (Figures 9.8 and 9.9) presented a history of the O-ring erosion and blow-by in the solid rocket booster joints of previous flights, presented the results of subscale testing by the contractor and the results of static tests of solid rocket motors.

PRIMARY CONCERNS

o   FIELD JOINT — HIGHEST CONCERN

   o   EROSION PENETRATION OF PRIMARY SEAL REQUIRES RELIABLE SECONDARY SEAL
      FOR PRESSURE INTEGRITY
      o   IGNITION TRANSIENT — (0-600 MS)
         o   (0-170 MS) HIGH PROBABILITY OF RELIABLE SECONDARY SEAL
         o   (170-330 MS) REDUCED PROBABILITY OF RELIABLE SECONDARY SEAL
         o   (330-600 MS) HIGH PROBABILITY OF NO SECONDARY SEAL CAPABILITY

   o   STEADY STATE — (600 MS - 2 MINUTES)
      o   IF EROSION PENETRATES PRIMARY O-RING SEAL — HIGH PROBABILITY OF
         NO SECONDARY SEAL CAPABILITY
         o   BENCH TESTING SHOWED O-RING NOT CAPABLE OF MAINTAINING CONTACT
            WITH METAL PARTS GAP OPENING RATE TO MEOP
         o   BENCH TESTING SHOWED CAPABILITY TO MAINTAIN O-RING CONTACT DURING
            INITIAL PHASE (0-170 MS) OF TRANSIENT

Figure 9.8   *The chart presented by the contractor's staff engineer summarizing primary concerns with the field joint and its O-ring seals on the boosters. (Source: Reference 1.)*

Joint Primary Concerns   SRM 25

■   A temperature lower than current data base results in changing primary O-ring sealing timing function

■   SRM 15A–80° ARC black grease between O-rings

■   SRM 15B–110° ARC black grease between O-rings

■   Lower O-ring squeeze due to lower temperature

■   Higher O-ring shore hardness

■   Thicker grease viscosity

■   Higher O-ring pressure actuation time

■   If actuation time increases, threshold of secondary seal pressurization capability is approached

■   If threshold is reached, then secondary seal may not be capable of being pressurized

Figure 9.9   *The chart presented by the contractor's staff engineer indicating concern about temperature effect on seal actuation time (handwritten). (Source: Reference 1.)*

During the teleconference, the contractor's vice president, Engineering, recommended that mission 51-L not be flown until the temperature of the O-ring reached 53°F, which was the lowest temperature of any previous flight. (The recommendation chart used by the vice president, Engineering, is shown as Figure 9.10.) The contractor's vice president, Space Booster Programs, was asked his opinion, and he stated that based on the engineering recommendation he could not recommend launch. Certain of the NASA participants expressed dissatisfaction with that recommendation, and after some discussion, the vice president for Space Booster Programs requested five minutes off-net to caucus.

The contractor's caucus at the Utah plant lasted about 30 minutes. Two of the engineers voiced objections to launch, and the vice president, Engineering, also expressed some reluctance to launch. The senior vice president, Wasatch Operations, expressed the need to make a management decision and asked the vice president, Engineering, to "put on his management hat." A final management review was conducted involving only the senior vice president and the three other vice presidents.

At approximately 11:00 P.M. (EST), the teleconference resumed, the contractor's management stating they had reassessed the problem, that the temperature effects were a concern, but that the data were admittedly inconclusive. The contractor's vice president, Space Programs, read the rationale recommending launch and stated that that was the contractor's recommendation. At NASA's request, the contractor's recommendation was confirmed in writing by telefax (see Figure 9.11).

The Commission reported the following findings about the contributing cause of the accident.

Findings

1.   The Commission concluded that there was a serious flaw in the decision-making process leading up to the launch of flight 51-L. A well-structured and -managed system emphasizing safety would have flagged the rising doubts about the solid rocket booster joint seal. Had these matters been clearly stated and emphasized in the flight readiness process in terms reflecting the reviews of most of the contractor engineers and at least some of the Marshall engineers, it seems likely that the launch of 51-L might not have occurred when it did.

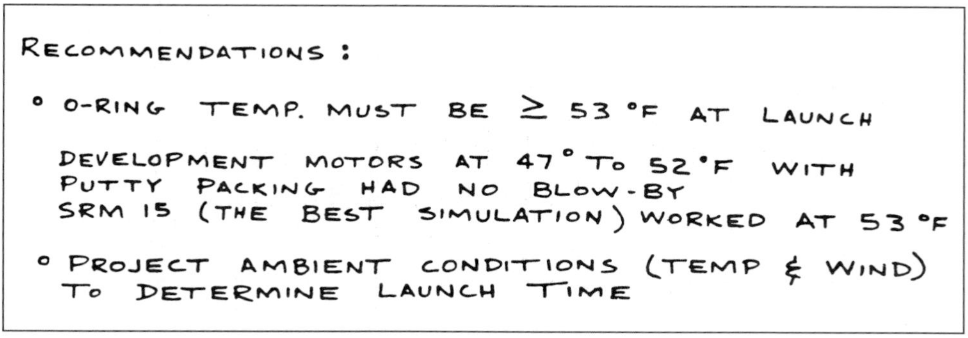

RECOMMENDATIONS :

o O-RING TEMP. MUST BE $\geq$ 53 °F AT LAUNCH

   DEVELOPMENT MOTORS AT 47° TO 52 °F WITH
   PUTTY PACKING HAD NO BLOW-BY
   SRM 15 (THE BEST SIMULATION) WORKED AT 53 °F

o PROJECT AMBIENT CONDITIONS (TEMP & WIND)
   TO DETERMINE LAUNCH TIME

Figure 9.10   *The initial contractor's recommendation chart presented by the vice president, Engineering, at the second teleconference prior to the contractor's caucus. (Source: Reference 1.)*

MTI ASSESSMENT OF TEMPERATURE CONCERN ON SRM-25 (51L) LAUNCH

O   CALCULATIONS SHOW THAT SRM-25 O-RINGS WILL BE 20° COLDER THAN SRM-15 O-RINGS

O   TEMPERATURE DATA NOT CONCLUSIVE ON PREDICTING PRIMARY O-RING BLOW-BY

O   ENGINEERING ASSESSMENT IS THAT:

    O   COLDER O-RINGS WILL HAVE INCREASED EFFECTIVE DUROMETER ("HARDER")

    O   "HARDER" O-RINGS WILL TAKE LONGER TO "SEAT"

        O   MORE GAS MAY PASS PRIMARY O-RING BEFORE THE PRIMARY SEAL SEATS (RELATIVE TO SRM-15)

            O   DEMONSTRATED SEALING THRESHOLD IS 3 TIMES GREATER THAN 0.038" EROSION EXPERIENCED ON SRM-15

    O   IF THE PRIMARY SEAL DOES NOT SEAT, THE SECONDARY SEAL WILL SEAT

        O   PRESSURE WILL GET TO SECONDARY SEAL BEFORE THE METAL PARTS ROTATE

            O   O-RING PRESSURE LEAK CHECK PLACES SECONDARY SEAL IN OUTBOARD POSITION WHICH MINIMIZES SEALING TIME

O   MTI RECOMMENDS STS-51L LAUNCH PROCEED ON 28 JANUARY 1986

    O   SRM-25 WILL NOT BE SIGNIFICANTLY DIFFERENT FROM SRM-15

JOE C. K   VICE PRESIDENT
SPACE BOOSTER PROGRAMS

M   T   INC.
Wasatch Division

Figure 9.11   *Copy of the telefax sent to Kennedy and Marshall centers by the contractor detailing the company's final position on the January 28 launch of mission 51-L.* (Source: Reference 1.)

2.   The waiving of launch constraints appears to have been at the expense of flight safety. There was no system that made it imperative that launch constraints and waivers of launch constraints be considered by all levels of management.

3.   The Commission is troubled by what appears to be a propensity of management at Marshall to contain potentially serious problems and to attempt to resolve them internally rather than communicate them forward. This tendency is altogether at odds with the need for Marshall to function as part of a system working toward successful flight missions, interfacing and communicating with the other parts of the system that work to the same end.

4.   The Commission concluded that the SRB contractor's management reversed its position and recommended the launch of 51-L, at the urging of Marshall and contrary to the views of its engineers in order to accommodate a major customer.

REFERENCES

1. *Report of the Presidential Commission on the Space Shuttle* Challenger *Accident,* Government Printing Office, Washington, DC, June 6, 1986.
2. *NASA, The First 25 Years, 1958–1983,* A Resource for Teachers, National Aeronautics and Space Administration, Washington, DC, 1983.
3. ALLAWAY, HOWARD, *The Space Shuttle at Work,* National Aeronautics and Space Administration, Washington, DC, 1979.

EXERCISES

9.1 Discuss the following questions:
   a. Why did NASA's Safety Program not detect and correct problems with the defective solid rocket booster joint?
   b. How did institutional pressures contribute to shortcuts and unnecessary risks to the shuttle and its occupants?
   c. What is an engineer's responsibility when confronted with management decisions that he or she believes to be a threat to human life? Did the engineers involved in the *Challenger* launch act in a responsible and professional manner?

9.2 Prepare a report describing the history of the design of the solid rocket booster joint. Use Reference 1, Chapter 6, as a primary reference source.

9.3 Prepare a report describing events that happened after the space shuttle *Challenger* accident. Address the following questions. What was the Reagan Administration's reaction to the Commission report? What effects did the accident have on NASA, the rocket booster contractor, and on future plans for space flight?

9.4 Examine newspaper and magazine articles published in the six-month period following the *Challenger* accident. From these sources, identify (by title) NASA and contractor personnel who have resigned or been reassigned in the aftermath of the accident.

9.5 Discuss the mechanism used (a Presidential Commission) to investigate the space shuttle *Challenger* accident. What other approaches could have been used? Under what circumstances is it appropriate to carry out such investigations by a presidentially appointed mechanism?

INDEX